Presented to

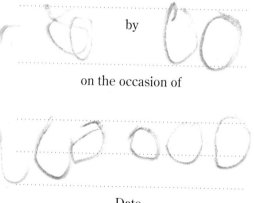

by

on the occasion of

Date

THE BOOK

FOR
children

KENNETH N. TAYLOR

Illustrated by
Richard and Frances Hook

Tyndale House Publishers, Inc.
WHEATON, ILLINOIS

Library of Congress Cataloging-in-Publication Data

Taylor, Kenneth Nathaniel.
    The Book for children / Kenneth N. Taylor ; illustrated by Richard and Frances Hook.
        p.   cm.
    Includes index.
    Summary: A collection of illustrated Bible stories, ranging from Genesis to Revelation.
    ISBN 0-8423-5177-9 (hardcover : alk. paper)
    1. Bible stories, English. [1. Bible stories.] I. Hook, Richard, ill. II. Hook,
Frances, ill. III. Title.
BS551.2.T373 2000
220.9′505—dc21   99-41422

Printed in Singapore

07 06 05 04 03 02 01 00
7   6   5   4   3   2

CONTENTS

The Book about Moses

The Book about One Kingdom

The Book about Two Kingdoms

The Book about People Far from Home

The Book about Coming Home Again

The Book about Jesus

The Book about Jesus' Friends

Dear Mom and Dad,

You have made an important decision—you want to share God's Word with your family. That's a very good decision, and God will help you follow through on doing what he has put in your heart to do.

This book actually contains ten books or sections of Bible stories, which will take you from Genesis to Revelation. The stories are based on *The Book,* which you may be reading yourself. It's an easy-to-read Bible translation for adults called the New Living Translation.

In *The Book for Children* the stories are written in a way that is easy for your whole family to understand. And there are many illustrations so that everyone can follow along visually as you read the stories. The pictures will also help your children remember what they hear.

May God bless you and your family as you read this book of Bible stories together.

KENNETH N. TAYLOR

How to Use This Book

Perhaps you have often wondered how to

- introduce your children to God and his Word
- help your children learn to know God's people
- teach your family to love and obey God
- help your children know all about Jesus
- explain the way to become a Christian

You can do all of these things by reading the Bible stories in *The Book for Children*. This library of books will take you and your family through the Old Testament as you read together

- The Book about the First People (Stories 1–6)
- The Book about Abraham's Family (Stories 7–27)
- The Book about Moses (Stories 28–50)
- The Book about a New Land (Stories 51–62)
- The Book about One Kingdom (Stories 63–76)
- The Book about Two Kingdoms (Stories 77–97)
- The Book about People Far from Home (Stories 98–107)
- The Book about Coming Home Again (Stories 108–113)

You'll be able to follow the events in the New Testament by reading

- The Book about Jesus (Stories 114–146)
- The Book about Jesus' Friends (Stories 147–170)

READING PLANS

Before you choose a way to read this book, you need to create a sandwich. But you don't need to go to the kitchen to prepare it! You just need to remember how important it is to "sandwich" Bible reading with prayer.

First, pray about how, when, and where you'll read this book of Bible stories. And you'll ask for wisdom regarding what reading plan to choose. God knows you, and he knows your family. Ask him to help you choose a plan that will work best for all of you at this time. You may choose one of the following approaches, or you may come up with your own plan. Your prayer of preparation is the first slice of "bread" for your sandwich.

Next, read *The Book for Children* with your family. The Bible reading is the "meat" for your sandwich.

After you've read a Bible story, pray again. It's a good idea to pray out loud with your children so they know that we can ask God to speak to us. But you'll want to continue praying silently throughout the evening and the next day. Pray that your children (and you, too) will learn about God and his love through each story. Pray that the lessons he wants to teach will come through. Those prayers will create the top "slice" for your Bible-reading sandwich.

Here are some of the reading plans you may want to consider.

1. *Look at the pictures and read the captions.* Begin by turning to the first picture in the book, which shows Adam and Eve in the Garden of Eden. Talk about the picture with your children and read the caption. If they are familiar with the story, let them tell what they know. And if they want to hear the story that goes with the picture, read it to them, pausing as you listen to their comments or answer their questions.

You may want to spend some time with this book, just looking at pictures and reading captions. You can show your young ones how to look at the "Contents" pages to discover where they will find pictures of Abraham, Joseph, Moses, Ruth, David, Mary, Jesus, and other familiar Bible characters. Whenever they show interest in hearing more about the story that goes with a picture, be sure to share it with them.

2. *Read familiar stories.* Check out the story titles to see which ones sound familiar. Or look in the back of this book to find the "Index of Important People in the Bible." Then choose some favorites to read after dinner or at bedtime.
3. *Read new stories related to familiar ones.* Perhaps your child has heard about prophets such as Elijah and Elisha but doesn't really know how they fit into the whole story of the people of Israel. How about taking the whole section "The Book about Two Kingdoms" and reading a story every day? This will help your child begin to see how God worked through different people to bring about his plans.
4. *Read the entire book from beginning to end.* You may at some point want to make a commitment as a family to read one story together each day, starting with "The Book about the First People" and continuing right through to "The Book about Jesus' Friends." If you read five stories a week, you'll finish the Old Testament in five to six months and the New Testament in less than three months.

You may want to take a break after that and read a family devotional book together. Then come back and read through the entire Bible again. If you do this several times, God's Word will become more and more real and understandable to your children. You'll find that each time you go through it, there will be new questions, comments, and insights. And as the facts become more familiar, the application will become more apparent—not just to you but to your kids as well.

ASKING QUESTIONS

If you want to go beyond just reading stories, here are several good questions that will get a family discussion started:

- Who were the people in the story?
- What did God do for the people?
- What did this story teach you about God?
- Did the people in the story obey him? love him? thank him?

- Would you want to be like anyone in the story? Why?
- Do you want to be different from anyone in the story? Why?

You may not always want to use all of the questions—perhaps instead you'll select the two or three that are most appropriate. If you wish, feel free to ask more specific questions related to the stories. You may even want to encourage your older children to create questions for the rest of the family.

EXPLAINING HOW TO BECOME A CHRISTIAN

The whole Bible contains stories about God and his people.

The Old Testament (Stories 1–113) focuses on *God the Father*—how he not only created people but stayed with them to teach them and lead them and help them. But the people did not want to obey—they needed a Savior who would die for them to take the blame for their sins. Then God, who is a perfect and holy God, could forgive their sins and make them part of his very own family. The Old Testament prophets told about the Savior who would come hundreds of years later.

In the New Testament (Stories 114–170) many stories are about Jesus, who is *God the Son* and who came to be our Savior. There are also many stories about people who learned how to turn away from their sins and follow Jesus. The people who did this were called Jesus' followers, and sometimes they were called believers. They were also called *"Christ*ians" because they belonged to Jesus *Christ*. Jesus came to this earth from heaven. He was born as a baby, grew up, and taught people about his Father in heaven. Then he died on the cross for our sins, came back to life, and went to live in heaven again. After he left this earth, he sent *God the Holy Spirit* to be with us all the time and help us live for Jesus.

To explain how to become a Christian, read some of the following stories and talk about what each person did:

- *Nicodemus* (Story 119) learned about being born again. Jesus explained that we can have "a new life from heaven. It's a life that will last forever."
- *Peter, Andrew, James, and John* (Story 121) left their fishing nets to follow Jesus. They became his disciples, learning how to be like him and help others as he did. We can be Jesus' followers too and learn to live the way he wants us to.
- *Zacchaeus* (Story 136) had done things that were wrong. "Jesus saw that Zacchaeus was sorry and was ready to do what was right. So he told Zacchaeus that his sins were forgiven."
- *Jesus* (Stories 141–146) died on the cross for our sins. Then he came back to life again and went back to heaven. We can trust Jesus to be our Savior—to save us from our sins.
- *Saul* (Story 149), who later became known as Paul the missionary, had been very much against Jesus' followers. He put them in jail and even killed some of them. But he saw a light from heaven and heard Jesus talking to him. Then he became a believer and helped many other people learn about Jesus. All of us who become Christians should be missionaries like Paul, even if we just tell others in our own families and neighborhoods about our Savior.
- *The jailer at Philippi* (Story 154) knew that God must have sent the earthquake that set Paul and Silas free from their chains. When he asked what he needed to do to be saved, Paul and Silas answered, "Believe in the Lord Jesus, and you will be saved."

Remember that your job is not to determine the time when your children will be ready to receive Jesus as Savior. Your job is simply to share the information they need to make the decision and to pray for your kids every day. God the Holy Spirit will move in your children's lives, and he will move in yours so that you recognize when they are ready to ask Jesus to be their Savior. When that time comes, have them pray a prayer something like this:

Jesus, I'm sorry about all of the bad things I've done. Please forgive me. I believe that you are God's Son and that you died on the cross to save me from my sins. I ask you to be my Savior. I want to be your follower now, and I want to live with you forever. Thank you for helping me to love you and please you every day. Amen.

THE
BOOK
about
the First
People

The first man and woman, Adam and Eve, lived in the Garden of Eden.

God Makes a Beautiful World

Genesis 1–2

Long, long ago—long before anyone can remember— God made the world. But it didn't look the way it does now, for there were no people, animals, birds, trees, bushes, or flowers. Everything was lonely and dark.

Then God made the light. He said, "Let there be light," and light came. God was pleased with it. He gave the light a name, calling it "day." And when the day was gone and the darkness came again, he called that darkness "night." God did these things on the first day of creation.

Then God made the space above the earth. He gave the space a name, too, calling it "sky." God did this on the second day of creation.

Next God said that the waters covering the earth should become oceans and lakes, and the dry land should appear. God also made the grass grow, and the bushes and trees. All this was on the third day of creation.

On the fourth day God let the sun shine in the daytime, and the moon and stars at night.

On the fifth day God made great sea monsters and all the fish. And he made the birds. He made some, like ducks and geese, to fly over the water and swim on it and live near it. He made others, like eagles, robins, pigeons, and wrens, to fly over the land and live in the woods and fields.

On the sixth day of creation God made animals that walk on land. He made those that are wild and live out in the forests, such as elephants, lions, tigers, and bears. He made those that are tame and useful, such as rabbits, horses, cows, and sheep. And he made little insects, such as ants that crawl around on the ground and bees that swarm in the air and make honey in trees.

Then God made someone very special. God made a man! This is how God made him. He took some dust from the ground and formed it into a man's body. God breathed into the body, and the man began to breathe and walk around. God named the man Adam.

Then the Lord God planted a beautiful garden as a home for the man he had made, calling it the Garden of Eden. In it God planted lovely trees full of delicious fruit. God told Adam he could eat any fruit in the garden except the fruit from one tree. That tree was the tree of the knowledge of good and evil. If Adam took even one bite from that tree's fruit, God said Adam would begin to die.

Adam was the only person in all the world, and he was lonely. God decided it wasn't good for him to be alone, so he made another person who would be with Adam and help him. This is how God did it. He put the man to sleep. And while Adam was sleeping, God took one of his ribs and made a woman from it. Then God brought the woman to Adam, and she became his wife. Adam named her Eve.

Then God looked at all he had made in those six days, and he was very pleased. So the earth and skies and all the plants and animals were finished in six days of creation.

On the seventh day, God rested. It was a quiet and different day from all the others—a holy day of rest.

STORY 2
The World's Saddest Day

Genesis 3

There was someone else in the Garden of Eden besides Adam and Eve and God. Satan was there, in the shape of a serpent. Satan is the wicked spirit who tempts us to sin. He came to Eve and told her to do something that was wrong. He asked her, "Did God really tell you not to eat the fruit of any of the trees in the garden?"

"We may eat any of it except from one tree," she replied. "We are not to eat the fruit of the tree in the middle of the garden. God said that if we do, we will start growing old and die."

"That's not true!" Satan told her. "It won't hurt you at all! Really, it's good and will make you wise!"

Eve should have gone away and should not have paid any attention to Satan. But instead, she went over and looked at the tree. It was beautiful, and the fruit looked so good! When she remembered that Satan had said it would make her wise, she ate some of the fruit. She gave some to her husband, Adam, and he ate it too.

After they had done this, they heard a voice calling to them. It was God's voice. But they didn't go to him. Instead, they hid among the trees, for now they were afraid of God. He called to them again.

"Where are you, Adam? Where are you?"

"I'm hiding," Adam finally replied, "for I'm afraid of you."

"Have you eaten the fruit I told you not to eat?" God asked.

Then Adam began to make excuses and blamed Eve. He said, "The woman you gave me brought me some of the fruit, and I ate it."

God asked Eve, "What is this you have done?"

"Satan fooled me," she said, "so I ate some of the fruit."

God was very angry. He told the serpent, "You will be punished by having to crawl on the ground in the dust all your life."

God told the woman, "When your children are being born, you will have pain."

God told Adam, "Because you listened to your wife and ate the fruit I told you not to eat, the ground will no longer grow lush crops. Instead, it will grow thorns and thistles. As long as you live, you will have to work hard to get enough food to eat. And someday when you die, your body will become dust again, like the dust you were made from."

God made clothes for Adam and Eve. Then he sent them out of the beautiful garden. He didn't want them to go back to live there anymore. So he sent angels with a sword made of fire to stop them from ever going back into the garden again.

But even though they had sinned, God made a way for Adam and Eve to be saved from punishment after they died. He promised to send a Savior who would be punished for their sins. God said that people would need to ask him to forgive them. And they would need to trust the Savior to save them. Then God said he would help people obey him and do what is right and good. And someday he would take them to heaven when they died.

When the Savior—Jesus—came, he died for Adam's and Eve's sins, for their children's sins, and also for ours. We are all sinners. But God forgives us if we ask him to, because Jesus died to take away our sins.

STORY 3
The First Family Fight
Genesis 4

After God sent Adam and Eve out of the Garden of Eden, he gave them two sons. Cain was the older one. Abel was the younger one. When the boys grew to be young men, Cain became a farmer, planting crops in his fields. Abel was a shepherd with a flock of sheep. They both had wicked hearts like their parents, so they sinned—they did things that were wrong. But Abel pleased God. That means he was sorry about his sins. And he must have believed God's promise to send a Savior.

One day Abel brought a lamb from his flock and offered it as a gift to God. He put the lamb on an altar, which was a pile of stones. This gift was called a sacrifice. By giving God his lamb, Abel showed God that he loved him.

God was pleased that Abel worshiped him like this. In many ways the lamb was like Jesus, the Savior. One day God would send his Son, Jesus, to die for people's sins. This Savior would be gentle and patient and innocent like the lamb. He would become a sacrifice just as the lamb was.

Abel's brother, Cain, did not please God. So he did not turn from his sins. He must not have believed God's promise to send a Savior. And the offering he brought was not a lamb, but some

Adam and Eve's older son, Cain, was angry because his brother, Abel, pleased God. After Cain killed Abel, God made Cain leave home forever.

things from his garden. God was not pleased with Cain or his offering.

When Cain realized that God had accepted Abel's sacrifice but not his, he was angry with God. But God spoke kindly to him and asked why he was angry. God said that if Cain would worship him in the right way, he would accept Cain's gift and be pleased with him.

Methuselah, the oldest man who ever lived, was 969 years old when he died!

Cain was angry with God but took his anger out on Abel. One day when they were in a field together, Cain killed Abel.

Then God called to Cain, "Where is Abel, your brother?"

"How should I know?" Cain answered. "Am I supposed to look after my brother?"

But God had seen what Cain did. So God said that for the rest of his life Cain would have to wander from place to place. When Cain planted a garden, it wouldn't grow well, so Cain would have to keep moving, trying to find different places where crops would grow. Cain was afraid that people would try to hurt him. But God still loved Cain and said he would never let anyone hurt him.

STORY 4

A Long, Long Time to Live

Genesis 5

Cain and Abel's father and mother, Adam and Eve, lived for many years after the fight between their first two sons. When Adam was 930 years old, he died. His body became dust again. That's what God had said would happen because Adam and Eve sinned in the Garden of Eden.

Before Adam and Eve died, they had many

children. The children grew up and had children too. Then those children grew up and had children until there were many, many people in the world.

One of those people was Enoch. He walked with God. That means he loved God and thought about God all the time. It was as if he and God walked together like friends. Enoch listened to what God said and always tried to please and obey him. When Enoch was 365 years old, God did a wonderful thing for him. God took Enoch right up to heaven! So he didn't die like other men. God just took Enoch away to live with him.

Enoch had a son named Methuselah who lived to be 969 years old. Methuselah is known as the oldest man who ever lived.

STORY 5

Noah Is Safe in a Boat

Genesis 6–8

As the years went by, the world became more and more wicked. People did all kinds of bad things. They didn't care about pleasing God and didn't even try to obey him. So God was angry with them and said he would punish them by sending a flood to cover the earth with deep water, drowning all living things.

But there was one good man whose name was

Noah. He loved God and always wanted to please him. God loved Noah, too. He told Noah about the flood he was going to send so that Noah could get ready for it.

God told Noah, "I want you to build a boat. Make it huge!" God said to make it as high as a three-story house, filled with many large rooms. It was to have a long window all around it and a big door in the side. God said that when the boat was finished, Noah and his family would live in it and float away safely when the flood came.

God also told Noah to bring into the boat a father and mother animal, bird, and even insect of every kind there was. Then, when the flood came, several of each kind of living thing would still be alive inside the boat. But everything outside would be drowned.

So Noah began to build the boat. It took him a long, long time—more than a hundred years. But as you know, at that time people lived much longer than they do now.

When the boat was finished, God told Noah to bring all his family and the birds and animals and insects into the boat. God said that in one week he would send a rain that would last forty days and forty nights. The flood would come, and everyone outside the boat would be drowned.

So Noah brought his wife and his three sons and their wives into the boat. And he brought in at least two of each kind of animal, insect, and bird. These were in pairs, a father and a mother of each kind. Two of some kinds came and seven of other kinds.

When all were safely inside, God closed the door.

Seven days later it began to rain. In fact, it poured. It rained without stopping for forty days and forty nights, just as God had said it would. The rain came down as if it were being poured from great windows in the sky. The creeks, the rivers, and the great oceans all began to rise, and water covered the land. After a while there was so much water all around the boat that it was lifted off the ground. Higher and higher the water rose, with the boat floating on it.

But what about those people who had refused to obey God? Now it was too late to get into the boat. All the earth was covered with water, and there was no land anywhere. Only the boat was floating upon the water.

All through that dreadful storm God took care of Noah and all those who were with him. God kept the boat and everyone inside safe. Finally the rain stopped, and the water began to go down again.

After Noah had been in the boat for 150 days— almost half a year—the boat rested on top of Mount Ararat. But Noah and his family stayed

At God's command, Noah brought animals of every kind to live in the huge boat he built. God saved Noah, his family, and the animals from the Flood.

inside, for God wasn't ready to let them out yet.
Two months later the flood had gone down even
more. By then the tops of other mountains were
peeping above the water.

Finally the ground was dry. So God told Noah
and his wife and his sons and their wives to come
out of the boat. He said to let out all the animals
and insects and birds, too.

Then Noah built an altar, as Abel had done, and
sacrificed animals and birds to the Lord. This was
Noah's way of thanking God for saving him and
his family from the Flood.

God promised that he would never send another
flood to drown all living things. As proof, he gave
Noah a sign—a beautiful rainbow in the sky that
Noah could often see when it rained. Whenever he
saw it, Noah would remember God's promise not
to send a flood like that again.

STORY 6

A Huge Tower

Genesis 11

Soon after the Flood ended, Noah became a
grandfather, for God gave children to Noah's
sons and their wives. These grandchildren grew
up and had children too, until after a while the
world was full of people again.

God wasn't happy about this tower because the people building it were trying to prove how great they were. They wanted to show God that they could get along without him.

Don't you suppose these people would have been very careful not to make God angry? They knew about the terrible flood and what had happened to all the people before. But no, they didn't care. They kept on doing all sorts of bad things. Their hearts were not filled with love for God. So they acted just like the people before the Flood, always sinning against God.

There was only one language in the world at that time. Today there are thousands of languages, like English, Spanish, French, Russian, Korean, Swahili, and Arabic. But in those days the people all talked alike, so everyone in all the world could understand everyone else!

One day the people said to each other, "Let's build a tower as high as heaven!" So they began to build it. The people were proud and wanted to show how great they were. They wanted to bring honor to themselves for being able to build such a high tower. But it is sinful to be proud, and God knew what they were thinking.

One day the Lord came down from heaven to see the tower, and he was not happy about it. He decided to stop the people from building it. So he made them begin to speak in different languages! Now they couldn't understand each other. One man would ask another for a hammer, but the other man couldn't understand him! This made them angry with each other, and soon they stopped working and went home.

The people didn't even want to live near each

other anymore. Only those speaking the same language wanted to live together. So the different groups of people moved away from those who didn't speak their language. That is why different languages are spoken in different parts of the world today.

When people began talking in different languages and couldn't understand each other anymore, they got all mixed up. The word *Babel* means "mixed up." So the tower was called the Tower of Babel, and it was never finished.

THE BOOK
about
Abraham's
Family

One day God told Abram to move to another country. Abram left with his family, his servants, and his animals.

STORY 7

A New Home for Abram

Genesis 11–12

Far away in the land of Ur (which was in the country we call Iraq), there lived a man named Abram. The people of Ur worshiped idols of wood and stone. This was very wrong of them, for God had said that they must worship only him. God told Abram, "Leave this country. I will show you another land where I want you to live."

So Abram left home with his wife, Sarai, his nephew Lot, and his servants. He left his other relatives and friends in Ur and began traveling. Even though he didn't know how far he would have to go or how long he would have to travel, he believed God would take care of him. Abram was 75 years old at that time.

It turned out to be a long, hard journey. Abram and the others had to cross wide rivers and a dry, lonely desert. Yet God took care of them and brought them safely to the Promised Land. It was called the land of Canaan. Today we call it Palestine.

"I will give all this land to you—this whole country," God told him. "It will belong to you and to

your children forever." Then Abram built an altar
and worshiped God by sacrificing an animal on the
altar.

Other people were living in the new land who
might have hurt him, but God made sure that they
didn't. There was also a famine when Abram
arrived. That means the crops didn't grow well in
the fields, so the people had little to eat. So Abram
and the others went away for a while to still another
country called Egypt, waiting until there was more
food in Canaan.

STORY 8

Abram Shares His Land

Genesis 13

After some time Abram and Lot and their families
returned to Canaan. Abram went to the place where
he had built an altar and worshiped the Lord again.

Abram was now very rich and owned many,
many cows, goats, and sheep. Lot had many
animals too. The men who took care of Lot's
animals quarreled with the men who took care of
Abram's animals. When Abram heard about this,
he talked to Lot about it. Abram could have said,
"This is my land, Lot, so you get out. God has given
it to me, and you must move away somewhere
else." But Abram didn't do that. He was very nice

Abram could have kept all the land for himself, but he offered to divide it with his nephew, Lot. And he gave Lot first choice.

to Lot and said, "Let's not have any fighting and quarreling between us."

Then Abram divided the land with Lot. Abram gave Lot first choice, even though he didn't need to—it was Abram's land, for God had given it to him.

Lot chose the best part of the country—the valley by the Jordan River. After Lot had moved away to his new home, the Lord said to Abram, "I will give you all of the good land Lot chose. Lot is living there now, but someday it will all be yours!"

God also said he would give Abram so many children and grandchildren and great-grandchildren that they would become a great nation. That promise has come true, and today we call Abram's family the Jewish people.

STORY 9

Abram Gets a New Name

Genesis 15–17

Abram knew that God was his friend. God had given him a new home in a new land and had promised to give him a big family. But Abram still didn't have any children. So he reminded his great friend that he wanted a son.

God took Abram out under the night skies and told him to look up at the stars. The Lord asked Abram whether he could count them. He couldn't do it because there were so many. Then God told him, "Someday your family will be like those stars—there will be too many people to count!"

God let Abram know that there would come a sad time for these people of his. They would be taken away to another country as slaves, where they would be treated cruelly for many years. "But afterward," God said, "I will punish those who hurt them. I will bring them back to the land of Canaan, and they will be very rich."

God also told Abram that he would live to be an old, old man. And he would die happy.

Soon after that, Abram had a son named Ishmael. But he was not the son God had promised to Abram and his wife, Sarai.

When Abram was 99 years old, God talked with him again. (Abram, knowing how great God is, lay with his face looking down toward the ground while God talked to him.)

God said again that he would give Abram many, many grandchildren and great-grandchildren—a whole country full of them—and some of them would be kings. God also made a very special promise to Abram and his children: "I will be your God," he said, "and you will be my people." Then God promised again to give the land of Canaan to Abram's family, the Jewish people.

God even gave Abram a new name! "Your name isn't Abram anymore!" God said. "From now on it is Abraham!" (Abraham means "the father of a whole country.") God gave Sarai a new name too. Her name became Sarah, which means "princess." So the Lord changed both their names, and he promised to give them a son whose name would be Isaac.

STORY **10**

God's Visit and Isaac's Arrival

Genesis 18; 20–21

One hot day Abraham was sitting at the entrance of his tent. He looked up and saw three men coming toward him, so he ran to meet them. He bowed his head down low, for that was the way to welcome strangers in that land.

Abraham invited the men to rest in the shade of a tree while he brought some water to soothe their tired feet. In those days people either went barefoot or wore sandals, so their feet became very dusty. One of the things a friendly man did for his guests was to give them water to wash their feet after a long, hot walk.

Abraham ran to the tent and told Sarah, "Quick, bake some bread." Next he ran out to where the cows were and selected a fat calf to be killed and cooked.

When the meat was ready, Abraham set it before the three men. He also brought them some butter and bread and milk. The visitors had a picnic

Abraham loved God very much. In the picture you can see him with his wife, Sarah, and his son Isaac.

beneath the tree while Abraham stood nearby to serve them.

"Where is Sarah?" they asked.

"My wife is in the tent," Abraham answered.

Then one of the visitors said, "Next year I'll come back around this time, and Sarah will have a son."

Sarah was still in the tent, but she heard those words. And she began to laugh. After all, she was a very old woman—around ninety years old. She was much too old to have a baby!

Now I must tell you that the three men were really not men at all. Two of them were angels, we believe, and the other one was God. Could God look and talk like a man? Yes, several times in the Bible he appeared in the form of a man and talked with someone.

When God heard Sarah laugh, he said to Abraham, "Is anything too hard for the Lord? Just as I said, I will return about a year from now. Then Sarah will have a son."

During the next year Abraham moved again, this time to a place named Gerar. While they lived there, God gave Abraham and Sarah a baby son, just as he had promised them. Abraham named him Isaac, for that is the name God had said to give him.

Abraham was one hundred years old and Sarah was over ninety years old when Isaac was born. What a happy day it was!

A Wife for Isaac

Genesis 22–24

Some time later the angel of God talked to
Abraham again about his family. God was greatly
pleased with Abraham for trusting him and for
being willing to obey. The angel of God said that
Abraham's family would someday be very large,
just as God had promised before. And his family
would help all the other people in the world. (The
angel said this because the Savior of the world
was going to be born into Abraham's family.)

Sarah, who was Abraham's wife and Isaac's
mother, died when she was 127 years old. Abraham
cried a lot because he missed Sarah. Isaac missed
her too. But now he had become a full-grown man
and wanted to get married.

Abraham didn't want his son to marry any of the
girls who lived near them. These girls worshiped
idols instead of worshiping God. So Abraham
wanted Isaac to marry a girl from the country where
their relatives lived. There the people obeyed God
and didn't worship idols.

But that country was far away. So Abraham
called for his oldest servant, the one who was in
charge of all his business. He asked the servant to
go to that faraway country and to bring back a girl
for Isaac to marry.

So the servant loaded ten of Abraham's camels with beautiful presents and began the long trip. After many, many days of hard travel he finally arrived at the town where Abraham's relatives lived. He made the camels kneel down by a well that was just outside the city.

It was evening when Abraham's servant arrived, and the young women were all coming out to draw water from the well. As the servant watched them, he asked God to help him find the right one.

This is how the old servant prayed. He told God that he would ask one of the young women to give him some water from her pitcher. Then he would wait to see if she answered him with a smile and said, "Yes, and I will water your camels, too." If she did, he prayed that she would be the one God had chosen to be Isaac's wife.

While he was still praying, a beautiful girl named Rebekah came. Carrying her pitcher on her shoulder, she went down to the well and filled it with water.

The servant ran over to her and said, "Please give me a drink from your pitcher."

"Certainly, sir," she replied. "And I'll water your camels, too!"

She set her pitcher down and gave the servant a drink. Then she ran back to the well and began drawing water for his camels!

After the camels had finished drinking, the old man gave Rebekah a gold earring and two gold bracelets. He asked her about her family. He also asked if there was room at her father's house for him and his men to spend the night. Rebekah told him who her father and her grandparents were. She also said that there was plenty of room.

Abraham sent his old servant to find a wife for Isaac. God helped the old man find the right one. Her name was Rebekah.

When the servant heard who her family was, he realized that she was the right one for Isaac. He bowed his head and worshiped the Lord, thanking God for helping him to find the right girl so quickly.

Rebekah ran home to tell her mother that the men were coming. When her brother Laban heard about it and saw the earring and bracelets, he ran to the well. He found the old man and brought him home. After Laban helped him unload the camels and feed them, it was time for supper. So Laban took Abraham's servant in to meet the family.

The servant told how he had come to the well and had prayed to find the right young woman to be Isaac's wife. Then the servant asked the family if they would let Rebekah go with him to marry Isaac. They said yes; since it was the Lord who had brought him, Rebekah could go.

When the servant heard this he was very happy and worshiped the Lord. He brought out other beautiful presents—silver and gold jewelry, and beautiful clothing—and gave them to Rebekah. He gave her mother and her brother presents too.

At last the servant and his men were ready to eat. Afterward they stayed at Laban's house all night.

Rebekah Says Yes

Genesis 24–25

In the morning Abraham's servant wanted to take Rebekah and leave at once to return to Abraham and his son Isaac. But her mother and brother said, "Let her stay with us a few days at least, and then she may go."

The old servant begged them not to delay him, for he felt that he should hurry back to his master.

The young woman's family said, "We'll call Rebekah and ask her if she is willing to go so soon."

She replied, "Yes, I'll go now."

So Rebekah's family sent her to marry Isaac. They knew she would be hundreds of miles away. But they prayed that she would be happy and have a big family.

After many long, hot days of travel on camels, Rebekah and the servant came at last to the land of Canaan. As the sun was going down, Isaac had gone out alone for a walk in a field. Perhaps he wondered if the servant would soon be back. Had God helped the old man find a young woman to be his wife? If so, what would she be like?

Just then Isaac looked up, and the camels were coming!

Rebekah looked up too. She saw Isaac walking in the field and asked the servant, "Who is that man coming to meet us?" The old man told her it was Isaac. So she took a veil and covered her face with it. When Isaac brought her into the tent that had been his mother's before she died, Rebekah became his wife. And he loved her.

Isaac's father, Abraham, made plans to give all that he had to Isaac when he died. Abraham lived to the age of 175. Then he was buried in the cave where he had buried his wife, Sarah.

Esau's Terrible Mistake

Genesis 25

After Isaac and Rebekah were married, God gave them twin sons! The babies' names were Esau and Jacob. Esau was born first, and Jacob was born a few minutes later. So Esau was the older one.

In those days the oldest son in every family had what was called the birthright. This meant he got more of the family's money and things when his father died. In fact, he got twice as much as the other children.

In Isaac's family Esau was born first and had the birthright.

When Esau and Jacob grew up to be men, Esau became a hunter. He went out into the fields and woods to kill deer. Then he brought the meat home to his father, Isaac. How his father loved that meat!

Esau made a terrible mistake. He sold his birthright to Isaac for a bowl of food.

Jacob stayed at home, where he probably helped to care for his father's sheep and goats.

One day Jacob was at home cooking some especially good food when Esau came in from his hunting. Esau was very tired and hungry, so he asked Jacob to give him the food. Jacob said he would give him the food if Esau would give him his birthright! Esau didn't care about his birthright at the time, so he told Jacob he could have it. Then Jacob gave him some food.

It was wrong for Esau to sell his birthright. God had given it to him, so he should not have sold it. It was wrong, too, for Jacob to take it.

STORY 14

Is It Jacob or Is It Esau?

Genesis 27–28

Isaac, who was getting very old and couldn't see, called for his oldest son, Esau. He told Esau to go out into the field and hunt for a deer.

"Cook the meat just the way I like it best," said Isaac. "Then I will bless you." He meant that he would ask God to be kind to Esau and give him many good things. So Esau went out into the field to hunt the deer for his father.

Rebekah heard what Isaac said, and she wasn't happy about it. She didn't want Isaac to give the special blessing to Esau, even though he was her oldest son. She wanted Jacob to have the blessing.

When Esau had gone to hunt for deer, Rebekah told Jacob to kill two of their goats and bring them to her. She cooked them so the meat tasted just like the deer meat Jacob's father loved so much. Then she got some of Esau's clothes for Jacob to put on. And she put goat skins on the back of his hands and neck. She told him to take the food to his blind father and to say that he was Esau.

So Jacob took the food to his father. Isaac was surprised that Esau had come back so soon. Because Isaac was blind, he asked if it really was Esau. Jacob said, "Yes, I'm Esau. And I have brought the deer meat you asked for."

His father put his hands on Jacob's hairy neck. (Remember, Jacob's mother had put a goat skin around his neck!) Then Isaac smelled the clothes Jacob was wearing. And he was convinced that it was really Esau, even though his voice sounded more like Jacob's. And of course, it was Jacob, and not Esau at all. Jacob had fooled his father. So his father ate the food and blessed Jacob. Isaac prayed that God would always help Jacob grow good crops in his fields. And he prayed for Jacob to be in charge of the family.

Jacob left the tent as soon as Isaac had blessed him. Right after that, Esau came in with the deer he had caught while he was hunting. He cooked the meat and took it to his father.

Isaac asked him, "Who are you?"

Esau answered, "I am Esau, and I have the meat you told me to get for you."

Isaac began to tremble. "Who was it, then," he asked, "who was just here? I gave him your blessing!" Isaac knew the answer to his own question. It was Jacob who had come in first and had stolen Esau's blessing.

Esau cried and begged his father to bless him, too. So Isaac did, but he had already promised the best things to Jacob. He couldn't take those things away from him.

Esau hated Jacob for what he had done. "My father will soon die," Esau said to himself. "Then I will kill Jacob."

When Rebekah heard what Esau was saying, she sent for Jacob and told him to leave home. She said he should go away to the country where she used to live, to the home of her brother Laban. Esau would not be able to hurt Jacob there.

But how could Jacob's mother get Jacob's father to agree? This is the way she did it. She reminded Isaac that the girls who lived nearby didn't love God—they prayed to idols. Rebekah said she would rather die than see Jacob marry a girl who didn't love God.

Isaac agreed that Jacob must not marry a Canaanite girl. He called Jacob to him and blessed him again. He told Jacob to marry one of his mother's relatives who lived far away in another country.

Then Isaac sent Jacob away to that far-off land

where his Uncle Laban lived. He sent him there to find a girl who would marry him. It was the same land where Abraham's servant had found Rebekah, Jacob and Esau's mother.

STORY 15

A Stairway to Heaven

Genesis 28

Jacob began traveling to the country where his Uncle Laban lived. When the sun went down, Jacob found a good place to sleep outdoors. Using a stone for a pillow, he went to sleep. During the night he had a dream. He thought he saw some stairs reaching to heaven, and angels were going up and down them. God stood at the top of the stairs. He told Jacob he was going to give this land to Jacob and his children. God said he would be with Jacob and take care of him wherever he went. And someday God would bring Jacob safely home again.

Jacob woke up and said, "God is here, and I didn't even know it!" Very early the next morning Jacob got up and worshiped the Lord. He called the place Bethel, which means "house of God."

Jacob Works Hard and Gets Married

Genesis 29–31

Jacob kept traveling a long, long time until he came to Haran, where his Uncle Laban lived. He saw a well in a field there. Three flocks of sheep were lying around it, and the shepherds were with their flocks. A large rock covered the well. When all the flocks arrived, the shepherds would roll away the stone and get water for the sheep. Afterward they would roll the stone back over the mouth of the well again.

Jacob asked the shepherds where they lived, and they told him at Haran.

"Do you know Laban?" he asked them. "Is he well?"

"Yes," they replied. "And look, here comes his daughter Rachel with his sheep."

Jacob went over to the well and kissed Rachel. Then he rolled away the stone and watered her sheep for her. When he explained that he was her Aunt Rebekah's son, she ran and told her father.

Laban ran out to meet his nephew. He gave Jacob a warm welcome and brought him home. After Jacob had been there about a month, Laban asked him to stay and work for him.

Jacob worked for Laban for many years so that he could marry Laban's beautiful daughter Rachel.

By this time Jacob was very much in love with Rachel. He told Laban he would work for him for seven years if he could marry Rachel afterward.

Laban was delighted. So Jacob worked for him for the next seven years. Even though it was a long time, the years went by in a hurry. They seemed like only a few days to Jacob because he loved Rachel so much.

But when the time was up, Laban would not let him marry Rachel. He said her older sister Leah should be married first, so Jacob had to marry her. Then he had to work seven more years for Rachel. This was very unfair of Jacob's uncle, but Jacob agreed to it because of his love for Rachel.

After many years Jacob had a very large family. He wanted to take his family back home to the land of Canaan. But Laban wouldn't let Jacob go.

One day Jacob heard Laban's sons talking angrily about him. They said he had stolen their father's sheep and that was why he was so rich. Jacob noticed that Laban was not as friendly to him as he used to be.

Then God told Jacob to return home to the land of Canaan. God said he would be with Jacob and keep him from harm.

Jacob sent word for Rachel and Leah to meet him out in the field where he was caring for his flock. He wanted to talk with them where Laban couldn't hear what he said. He told them that their father wasn't friendly to him anymore and that the Lord had told him to go back to Canaan.

Rachel and Leah both agreed he must do whatever the Lord wanted him to do.

Jacob's Secret Escape

Genesis 31–32

Jacob was ready to return home. He put his family on camels and took everything that belonged to him. Then he started back toward the land of Canaan, driving his sheep and goats ahead of him.

Laban was away when Jacob left, for Jacob had kept it all a secret. But three days after Jacob was gone, someone told Laban about it. Laban quickly set out after him. He was angry, for he didn't want Jacob to go. But that night, in a dream, God spoke to Laban. God told him not to harm Jacob or even speak roughly to him.

It took seven days for Laban to catch up with Jacob. In the hills Laban finally found him. Laban said, "Let's be friends and promise that we will never hurt each other."

Jacob agreed, and they made a huge pile of stones to remind them of their promise. If they were ever angry and set out to harm each other, they would see that heap of stones. Remembering their promise, they would go back home again.

Jacob then built an altar and offered up a sacrifice. Afterward he and Laban and the men who were with them ate together and camped together that night.

Early the next morning Laban kissed Rachel and Leah and their children good-bye and blessed them. Then he went back home.

As Jacob and his family traveled on toward Canaan, some angels met them. Jacob knew then that God was still with him, just as he had promised he would always be.

Jacob sent messengers to tell Esau about all that had happened while he was away. Jacob was afraid, even though it had been twenty years since he had stolen Esau's blessing. If Jacob still remembered his sin, wouldn't Esau remember too? What might Esau do to him?

Jacob's messengers returned with the scary news that Esau was coming to meet him with four hundred men. Jacob's heart sank. He divided all his sheep, goats, camels, and men into two groups. If Esau attacked one group, the other group might be able to escape.

Jacob prayed and asked God to save him from Esau, for he was afraid Esau would kill him and his family. He thanked the Lord for being so very kind to him before. He admitted he did not deserve the good things God had given him. When he had left Canaan twenty years before, he had owned only the staff he carried in his hand. He had been very poor, but God had made him very rich. He thanked God for this.

The next morning he sent some of his animals as a present to Esau—220 goats, 220 sheep, 30 camels with their colts, 40 cows, 10 bulls, and 30

These two brothers haven't seen each other for so many, many years. The one with the bow and arrows is Esau. And the other one is Jacob.

donkeys. Jacob hoped these gifts would make Esau so happy that he wouldn't hurt Jacob and his family or steal the rest of his animals.

Is Esau Still Angry?

Genesis 32–33

The same night after sending many of his animals as a present to Esau, Jacob woke up. He got up, awakened his family, and sent them across the river. When he was all alone, a man came and wrestled with him. Jacob was strong and kept on wrestling until the man touched Jacob's thigh. Just by that touch Jacob's thigh was put out of joint, and he became lame.

The man said, "Let me go, for the sun is coming up."

But Jacob replied, "I won't let you go until you bless me."

"What is your name?" the man asked.

So Jacob told him. (Jacob's name meant "tricky" or "unfair.")

The man said, "I am giving you another name. You are no longer Jacob, but Israel." (That name meant "prince of God" or "someone who has struggled with God.")

Who was this man? He was the same person who had visited Jacob's grandfather, Abraham, telling him that his wife would have a baby within a year.

This man was the Lord. The Lord was glad that Jacob wanted God's blessing so much that he kept on asking for it all night.

Jacob said to the man, "Now tell me your name."

But the Lord answered, "Do not ask!" And the Lord blessed Jacob there.

The sun was rising as he limped back across the stream. Jacob limped for the rest of his life because the Lord had touched him. Probably the Lord did this so he would always remember that God had blessed him.

When Jacob saw his brother Esau coming with four hundred men, Jacob divided his family into groups. If Esau attacked, perhaps some of them could run away and escape.

Then Jacob went on ahead by himself to meet his brother. He bowed low before him seven times. Esau ran to meet his twin brother. He put his arms around Jacob and kissed him on the cheek, as men did in that country when they met friends. Then they both started crying.

Esau asked, "Who are these people with you?"

"They are my family," Jacob replied. Then all the family members came, and the children met their Uncle Esau for the first time.

Esau asked Jacob, "Why did you give me all of these sheep and goats?"

"They are a present for you," Jacob replied.

"No, you shouldn't give these animals to me," Esau said. "I have enough, my brother. Keep them."

But Jacob said, "Please accept my present." He kept begging him to do it until Esau finally did.

Esau suggested to Jacob that they travel together as they returned home, but Jacob told Esau to go on ahead while he followed more slowly. "Some of the children are too little to go very far at a time," he explained. "And the sheep and goats cannot be driven too fast or they will get sick and die."

Esau agreed and offered to leave some of his men with Jacob. He said they could help him and protect him from robbers. Jacob was thankful but said he didn't need them. So Esau went back home.

Both brothers were glad to be friends again.

STORY 19

The Place Where Jacob Had a Dream

Genesis 33; 35–36

After Esau had gone, Jacob traveled to a place called Succoth. Here he stopped and rested his cows before he went on to the land of Canaan.

God spoke to Jacob again. He told him to go to the city of Bethel and to build an altar there. Bethel was the place where Jacob had dreamed a special dream more than twenty years before. It was about a stairway reaching to heaven, with angels going up and down on it. In that dream God had stood at the top of the stairs. He had promised to be with Jacob wherever he went and to bring him back safely. Now God had done this.

So Jacob said to his family, "Let's go to Bethel and build an altar there to worship God." Jacob talked about how kind the Lord had been to him many years before. (That's when he was running away from his brother, Esau.) He told them how the Lord had been with him ever since and had taken care of him.

On the way to Bethel they passed through cities where the people might have robbed them or hurt them. But God made the people afraid to do that, so they didn't try to harm Jacob or his family in any way.

Arriving safely at Bethel, Jacob built an altar and worshiped God. Then God spoke to Jacob, blessed him, and told him again, "Your name isn't Jacob anymore, but Israel." (Remember, Israel means "prince of God" or "someone who has struggled with God." This new name showed how much God loved him.)

God said again that he would give all the land of Canaan to Jacob and his children and his children's children. God promised that they would become a great nation and that some of them would be kings.

Then Jacob set up a great pile of stones at Bethel. He did it to mark the place where God had spoken to him. Now everyone would always remember that this was the place!

Afterward Jacob and everyone with him, including all of his children, started off to Bethlehem. Before they arrived, Rachel had another baby, and they named him Benjamin. Now Jacob had twelve sons! But Rachel died soon afterward. Jacob was terribly sad, for he loved Rachel very much. He piled stones over her grave to show where she was buried, and the stones stayed there for hundreds of years.

Finally Jacob came to Hebron, where his father lived. Yes, Isaac, his father, was still alive, even though he had become old and blind many years before. God had kept him alive until Jacob came home again.

But Isaac died soon afterward, and his sons, Jacob and Esau, buried him. They put his body in the cave where his parents, Abraham and Sarah, were buried. He was 180 years old at the time of his death.

Then Esau moved to the land of Edom. He took his wives, his children, his cows, and everything else he owned. He needed to move, for he and Jacob had many animals. There was not enough food for all of them to live together in the same part of the country.

Joseph's Dreams

Genesis 37

One of Jacob's twelve sons was named Joseph. He was the youngest in the family, except for Benjamin.

When Joseph was seventeen years old, he went out into the fields one day. He went to help his ten older brothers, who were taking care of the sheep and the goats. But while he was there he saw his brothers do something they should not have done. That night when he got home, he told his father. This was a good thing to do, for his father could talk to his brothers about what they had done. Then maybe they would not do it again. But of course his brothers were angry with him for telling on them.

Joseph was his father's favorite son, so his father gave him a beautiful coat. But this made his brothers jealous.

One night Joseph had a strange dream, and the next morning he told his family about it.

"In my dream," he said, "all of us were out in the field tying bundles of grain stalks. Then your bundles stood around mine and bowed to it!"

This dream made his brothers even angrier. They thought Joseph was saying that they should bow to him as though he were their king.

Then Joseph had another dream. This time he dreamed that the sun, the moon, and eleven stars all bowed to him. His brothers were angrier than ever. They knew Joseph was talking about them when he talked about the eleven stars. And the sun and moon must have meant their father and mother.

When Joseph told his father about the dream, his father scolded him.

"Do you think your mother and brothers and I are going to bow to you?" he asked. "Don't be foolish!"

Soon after this his brothers took their father's sheep to Shechem to find grass for them to eat. It took several days to walk there.

Some time later Jacob said to Joseph, "Go and find your brothers. See how they are getting along and how the sheep are." So Joseph went to find them.

But his brothers weren't at Shechem. He was wandering around in the fields looking for them when he met a man who told him, "Your brothers are at Dothan. I heard them say that they were going there." So Joseph went on to Dothan.

When his brothers saw him coming, they began talking to each other about killing him.

"Here comes that dreamer," they said. "Come on, let's kill him and throw him into a well. We'll say

Joseph was Jacob's favorite child. Jacob gave Joseph a beautiful coat, but this made Joseph's brothers jealous and angry.

some wild animal has eaten him. Then we'll see what happens to his dreams!"

When Joseph's brother Reuben heard the others talking like that, he didn't like it at all. He wanted to save Joseph, so he talked his brothers into putting Joseph in the well without hurting him. Reuben planned to come back and take Joseph out of the well.

Joseph came, and his brothers grabbed him. They took away his beautiful coat and put him into a well that did not have any water in it.

As they sat down to eat their lunches, they saw some men coming along on camels. These men were merchants who were taking things to sell in the country of Egypt. When Joseph's brother Judah saw them, he said, "Let's sell Joseph to those men! We'll get rid of him and get some money, too."

The other brothers thought this was a good idea. So they pulled Joseph out of the well and sold him for twenty pieces of silver. The merchants put him on a camel and took him far away to the land of Egypt.

Reuben was not there when Joseph was sold. When he came back to the well to get Joseph out, he was very sad.

"Joseph is gone!" he exclaimed. "What shall I do now?"

The brothers killed a young goat and dipped Joseph's coat in the blood. They took the coat to their father and told him they had found it on the ground.

Joseph dreamed one night that all of his brothers would bow down to him as if he were their king. This dream came true many years later.

"Is it Joseph's coat?" they asked.

Jacob knew it was and began to cry. "Yes," he said, "it is Joseph's coat. A wild animal must have eaten him. Joseph is dead." Jacob said that he would be sad and cry about his boy all the rest of his life.

STORY 21

Strange Dreams in a Jail

Genesis 39–41

The men who took Joseph to Egypt sold him to a man named Potiphar. He was an Egyptian army officer. Joseph became his servant and lived in his house.

The Lord helped Joseph work hard. His master was pleased with him and put him in charge of all his other servants. God blessed Potiphar because Joseph was in his home.

But after a while Potiphar's wife wanted Joseph to do something very wrong. Joseph said no, and that made her angry. She decided to get even with him, so she told her husband a lie. She said that Joseph had tried to hurt her. Her husband believed her and put Joseph in jail.

One day Pharaoh, the king of Egypt, became angry with two important men. One of them was his baker. The other was the man who brought him wine whenever he wanted a drink. Pharaoh put them both in the jail where Joseph was.

While they were in jail, both of these men had dreams one night. When Joseph saw them the next morning, they looked very sad.

"What's the matter?" he asked. "Why are you so sad this morning?"

"We had strange dreams last night," they told him. "But there is no one to tell us what they mean."

"Tell me your dreams," Joseph said, "and I'll ask God what they mean."

So they did, and Joseph was able to tell them what their dreams meant. He said to the wine officer, "When you get out of jail, ask the king to let me out too."

Both dreams came true just as Joseph said. The king sent a messenger to the jail to bring back the man who was in charge of his wine. I'm sorry to say that the man promptly forgot all about Joseph. The man didn't bother to tell Pharaoh about Joseph or try to get him out of jail.

Two years later the king had a dream. Pharaoh saw himself standing beside the Nile River. He saw seven cows coming up out of the water. They were fat and healthy, and they went into a meadow to eat grass. Then seven more cows came up out of the river. These cows were thin, and they ate the fat cows! Just then Pharaoh woke up.

Soon the king went back to sleep and had another dream. This time he thought he saw seven pieces of grain growing on one stalk. They were plump pieces, filled with grain for making bread. But afterward seven pieces of dried-up grain grew on the stalk. They ate up the seven good pieces! Then Pharaoh woke up and realized it was a dream.

The dreams bothered the king so much that he sent for all the wise men of Egypt. He told them his dreams, but they couldn't tell Pharaoh what his dreams meant.

Then the man in charge of the king's wine remembered the young man in jail. He remembered that Joseph had told him and the chief baker what their dreams meant. The man told Pharaoh that the dreams came true just as Joseph had said.

So the king sent for Joseph, who quickly shaved and put on other clothes. When he was brought to Pharaoh, the king said to Joseph, "I had a dream last night. No one has been able to tell me what it means, but I'm told that you can."

Joseph said he could not do it, but that God would. So Pharaoh told Joseph the dream about the cows and the dream about the stalks of grain.

Joseph told the king that both dreams meant the same thing. God was telling Pharaoh what was going to happen. The seven fat cows and the seven good pieces of grain meant that there would be seven years of wonderful crops. Everyone's gardens and all the crops in the fields would grow. The seven thin cows and the seven dried-up pieces of grain meant there would be seven bad years. Nothing would grow at all. People would be hungry, for nothing would grow in their gardens and fields.

Joseph told Pharaoh to put someone in charge of saving food. This person should make the people of Egypt save part of their crops during the seven good years. Then, during the bad years, the people would have enough food. The king thought this was a good idea, and he put Joseph in charge!

STORY 22

Joseph's Dreams Come True

Genesis 41–42

Pharaoh didn't send Joseph back to jail but made a great man of him instead. The king took off his own ring and put it on Joseph's finger. Pharaoh dressed him in beautiful clothing and put a gold chain around his neck. Joseph was in charge of all the land of Egypt and was almost as great as the king.

During the next seven years all the farms had good crops, just as Joseph had said. He went to all the farmers and made them give some of their grain to Pharaoh. Joseph took this grain and stored it in the nearby cities.

Then the seven years of good crops ended, and the seven years of poor crops began. Soon everyone was hungry because there was so little to eat. When all their food was gone, the people came to Pharaoh to ask for something to eat.

"Joseph is in charge," Pharaoh said. "Go to him, and he will tell you what to do."

Then Joseph opened up the buildings where the grain was kept and sold it to the people.

Joseph's brothers were still living in the land of Canaan when the famine came. Soon their grain was gone, and they needed food for their father, Jacob, and for their families.

Jacob said to them, "I hear there is grain in Egypt. Go and buy some for us so we won't starve to death."

So Joseph's ten older brothers got on their donkeys and rode for many days until they came to Egypt.

Since Joseph was the governor of Egypt, he was in charge of selling grain. His brothers bowed down to him. They didn't recognize him in his Egyptian robes, but Joseph knew them right away.

Imagine Joseph's surprise and joy to see his brothers again, even though they had been mean to him. But he pretended he didn't know them at all. He spoke loudly to them and asked, "Where are you from?"

"From the land of Canaan," they said. "We have come to buy food."

Then Joseph said, "No, you are spies. You have come here to see if we are weak, so that you can bring an army and attack us."

"Oh no, sir," his brothers answered. "We have

Joseph said that there would be seven years of good crops. Then there would be seven years of famine when no crops would grow. The Egyptians saved their grain during the seven good years.

come to buy food. We are all one man's sons. We are men who speak the truth. We are not spies." They said their youngest brother was with their father, far away in the land of Canaan, and one brother was dead.

Joseph still pretended not to know them. He said he would find out if they were telling the truth or not. He would send one of them back to Canaan to get their youngest brother. All the others would have to stay in Egypt during that time. If there was no younger brother, he said, he would know they were spies.

Then he put them in jail for three days.

On the third day Joseph talked with his brothers again. This time he said that only one of them had to stay. All the others could go home and take food to their families. One had to stay so that the others would come back again with their youngest brother.

When his brothers heard this, they were very sad. They said to each other that God was punishing them for selling Joseph long ago. Reuben, who had planned to take Joseph out of the well, said to his brothers, "Didn't I tell you not to do it? But you wouldn't listen to me."

Joseph listened to them talking to each other. They didn't know he could speak their language, for he had not been talking directly to them. Another person had been explaining what they were saying. But of course Joseph understood every word they said.

He turned away to cry. Then he had Simeon tied up while all the others watched. Simeon was the one he chose to stay in Egypt while the others went home for their youngest brother, Benjamin.

Then Joseph told his servants to fill his brothers' sacks with grain. He said to put at the tops of their sacks the money they had paid for the grain. But he didn't tell his brothers that the money was there.

Finally their donkeys were loaded, and all except Simeon started traveling back home to Canaan. That night when they stopped to eat, they opened a sack to get some food. There was the money right at the top of the sack! They were afraid, for they didn't know how it got there.

STORY 23

Will Benjamin Be Safe?

Genesis 42–43

After many hard days of travel Joseph's older brothers finally returned home. When they got there they told their father what had happened in Egypt.

As they unloaded their donkeys and emptied the grain out of their sacks, what a surprise they discovered! Each of them found his money at the top of his sack, lying right on top of the grain. The money wasn't in just one sack—it was in all of them!

When Jacob saw the money, he was afraid. He

didn't know what was going to happen to his family. He said, "Joseph is gone, and Simeon is gone. And now you want Benjamin, too."

Then Reuben said to his father, "I'd give up my two sons if I wouldn't be able to bring my little brother, Benjamin, back home! I will take care of him."

But Jacob said Benjamin couldn't go because Joseph was already dead. If anything happened to Benjamin, it would be too much to bear.

The famine became worse and worse. There was no food anywhere. Soon the grain from Egypt was almost gone. So Jacob said to his sons, "Go back to Egypt and buy us a little more food."

But Judah told his father they couldn't go unless Benjamin was with them. The governor had told them, "You must not return without your brother."

"I'll see that nothing happens to him," Judah said. "If I don't bring him back safely, I will be to blame forever. We should not have stayed at home so long, for we could have gone to Egypt and been back by now."

Finally their father agreed. He told his sons to take presents to the governor. He said to take honey and nuts and spices. They were to take money, too. Then Jacob prayed for his sons. He begged God to have the governor be kind to them, for if his children were taken away from him, he would be so sad he would die.

The brothers took the presents, the money, and their brother Benjamin and went back to Egypt.

Joseph and His Little Brother

Genesis 43

Soon Joseph saw his brothers standing in front of him again. When Joseph saw Benjamin with them, he said to his servant, "Take these men home to my palace. Get dinner ready for them, for they are going to eat with me."

Joseph's brothers were afraid when they saw where the servant was taking them. They thought Joseph was going to keep them as his slaves and never let them go home again. They thought it was because of the money that was found in their sacks.

Joseph's servant told them not to worry. He said there was nothing to fear. Then he brought their brother Simeon to them. Simeon was the one who had been left as a prisoner while the other brothers went home for Benjamin.

When Joseph arrived, they gave him the presents they had brought. And they bowed down low in front of him. It was just the way Joseph had dreamed they would do someday.

Joseph spoke kindly to them. He asked, "Is your father well—the old man you told me about? Is he still living?"

They answered, "Yes, he is still alive and in good health." And they bowed to him again.

When Joseph saw his brother Benjamin he said,

"This must be your youngest brother. May God be good to you, my son."

Then Joseph hurried away to find a place where he could be alone. He went into his bedroom and started crying because he was so happy to see his little brother again. But then he washed his face. And when he came out again, he kept back the tears so that his brothers didn't know he had been crying.

"It's time to eat!" said Joseph. He ate by himself at one table, and his brothers sat at another table. That's because Egyptians never ate with God's people, and everyone thought Joseph was an Egyptian!

Joseph seated the oldest brother at the head of the table. He told the next oldest to sit next to that brother. And he continued in the same way down the line according to his brothers' ages. Who could have told him their ages, they wondered! But you and I know that no one had to tell him, for he knew it all the time!

Joseph had waiters take food from his table to the table where the brothers were. He had them give Benjamin five times as much as any of the others! You see, Joseph loved Benjamin more than the rest because he and Benjamin had the same mother, Rachel. She died when Benjamin was born. (All the brothers had the same father, Jacob, but there were four different mothers.)

A Big Surprise

Genesis 44–45

Joseph told one of his servants to fill his brothers' sacks with grain. He said to put back their money in the top of the sacks, just as he had said to do before.

"And," said Joseph, "put my silver cup in the sack of the youngest boy, Benjamin." So that is what the servant did.

In the morning, as soon as it was light, the men got on their donkeys and started back to Canaan.

But they were hardly out of the city when Joseph told his servant to chase after them. He said to stop them and ask them why they had stolen his silver cup. So the servant hurried and caught up with them.

The brothers were very surprised. They wondered what the servant was talking about when he asked them about the cup.

"We would never do such a terrible thing as to steal the governor's cup," they said.

"If one of us stole it, let him die," they said. "And all the rest of us will go back to Egypt and be slaves."

The servant said, "Only the one who stole the cup will be a slave. The rest of you may go home."

Then the brothers took down their sacks from

the backs of their donkeys. They opened the sacks so the servant could look. He began with the sack of the oldest, but the cup wasn't there. He went on down the line, but none of them had the cup. Then he came to Benjamin. And there was the cup, right at the top of Benjamin's sack.

Now the poor brothers didn't know what to do. They tore their clothes because they were so sad and upset. Finally they loaded up their donkeys and went back to the city with Benjamin and the servant.

When they saw Joseph they all bowed way down in front of him. Joseph pretended that he thought Benjamin had really stolen his cup. He said they should have known that he would find out about it.

Judah stood up and spoke to Joseph for all of them. "Oh, what shall we say to you, my lord?" he asked. "God knows about our sins. Now we are all your slaves."

"No," Joseph said. "Only the one who stole the cup will be my slave. The rest of you may go on home to your father."

Judah begged Joseph not to keep Benjamin. He explained that Jacob, his father, had said that if anything happened to Benjamin, he would be so sad he would die. Then Judah begged Joseph to let him stay and be a slave instead of Benjamin. He asked Joseph to let Benjamin go home to his father.

Joseph couldn't stand it any longer. He ordered all of his servants to leave the room. When Joseph was left alone with his brothers, he began to cry. His brothers watched in surprise.

Finally, when he could speak, he told them, "I am Joseph! Oh, tell me more about my father!"

His brothers were too surprised and afraid to say anything. Then Joseph called them over to him.

"I am your brother Joseph!" he said again.

Then at last they realized what he was saying. How excited they were as they all hugged and kissed each other!

Joseph told them to stop being sad about what they had done to him, because God had turned it all into good. Joseph explained that the famine would last another five years, for God had said that there would be no crops for all that time.

"Hurry back to my father," he said. "Tell him that his son Joseph says, 'God has made me ruler over all of Egypt. Come down to me, and you will live in the best part of the land. Bring your children, your sheep and your goats, and everything else you have, and I will take care of you.' Tell my father how great I am in Egypt, and tell him about all you have seen. Hurry home and bring my father here."

Then Joseph hugged his brother Benjamin and cried again, for he was so glad to see him. Benjamin cried too, and so did all the brothers. Then they talked happily together, for their tears were happy tears.

Back Together Again

Genesis 45–47

When Pharaoh heard that Joseph's brothers had come, he was very glad. He told Joseph to have them go and get their father and their wives and children. He said to bring them all to Egypt, where there was plenty to eat.

"Take some of my wagons for your wives and little ones to ride in," Pharaoh said. "Don't bother to bring any of your things, for I will give you everything you need."

Then Joseph gave new clothes to each of his brothers, giving Benjamin more than any of the rest! And he sent his father twenty donkey-loads of food and other good things.

When they finally arrived home, how happy everyone was!

"Joseph is alive!" the brothers shouted. "He is governor over all the land of Egypt!"

Jacob did not believe them at first—it seemed too wonderful to be true. But when he saw Pharaoh's wagons, he knew that his sons were telling the truth.

"Joseph is alive!" he said at last. "I will go and see him now before I die."

So Jacob and his sons and their families all left their homes in Canaan and started off for the land of Egypt. Jacob stopped to worship God at Beersheba, where his father, Isaac, had built an altar many years before.

That night God said to Jacob, "Don't be afraid to go down to Egypt. While you are there I will make your family grow into millions of people." God said that he would take care of Jacob in Egypt. And when the time came for him to die, Joseph would be by his side.

So Jacob and his sons and their families left Beersheba and went on to Egypt. They took their cows with them and everything else that belonged to them.

Jacob sent Judah ahead to tell Joseph that his father was on the way. When Joseph heard this, he jumped into his chariot and raced out to meet him. He and his father cried for joy when they finally saw each other again. They had been apart for many years.

Israel (that was Jacob's other name, remember?) said to Joseph, "Now I can die in peace, for I have seen you again. To think that you are still alive!"

Then Joseph invited some of his brothers to come with him to meet Pharaoh and to tell him that they had arrived with their sheep and cows. When Pharaoh asked them what kind of work they did, they told him they took care of sheep and cows just as their grandfathers had done. Joseph told them to say this because it was the truth. Also Joseph wanted Pharaoh to let them live in Goshen, which was the best part of the land of

Egypt for raising animals. That's just what Pharaoh did. He said, "Let your family live in Goshen."

Then Joseph took his father to meet Pharaoh. And Jacob blessed the king.

STORY *27*

Jacob Blesses His Children

Genesis 48–50

Jacob lived in the land of Goshen with his children and their families for seventeen years. But at last the time came for him to die. He became very sick and sent for his son Joseph.

So Joseph took his two boys, Manasseh and Ephraim, and went to visit his father. Jacob sat up in bed and told them how kind God had been to him during his long life. He told them about the time when God had spoken to him in a dream. It was the dream about a stairway going up to heaven, with angels walking up and down on it.

Then Joseph told his father that he had brought his two boys with him so that Jacob could bless them. Jacob put his arms around them and kissed them. And he asked God to do good things for them. What a happy day that was for Jacob and Joseph and the two boys!

Then Jacob, also known as Israel, called in all his other sons and blessed each one of them. He told them he was gong to die, but that God would be with them and bring them back to the land of Canaan. He told his sons where to bury him. He said to bury his body in the cave where his grandparents (Abraham and Sarah) and his parents (Isaac and Rebekah) were buried.

When Jacob had finished all he had to say to his sons, he lay back on the bed and died. Joseph kissed his father and cried. Then he told his servants to get his father's body ready to be buried. For seventy days all the Egyptians showed how sad they were that Jacob had died.

Joseph told Pharaoh that he had promised to bury his father back in Canaan. So Pharaoh let Joseph leave the country with his brothers for a while.

After the funeral, Joseph's brothers were afraid. Now their father was no longer able to help them. So they thought that Joseph would get back at them for all the bad things they had done to him. But he told them not to be afraid. He said he knew they had wanted to hurt him by selling him as a slave. But God had turned what was bad into something good. God had put him in Egypt, where he could save many people from starving during the famine. Joseph's kind words made his brothers feel better.

Joseph stayed in Egypt the rest of his life. He lived long enough to see his great-grandchildren! But after many years he told his brothers that the time had come for him to die. He asked that his bones be taken back to Canaan when God took the people of Israel back there again. Then Joseph died. He was 110 years old.

It wasn't until four hundred years later that the people of Israel went back into the Promised Land of Canaan. When they did, they took along Joseph's bones just as Joseph had asked.

THE
BOOK
about
Moses

A princess found a baby boy in the little boat his mother made for him. The princess brought him to the palace and named him Moses. He became her son—a grandson of Pharaoh, Egypt's king!

STORY 28

A Princess Finds a Baby

Exodus 1–2

Jacob had died, and his son Joseph had died. As time went on, Joseph's brothers grew old and died too. After hundreds of years, Jacob's grandchildren and their children became a great nation in Egypt. There were so many of them that they filled the land.

Then a new king began to rule over Egypt. He didn't care at all about Jacob's family. He didn't care about all that Joseph had done to save Egypt. When the new king saw how many people from Jacob's family there were in the land, he was afraid of them. He thought that if his enemies came to fight against him, Jacob's huge family would help his enemies. Then they might run away. He didn't want that to happen. He wanted them to stay in Egypt to do his work.

So this wicked king got his Egyptian people to be very unkind to Jacob's family (now known as the Israelites or the people of Israel). The Egyptians made slaves of them. The Israelites had to build houses for the Egyptians and work in their fields.

But the worse the Israelites were treated, the bigger their families grew to be. God had promised Abraham and Isaac and Jacob that their children would become a great nation. And now God was doing as he had promised.

Pharaoh told his people that whenever they saw a baby boy among the Israelites, they must not let him live. What a mean king he was! But God kept his people safe from this evil king.

Now I'm going to tell you what happened to one of the little Israelite babies. He was a baby boy who became one of the greatest men in all the world when he grew up.

His mother and father loved him very much, and they were afraid of the Egyptian king. So the baby's mother hid him at home for three months after he was born. Then she made a little basket from the long weeds that grew by the river. She smeared the outside of it with tar to keep the water out. It was a little boat that would float safely on the water.

The mother put her baby boy in the little boat. Then she floated it out among the bushes at the edge of the river. The baby's sister, whose name was Miriam, hid there and watched to see what would happen to her little brother. She was ready to help him in any way she could.

Soon a princess came along. Pharaoh was her father. She had come to wash herself in the river. As she and her maids were walking along the edge of the river, she saw the little boat in the bushes. She sent one of her maids to get it and bring it to her. The princess wanted to open the basket and see what was inside. When she did, there was a little baby boy! She felt sorry for him and wanted to adopt him as her own son.

"This must be one of the Israelite children," she exclaimed. Miriam, the baby's sister, went over to the king's daughter. The girl asked, "May I go and get one of the Israelite women to take care of the baby for you?" The princess said yes, so Miriam ran home to get her mother! When her mother came, the princess said to her, "Take care of this baby for me, and I will pay you well!"

So the baby's mother took him home again!

When the little baby was older, the princess sent for him to come and live in her palace and be her son. That made him a prince. She called him Moses, an Egyptian word that means "taken out," because she had taken him out of the water. Moses lived in the palace for many years.

STORY 29

Moses Runs Away

Exodus 2

One day when Moses was grown up, he went to visit his own people, the Israelites. He wanted to see how they were getting along. While he was with them, he saw an Egyptian hitting an Israelite. Of course this made Moses very angry, for he was an Israelite, too. Moses looked to see if anyone was watching. Then he killed the Egyptian and hid his body in the sand.

The next day as he was walking around, Moses saw two Israelites quarreling. He scolded the man who was in the wrong, asking him why he had hit the other man. This made the man who had done wrong very angry.

"You can't tell me what to do," he shouted. "Are you going to kill me the way you killed that Egyptian yesterday?" Then Moses was afraid. He understood that someone had seen him kill the Egyptian and that everyone knew about it.

When Pharaoh heard what Moses had done, he wanted to have Moses killed. But Moses ran far away to the land of Midian. He sat down beside a well, where he tried to think what to do next. Soon some girls came to get water. There were seven of them, all sisters. They wanted to water their father's sheep, but some shepherds who were standing beside the well told them to go away.

Moses told the shepherds to be quiet, and he helped the girls water their sheep. When the girls got home, their father asked why they had come back so quickly. They told him that an Egyptian had saved them from the shepherds. And he had helped them get the water.

"Where is the man?" their father asked. "Why didn't you bring him home with you?" He told them to go back and find the man and invite him home for dinner. So they did, and Moses went home with them. He liked the family so much that he stayed and helped them. He even married one of the girls and lived there for many years, caring for their father's sheep.

STORY 30
A Voice in a Burning Bush

Exodus 2–4

While Moses was living in the land of Midian, the Egyptians were being very hard on the people of Israel. Finally the Israelites cried to God because they had to work so hard. God heard them and looked down from heaven and felt bad for them. Soon after that, God gave Moses a job to do. This is how it happened.

One day Moses was taking care of his family's sheep out in the country near Mount Sinai. Suddenly he saw fire coming out of a bush. Moses ran over to the bush and saw a strange thing. The bush was on fire but didn't burn up! Just then God called to him from the bush, "Moses! Moses!"

We can hardly imagine how surprised and frightened Moses was. But he said, "Yes, Lord, I am listening."

God told him, "Don't come any closer. But do take off your sandals, because the place where you stand is holy ground." The ground was holy because God was there.

God said, "I am the God of your people, the people of Israel—the God of Abraham, Isaac, and Jacob." Moses hid his face, for he was afraid to look at God.

Then the Lord told Moses that he had seen how sad the Israelites were. He had heard their cries for help. And he had come down from heaven to set them free from the Egyptians.

There was a new king in Egypt by this time. The new king was called Pharaoh just like all the other kings of Egypt. The Lord told Moses to go to Pharaoh and tell him to stop hurting the people of Israel. And God told Moses he was to lead the people out of Egypt. They were to go back to Canaan, and it would become their very own land. On the way, they were to stop right at this mountain where God was talking with Moses.

But Moses said he was sure that his people would not listen to him. No one would believe that the Lord had really sent him.

God told Moses to throw his shepherd's rod on the ground. Moses did, and God changed it into a snake! Moses was afraid of it and ran away.

Then the Lord said, "Grab it by the tail." Moses did, and it changed back into a shepherd's rod again!

God said to Moses, "Now put your hand inside your coat." When Moses took it out, his hand had turned white! It was covered with white spots from a disease called leprosy.

"Put your hand back inside your coat again," God

Moses was surprised to see a bush on fire that kept burning and burning. It didn't burn up because God was there!

said. When Moses took it out this time, it was well again!

God gave Moses power to do these two wonderful miracles. He did it so that when the Israelites saw him do them, they would believe that God had sent him. But if they still would not believe him, Moses was to take some water out of the Nile River and pour it on the ground. The water would change to blood!

Moses had a brother whose name was Aaron. God said that Aaron could go with Moses and make the speeches to Pharaoh and the people of Israel. God would tell Moses what to say, and Moses would tell Aaron what to say. Then Aaron would tell the Israelites and the king what God wanted them to know.

When the Lord had finished talking with him from the burning bush, Moses went back home. He asked his father-in-law, whose name was Jethro, if he could return to Egypt to visit his people. Jethro said yes.

STORY 31

Bricks without Straw

Exodus 4–7

The Lord told Moses' brother, Aaron, to go and meet Moses out in the desert. When Aaron got to Mount Sinai, Moses told him about everything that had happened. And he told his brother what God wanted them to say and do.

Moses and Aaron went to Egypt together. Aaron talked with the Israelite leaders, and Moses showed them the two miracles. Moses threw down his shepherd's rod, and it became a snake. Then he put his hand inside his coat, and it became white with leprosy. When the leaders saw these two miracles, they believed that God had sent Moses and Aaron. They believed that Moses was to lead them out of Egypt.

Then Moses and Aaron went to Pharaoh. They told him, "The Lord God of Israel says, 'Let my people leave Egypt and worship me in the desert.'"

"Huh!" Pharaoh said. "Who is the Lord, and why should I obey him? I've never heard of that god, and I certainly won't let you keep these Israelite people from working."

One of the jobs of the Israelite slaves was to dig clay and make bricks by drying the clay in the sun. They mixed the clay with pieces of straw to make the bricks strong.

Pharaoh's leaders had been giving them this straw. But Pharaoh became so angry that he said from now on they must get their own straw. And they still had to make just as many bricks as before. Pharaoh said the people were lazy. That was why they wanted time to go and worship their God.

So the people of Israel had to go out into the fields and gather straw. They worked very hard, but they could not make as many bricks as when the straw was brought to them. The Egyptians who were in charge beat the Israelite leaders.

These leaders of God's people told Pharaoh that he wasn't being fair. How could he expect them to make as many bricks, now that he was not giving them the straw?

He replied, "You're lazy! That's why you say, 'Let us go and worship the Lord.'" He told them to get to work, and he said they wouldn't get any more straw.

Then the Israelites saw that they were in real trouble. The leaders went to Moses and Aaron and accused them of making things worse for them instead of better.

Moses told God how upset he was. He asked, "Why did you send me, Lord?" Then Moses said he had only made things worse for the people since he came. The Egyptians were harder on the Israelites than before.

"Just wait," the Lord told Moses, "and you'll see what I am going to do. Tell my people that I will set them free—they will no longer be slaves. They will be my special people, and I will be their God. I will lead them into the land I promised long ago to Abraham, Isaac, and Jacob."

Moses told the Israelites what God said, but they wouldn't listen to him anymore.

Then the Lord sent Moses and Aaron to talk to Pharaoh again. "When Pharaoh tells you to do a miracle, throw your shepherd's rod on the ground," the Lord said. "It will change into a snake, just as it did before."

So Moses and Aaron went to Pharaoh. Aaron threw down his rod, and sure enough, it changed into a snake. Then Pharaoh called for his people who did magic. They brought some shepherds' rods and threw them down. And their rods changed into snakes too. But Aaron's snake swallowed up all the other snakes! Even so, Pharaoh wouldn't let the people go.

STORY 32

The Terrible Troubles Begin

Exodus 7–8

The Lord told Moses to go to Pharaoh the next morning when he would be taking a walk beside the river. When Pharaoh came along, Moses was to go up to him. He was to say, "The God of the Israelites has sent me to tell you, 'Let my people go. They must worship me in the desert.'" Then God told Moses more things that he and Aaron were to do.

The next morning Moses and Aaron went to the river. Sure enough, Pharaoh was out for a walk, so Moses told Pharaoh what the Lord had said. But Pharaoh refused to let the people go.

Then Moses hit the Nile River with his shepherd's rod while Pharaoh and his men were watching. When Moses did this, the water in the river changed to blood! Then Aaron pointed his shepherd's rod toward other streams and ponds. Suddenly all the water in Egypt changed to blood! So the fish died, and the Egyptians had no water to drink.

The Egyptians dug holes in the ground near the river. They needed to get water good enough to drink, for the blood stayed for seven days.

The Lord now told Moses what to say to Pharaoh next. Unless he let the people go, God would send millions of frogs to cover Egypt. They would get inside the Egyptians' houses and even jump into their beds.

Pharaoh wouldn't let the people go.

So God told Aaron to point his shepherd's rod over the rivers of Egypt. Suddenly, millions of frogs came up out of the water.

Now Pharaoh and the people of Egypt were in real trouble. Frogs were everywhere. He called for Moses and Aaron and asked them to pray that God would take the frogs away. "If you do," Pharaoh said, "I'll let the people go to give sacrifices to your God."

"When do you want the frogs to die?" Moses asked.

Pharaoh replied, "Tomorrow."

So the next day Moses prayed to the Lord, and the Lord did as Moses asked. The frogs in the houses and towns and fields all died, and the people gathered them in great heaps. The smell of dead frogs was all over the land. It was terrible!

But when Pharaoh saw that the frogs were dead, he wouldn't let the people go.

Then the Lord commanded Aaron to strike the

dust on the ground with his shepherd's rod. And the dust changed into very small biting insects called lice, which covered the people and the cows.

But Pharaoh's heart was wicked. He wouldn't let the people go.

STORY 33
Flies, Boils, and Hail
Exodus 8–9

The Lord told Moses to get up early again the next morning to meet Pharaoh as he went down to the river. Moses was to tell him again to let the people go. If he still refused to let them go, the Lord would send flies all over Egypt.

Moses did as God said. But again Pharaoh said no, he wouldn't let the people go. So God sent the flies, and they covered the whole country.

But in the land of Goshen, where the Israelites lived, there were no flies at all. That's because the Lord did not send them to the place where his people were.

Pharaoh was very upset about the flies, just as he had been about the frogs. He called for Moses and Aaron. And he told them, "All right, the people of Israel can sacrifice gifts to their God. But they must stay in Egypt to do it."

Moses told Pharaoh that God's people had to travel for three days into the desert to sacrifice gifts to the Lord. That is what God had told them to do. So Pharaoh said they could go, but not that far.

"Now please," he begged Moses, "pray to your God for me." Moses said he would. Then he warned Pharaoh not to change his mind again about letting the people go. But that's just what Pharaoh did. When he saw that the flies were gone, he wouldn't let the people go!

Next the Lord had Moses tell Pharaoh that a sickness would kill the animals of the Egyptians. But the Israelites' animals would not be hurt at all.

Pharaoh still said no, the people could not go.

So the Lord sent the sickness. The Egyptian cows and horses and camels and sheep began to die. Pharaoh sent some men to see if any of the Israelites' animals were dead, but not one of them was even sick! When Pharaoh heard this, his heart grew even harder and more wicked than before, and he would not let the people go!

Then the Lord told Moses and Aaron to stand where Pharaoh could see them. God said to toss ashes into the air. When Moses did that, sores broke out on the Egyptians and their animals.

But Pharaoh's heart was still wicked, and he wouldn't let the people go!

So the Lord told Moses to get up early again the next morning. He said to tell Pharaoh that God would send a hailstorm such as there had never been before. Moses told Pharaoh to get all his animals in from the fields quickly, for everything out in the storm would die.

Flies, flies everywhere. They filled the houses and filled the air outside. No one could get away from them.

Then the Lord told Moses to point his hand toward heaven. Suddenly a terrible hailstorm began, and lightning kept flashing in the sky. Never before had there been such a storm in Egypt. The hail beat down everything in the fields, killing both people and animals.

But in the land of Goshen, where the people of Israel lived, no hail fell at all!

Then Pharaoh sent for Moses and Aaron and said, "I have sinned. The Lord is good, and my people and I are wicked. Beg the Lord to stop the terrible thunder and hail, and I will let you go right away."

Moses said that as soon as he was out of the city, he would ask the Lord to stop the thunder and hail.

So Moses did that. When he prayed, the thunder and hail stopped. But when Pharaoh saw that it had stopped, he changed his mind and wouldn't let the people go!

STORY 34

Locusts and Darkness

Exodus 10

Moses and Aaron went to Pharaoh again. They told him that if he wouldn't obey the Lord, the next day the Lord would send locusts. They would eat everything that was left. Locusts are like grasshoppers, but they eat gardens and crops.

Pharaoh said, "All right, go and worship the Lord

your God. But which of the people do you want to go?" Moses answered that all of the people of Israel were to go and have a religious holiday. He would take young and old, sons and daughters, sheep and cows.

Pharaoh said that only the men could go—the women and children had to stay in Egypt. Then the king had his men drag Moses and Aaron away.

The Lord told Moses to lift his hand toward heaven and the locusts would come. Then the Lord sent an east wind. It kept blowing all that day and all night, too. In the morning the wind brought so many locusts that they filled the sky and covered the ground! They were all over Pharaoh's palace and in the houses of all the Egyptians. The locusts ate everything that the hail had left.

Pharaoh quickly called for Moses and Aaron and said, "I have sinned." He asked Moses to forgive him only this one more time and to pray that God would take the locusts away.

So Moses went out and prayed. The Lord sent a strong west wind that blew the locusts into the Red Sea, where they drowned.

But when Pharaoh saw that the locusts were gone, he wouldn't let the people go!

The Lord told Moses to hold up his hand toward heaven again. Then it became dark all over the land. The Egyptians couldn't see one another for three days—they couldn't even leave their homes.

But in the houses of the Israelites, it was as light as usual.

Then Pharaoh called for Moses and said, "All right, go and worship the Lord! Take your children with you, but not your sheep and cows." But Moses told him they needed their animals as gifts to God. That made Pharaoh angry. He told Moses to get out of his sight and never come back again. If he did, Pharaoh said he would kill him.

STORY 35
The Worst Punishment of All
Exodus 11–12

Moses had one more message for Pharaoh. He said that God was going to send one last terrible punishment. The Lord himself was soon coming to Egypt in the middle of the night. He would cause the oldest son in every Egyptian home to die. Even Pharaoh's oldest son would die. There would be a cry of great sadness all through the land. But not one of the Israelite children would be hurt in any way. Then Pharaoh would know that he and his people were the ones the Lord was punishing, and not the Israelites. Moses told Pharaoh that after this punishment the Egyptians would beg Moses to take God's people and leave the country.

Moses left in great anger, letting Pharaoh sit there.

Then the Lord told the Israelites to get ready to leave Egypt. He told them to ask the Egyptians for silver and gold jewelry to take with them. And the Lord made the Egyptians want to give their jewels to the people of Israel.

The Lord said that each family in Israel should get a lamb on the tenth day of the month. They should kill it on the fourth evening after that. Then they were to sprinkle the lamb's blood on each side and on top of the door to their home. They were to stay in their houses and not come out again until morning. That night the angel of the Lord would come and kill the oldest child in every home that didn't have blood on the door.

On that fourth evening the people were to roast the lamb, God said. And everyone in the house was to eat some of it. As they ate they had to be dressed to travel, with their shoes on and their walking sticks in their hands. And they were to eat in a hurry, for the Lord would go through the land that night. When he caused the oldest sons of the Egyptians to die, at last Pharaoh would really let them go.

God promised that he would pass over the houses with blood on the door. He would not hurt anyone inside. So the Israelites' lamb supper that night would always be called the Lord's "Passover."

At last the terrible night came. In the middle of the night the Lord passed through the land. Wherever he saw the marks of blood, he passed over that house and no one there was harmed. But there were no marks of blood on the houses of the Egyptians. The Lord caused the oldest son in every one of those homes to die. Even Pharaoh's oldest son died that night.

The king got up in the night with all his people. There was a cry of great sadness through all the land, for in every home the oldest son was dead.

Pharaoh called for Moses and Aaron and told them to leave Egypt at once and to take all the people of Israel with them. "Take all your sheep and cows," he begged, "and leave tonight." All the Egyptians begged them to go quickly, for they were afraid the Lord would kill every one of them.

So God's people left Egypt that night, carrying their clothes on their shoulders. The Egyptians gave them silver and gold jewelry, and fine clothes, too. So they went away with great riches. Many Egyptians went with them.

The lamb that was killed in every Israelite home that night was in some ways like Jesus, our Savior. The lamb died for the people, and its blood saved them. That is what happened again many years later, when Jesus came as the Lamb of God. He died for each of us.

And just as God did not punish those who had lamb's blood on their houses, so it will be when Jesus comes again. He will not punish those whose hearts have been made clean from sin. Those who love Jesus are clean because of the blood he gave when he died.

As the Israelites left Egypt, they took the body of Joseph with them. After four hundred years, his dying wish was being fulfilled.

A Path through the Sea

Exodus 13–15

At last the people of Israel were free. What a wonderful feeling it must have been to no longer be Pharaoh's slaves!

The Lord led them toward the Red Sea. When they came to the edge of the desert, they set up their tents and made camp.

As they traveled, the Lord was very kind to them. He went ahead of them in a cloud to show them the way. The cloud was shaped like a pillar reaching up toward heaven. In the daylight it looked like a cloud, but at night it became a pillar of fire. It gave them light at night so they could travel whenever the Lord wanted them to, day or night.

Almost as soon as the Israelites left Egypt, Pharaoh and his officers were sorry they had let them go. "Why did we ever let them get away from us?" they asked.

Then Pharaoh and his army got into their chariots and chased after the people of Israel. They caught up with them as they were camping by the Red Sea. The Israelites saw the Egyptians coming and were afraid. They cried out to God. Then they turned against Moses and blamed him for getting them into this trouble. They said it would have been better to stay and be slaves to

God led Moses and the people by a cloud in the sky. When the cloud moved ahead, the people followed. But when it stood still, they stopped for a while.

the Egyptians than to be killed in the desert. But Moses told them not to be afraid. "Wait and see what the Lord will do for you," he said. "For the Egyptians you have seen today will never be seen again. The Lord will fight for you, so you won't need to do a thing."

When Pharaoh and his army had almost caught up with them, the cloud in front of God's people moved behind them. It came between them and Pharaoh's army. During the night the cloud was dark on the side where Pharaoh was, and no one in his army could see. But the side of the cloud that faced Israel was as bright as fire! It gave the people light in their camp.

The Lord said to Moses, "Tell my people to start marching to the sea. When they get there, point your shepherd's rod toward the sea. And a path through the water will open up in front of you. Then my people will go across on dry ground!"

So Moses pointed his rod toward the sea, as the Lord had told him to. And the water opened up ahead of them, making a path across the bottom of the sea. The water was piled high like walls on each side of the people, so they could walk across on dry ground. Soon they were safe on the other side!

The path through the water was still there the next morning. So when Pharaoh saw what had happened, he and his army started across between the walls of water. But the Lord made the wheels come off the Egyptian chariots, so they came to a quick stop.

"Turn around! Let's get out of here!" the Egyptians shouted. "The Lord is fighting against us. He is for the Israelites."

But before they could get out, the Lord told Moses to point his rod toward the sea again. When he did, the water came together. It covered the Egyptians, drowning the entire army.

Moses and all of the Israelites were safe on the other side of the Red Sea. There God's people sang a song of praise to the Lord for saving them from Pharaoh.

STORY 37

Food from Heaven and Water from a Rock

Exodus 15–17

The Israelites now found themselves in a big desert. It was between Egypt and the Promised Land of Canaan, where God was leading them. Soon their water was gone, and they were thirsty. They finally arrived at a place called Marah. There they found water, but it was too bitter to drink. Instead of asking the Lord to help them, they got upset with Moses.

Moses prayed to the Lord about it, and the Lord showed him the branch of a tree and told him to throw it into the water. He did, and suddenly the water was no longer bitter—the people could drink it!

They traveled on and came to Elim, where they found twelve wells and seventy palm trees. Going on farther they came to another desert. The people got upset again because they were hungry. They said that when they were in Egypt they had plenty of food. Now they wished God had killed them there instead of bringing them out into the desert to die.

God heard the people. He told Moses he would send meat for everyone that evening and as much bread as they wanted in the morning. Then the people would know that the Lord their God was taking care of them.

The Lord did as he promised. That evening, about the time the sun was going down, huge flocks of birds called quail flew into camp. The people ate them for supper.

The next morning after the dew was gone, small white flakes were all over the ground. The flakes tasted like bread made with honey. No one knew what it was, so the people called it "manna," which in their language meant "What is it?"

"This is the bread the Lord promised you," Moses told them.

The Lord told the people to go out each day and gather as much as they wanted. He told them not to take more than they needed for one day, since there would be a fresh supply each morning. The Lord wanted them to trust him one day at a time for their daily bread. Some of the people didn't obey. They gathered enough for two days instead of one. The next morning the extra manna was spoiled, with worms crawling around in it.

Each morning when the sun warmed the ground, the manna melted away and disappeared. But early the next morning there was always more waiting for them.

On the sixth day there was twice as much as other days. That was because the next day was the Sabbath day when God told the people not to work. On that day there was no manna on the ground. So the sixth day was the only time when the manna the people saved for the next day didn't spoil. Some of the people went out on the Sabbath anyway to try to get food, but there wasn't any. The Lord was angry, so they didn't do it anymore. They rested on the Sabbath day as the Lord had told them to.

Moses told Aaron to get a bottle and fill it with manna. He wanted to keep it forever, so that the children who weren't even born yet would be able to see it. Then they would know how God fed his people in the desert. Aaron did this, and God kept the manna from spoiling.

The Israelites ate manna every day for forty years as they traveled to the land of Canaan.

God rained down food from heaven! This food was called "manna."

One day while they were traveling they came to another place where there was no water. So they complained again. "Get us water," they demanded of Moses.

"Why blame me?" Moses asked.

"Because you brought us here," they replied.

Then Moses cried out to the Lord and said, "What shall I do? The people are almost ready to stone me."

By this time they were close to Mount Sinai, where God had talked to Moses through a fire burning in a bush. Now God told him to lead the people to a rock at Mount Sinai and to strike the rock with his walking stick. Moses did as the Lord said, and water poured out of the rock, giving everyone enough to drink!

STORY 38

A Meeting on the Mountain

Exodus 17; 19

Then some soldiers from the country of Amalek attacked the Israelites. There was a brave man among the people of Israel whose name was Joshua. Moses said to him, "Choose the men you want, and go out tomorrow to fight with the army of Amalek. I will stand on top of the hill with the staff of God in my hand."

Joshua did as Moses told him to. As Joshua's men fought with the Amalekites, Moses, Aaron, and a man named Hur went up to the top of a hill where they could watch. Moses pointed his shepherd's staff toward the men fighting in the valley below. As long as he held it up, the people of Israel kept winning. But whenever he let it down, the enemy began to win. Soon Moses' arm became very tired. So Aaron and Hur rolled a rock over to where he was standing, and he sat on it. They stood on each side of him and held his hands up all day until the battle finally ended at sunset. So God gave the victory to his people.

God was angry with the Amalekites for fighting against his people. He said the time would come when there would be no Amalekites left.

The Israelites arrived at Mount Sinai two months after leaving Egypt. They camped at the bottom of the mountain while Moses went up and talked with God. The Lord said to remind the people of how he had kept them safe from the Egyptians. He said that he would love them more than any other people if they would obey his commandments.

Then God told Moses to go down and call the people together. In three days God would return to the top of the mountain to talk with Moses there, and all the people would hear him. Moses was to have the people get ready for God's visit by washing their clothes and being very careful not to sin. None of them was allowed to go up onto the mountain, for anyone who did would die. A loud trumpet blast high up on the mountain would be the signal for everyone to gather quickly at the bottom and wait there for God to speak.

Moses went down to tell the people what God said. Afterward they put on fresh, clean clothes for the awesome occasion. On the morning of the third day there was loud thunder and bright lightning. Then the Lord came to the top of the mountain in a thick cloud. And there was a trumpet blast so long and loud that the people trembled with fear.

But Moses led the people out of the camp to the foot of the mountain. The whole mountain was covered with smoke because the Lord was there. The smoke went up into the sky, and the mountain shook. The trumpet blast grew louder and louder. Moses talked to God, and God answered him, calling him to the top of the mountain.

STORY 39
The Ten Commandments
Exodus 20–24

Then God gave the people of Israel the Ten Commandments:

1. YOU MUST NOT HAVE ANY OTHER GOD BUT ME. This means that we must love God more than anyone or anything else, for anything we love more than God becomes our god instead of him.

2. YOU MUST NOT MAKE ANY IDOL, OR BOW DOWN TO ONE, OR WORSHIP IT.

Many people in the world make statues, or idols, and believe that they are gods that can help them. But in this commandment God does not allow making such statues or bowing down to them or worshiping them. God is the one who created us, and he is the only one who can save us from our sins. We are to worship no one but him. This commandment also means that we are not to think of money, or clothes, or anything else as more important than God.

3. YOU MUST NOT USE THE NAME OF THE LORD YOUR GOD IN THE WRONG WAY.
   Whenever we speak God's name, we must do it reverently, remembering how great and holy a name it is. If we speak it carelessly or thoughtlessly, we offend God. This commandment teaches us not to swear.

4. REMEMBER TO KEEP THE SABBATH DAY HOLY.
   In this commandment, God instructs his people not to work on the Sabbath. This is because God rested on the seventh day after his six days of work when he created the heavens and the earth.

5. HONOR YOUR FATHER AND YOUR MOTHER.
   Next to obeying God, the most important people to obey are our parents. We should honor them by doing what they tell us to right away, or by doing what we know they want us to do even without waiting to be told.

6. YOU MUST NOT KILL.
   We break this commandment by murdering,
   but we also break it when we are so angry with
   someone that we wish that person was dead. For
   then God sees murder in our heart.

7. YOU MUST NOT COMMIT ADULTERY.
   When a married man lives with another woman
   as if she were his wife, it is adultery. God says we
   must never do this. And a man and a woman who
   are not married must never sleep together, for
   God commands us to be pure in all our thoughts,
   words, and actions.

8. YOU MUST NOT STEAL.
   You must not take anything that belongs to
   someone else. If you have ever done this, whether
   by mistake or on purpose, God commands you to
   give it back or pay for it.

9. YOU MUST NOT TELL LIES.
   This means you must never say anything about
   another person that isn't true. And when you are
   saying what *is* true, you must be very careful how
   you say it. Don't leave out a little or add a little to
   make it different from the real truth.

10. YOU MUST NOT WISH YOU HAD ANYTHING THAT IS
    YOUR NEIGHBOR'S.
    We must not be upset when we can't have all the
    things God gives to other people. God, who knows
    best, gives to each of us just what he wants us to
    have.

God called Moses to the top of Mount Sinai, where he gave him the Ten Commandments written on two tablets of stone.

The people heard the loud thunder and trumpet blast. They saw the lightning and smoke. And they were terrified. They said to Moses, "You tell us what God wants, and we will do it. But don't let God speak to us, or we will die." Moses told them God hadn't come down to hurt them—he just came to show his power. The people were not to be afraid of God, but they *were* to be afraid to sin against him.

Everyone stood a long way off from the mountain while Moses climbed up to the dark cloud where God was. There God talked with him and gave him more rules that would help the people know how to obey.

When the people heard these rules, they promised to obey all of them.

Then God told Moses to come up to the top of Mount Sinai again, so that he could give him two tablets of stone with the Ten Commandments written on them. So Moses went up, along with Joshua, his assistant.

A Special House for God

Exodus 25–28

While Moses was on Mount Sinai, the Lord told him that the people should build a Tabernacle. This would be like a church, where they could worship him. He gave Moses a pattern of the building so Moses would know just what it should look like. The Tabernacle would be easy to take apart and put together again, for the people were to carry it with them on their journey to the land of Canaan.

God also commanded Moses to make an Ark to be placed inside the Tabernacle. This Ark was to be a beautiful box made of wood, then covered inside and outside with pure gold.

God said that when the Ark was finished, Moses was to put into it the two stone tablets God would give him—the tablets with the Ten Commandments written on them.

The Ark was to have a cover of solid gold, with two gold angels called cherubs on it. One cherub was to be at each end so they would face each other with their wings spread out.

There was also to be a table made of wood and covered with gold to stand in the Tabernacle. And a gold lampstand would give the Tabernacle light.

The frame of the Tabernacle was to be made of boards covered with gold. The whole Tabernacle would be covered with heavy sheets of cloth. And a beautiful curtain, called the veil, would hang across the inside of the Tabernacle, dividing it into rooms. Moses was to place the Ark in the inner room. The gold table and the gold lampstand would go in the outer room.

There was to be a little yard all around the Tabernacle and a wall of curtains to protect the yard. An altar would stand in the yard in front of the entrance to the Tabernacle. It would be made of wood covered with bronze, large enough to sacrifice oxen, sheep, and goats on it.

The Lord said that Aaron and his sons would be God's priests. They would sacrifice to God the animals brought to the Tabernacle by the people of Israel. Aaron would be the high priest. He would be in charge, and his four sons would be his assistants.

God told Moses to have Aaron wear a robe made of embroidered linen. Over the linen robe he would have a long, sleeveless blue coat. Hanging from the lower edge of this outer robe would be blue, purple, and scarlet yarn decorations made to look like fruit.

Over the blue robe, Aaron was to wear a many-colored vest. On the front of this vest would be a square piece of embroidered cloth with twelve beautiful jewels on it.

On his head Aaron would wear a linen turban

The Ark was the most important part of the Tabernacle. Its cover had two cherubs on it. Inside were the stone tablets with the Ten Commandments written on them.

with a band of gold fastened to the front of it. These words were to be written on the gold band: "Set apart as holy to the Lord." This would remind Aaron that God commanded him to be holy, and it would remind the people to honor Aaron as God's high priest.

Aaron Makes a Gold Calf

Exodus 29–32

The Lord told Moses to bring Aaron and his sons to
the entrance of the Tabernacle. Then he was to put
their special robes on them and pour olive oil on
Aaron's head, anointing him as God's high priest.
Afterwards Moses would give sacrifices to God on
their behalf.

As priests, Aaron and his sons were to be given
the job of sacrificing two lambs every day on the
big bronze altar. The lambs would be sacrificed for
the sins of the people.

God told Moses to make a smaller altar of wood
covered with gold. This altar was for burning sweet-
smelling incense.

The animals to be sacrificed on the bronze altar
would represent Jesus, the Savior, being offered as
a sacrifice for our sins. The incense sending up its
sweet smoke from the gold altar would represent
the prayers of God's people.

When the Lord had finished talking with Moses,
he gave him the two tablets of stone on which he
had written the Ten Commandments. Moses had
been with God on Mount Sinai for forty days and
forty nights learning about all the things God
wanted made.

Meanwhile, the people of Israel were in their

camp at the foot of the mountain. They became impatient when Moses stayed so long. They went to Aaron and said, "We don't know what has become of Moses. We want to worship idols, like all the other nations do."

"All right," Aaron said. "Bring me the gold earrings that belong to your wives and children." Aaron melted the earrings in a fire and poured out the gold into a big lump, which he made into the shape of a gold calf.

The people bowed to the calf and said it was their god, who had brought them out of the land of Egypt. Aaron built an altar in front of it and told the people to come back the next day for a big celebration. Early the next morning, they sacrificed burnt offerings to the calf instead of to the Lord. They had a big party, eating and getting drunk and dancing around the calf.

Moses was still on the mountain. "Quick! Go on down," God told him. "The people have done a very wicked thing. They made a calf and worshiped it. They called it their god."

Moses hurried down the mountain with the two tablets of stone in his hands. Joshua was with him. As they came near the camp, they heard the noise of the people shouting.

Joshua said to Moses, "It sounds as if they are getting ready for war."

"No," Moses said. "It isn't the noise of war—they are singing."

When Moses saw the people dancing in front of

the gold calf, he could hardly believe it. In great anger he hurled the two tablets of stone down the mountain, and they broke in pieces as they smashed against the ground.

STORY 42

The Idol Is Smashed

Exodus 32–34

Moses ran all the rest of the way down the mountain. He smashed the calf and ground it into powder. Then he threw the powder into the water and made the people drink it.

Moses turned to Aaron and asked, "Why have you helped the people sin in this terrible way?" Aaron tried to excuse himself. He said the people told him to make the calf or they would hurt him. They brought him their gold, he said. And when he put it into the fire, it just happened to come out in the shape of a calf. What a wicked thing for Aaron to say!

A terrible punishment from the Lord came upon his people because of their sin. About three thousand of them died that day.

The next day Moses told the people that he would pray for them, and perhaps their sin would be forgiven. So he talked with the Lord about it. He confessed that the people had sinned terribly because they had made the idol and worshiped it, but he begged God to forgive them. God said no, he would punish those who had sinned. He would not go with them to the Promised Land of Canaan, and he would not send the cloud to lead them anymore.

Moses begged God to stay with his people. The Lord listened to his prayer and finally promised that he would.

Then God told Moses to make two stone tablets like the ones he had broken. God said he would write the Ten Commandments on them again. He told Moses to come up alone to the top of the mountain in the morning. No one else could be anywhere near the mountain, and no sheep or cows were to graze there.

So Moses chipped out two tablets of rock, just like those he had broken. He went up to the top of Mount Sinai early in the morning, carrying the tablets. And the Lord came down in the cloud and passed in front of him. When Moses heard his voice, he bowed quickly to the earth and worshiped. He prayed again that the Lord would forgive the people of Israel and would let them be his people again.

God accepted Moses' prayer and took the people back again as his own. He promised that he would do wonderful things for them. He would drive out the wicked people of Canaan to make room for his people to live there instead.

Workers Build the Tabernacle

Exodus 35–40; Leviticus 16

Now Moses invited the people to bring their gifts of gold, silver, bronze, wood, and whatever else was needed to begin building the Tabernacle. The people gladly brought their gold and silver bracelets and earrings and other ornaments. Some brought jewels for the front of the high priest's vest. Others brought olive oil for the lamp. They kept on bringing more and more gifts. Finally there was enough, but still the people kept on bringing things. Moses had to tell them to stop! He handed their gifts to the workers chosen and trained by the Lord to do the work.

These men made curtains to spread over the top of the Tabernacle as its roof. They also made a beautiful curtain to hang inside the Tabernacle, to divide it into two rooms, and a curtain for the entrance. They made frames from boards covered with gold. They covered the whole Tabernacle with heavy sheets of cloth.

Then the workers made Aaron's beautiful clothes—his linen coat and the vest with twelve beautiful jewels attached to it. Aaron wore the jewels over his chest.

These children are bringing their gifts to the Tabernacle. God is pleased because they want to help.

The robe under the vest was all blue, and around its lower edge hung what looked like blue, purple, and red fruits. Between the fruits were gold bells that tinkled as Aaron went in and out of the Tabernacle.

Special clothes were made for Aaron's sons, too. And there was a turban for Aaron's head. It had a gold band on it that read: "Set apart as holy to the Lord."

One of the workers made the Ark. He covered a

wooden box inside and outside with solid gold. He made the cover of pure gold. Then he made two gold angels called cherubs, one for each end of the cover. Their faces were turned toward each other, and their wings were spread out. The Ark was the most important part of the Tabernacle because God was there.

At last the different parts of the Tabernacle were finished and ready to be put together. The workers brought them to Moses, and he inspected them to be sure everything was just as God had said.

God told Moses to go ahead now and put the parts together. Soon the Tabernacle was finished, with the yard around it and everything in place inside.

Then the cloud pillar that led the people of Israel as they traveled came down. It stood over the Tabernacle and covered it. And the glory of the Lord filled the inside of the Tabernacle so that Moses couldn't go in.

The inner room in the Tabernacle was where Moses put the Ark. So that room was the most holy part of the Tabernacle. It was called the Most Holy Place. The Lord told Moses that no one but Aaron, the high priest, could ever go in there. Even Aaron could go there only once every year.

Before going in, he offered sacrifices for his own sins and for the sins of all the people. What did it mean when the high priest did this? He was showing what the Savior would do for all who trust in him. The high priest went into the most holy place on earth to pray for the people. Jesus, the Savior, after he was crucified, went up to heaven to pray for us. Aaron is dead and cannot ask God to forgive us, but the Savior is alive in heaven and is there every day asking God to forgive us.

Three Holidays

Leviticus 23

The Lord told the people of Israel to have several religious holidays each year. Here are three of them.

The first was called the Passover. This celebration was to remind God's people of the night they came out of Egypt, for it was a great victory over the Egyptians. Each year when they celebrated this event, the people ate a lamb during the night, just as they had done that first time. For seven days afterward they ate bread made without yeast. God wanted the people to have this celebration each year. He wanted them to always remember how he had punished Pharaoh until that Egyptian king finally let the people of Israel go.

Seven weeks after the Passover, there was the Harvest Festival. This lasted only one day and came after the grain had been gathered into the barns. The people thanked God for sending the

These children and their parents are celebrating one of Israel's three great holidays. Each holiday was a time of joy and thanksgiving.

rain and the sunshine that made their crops grow out in the fields. They thanked him for giving them food enough for another year.

At the end of the year there was the Festival of Shelters. This celebration lasted seven days. During that week all the people of Israel moved out of their homes. They lived in huts made from branches of trees. That's because the Israelites lived like that for forty years while they were traveling through the desert. The Lord wanted them to remember this when they arrived in Canaan and were living in houses again.

STORY 45

Always Complaining

Numbers 10–12

Now it was time for the Israelites to leave Mount Sinai, for the Lord told them they had been there long enough. They should move on toward Canaan, he said. So the cloud rose from the Tabernacle and moved ahead of the people. They followed it for three days until they came to the wilderness of Paran. There it stopped, and there they camped.

Were the people thankful to God for the cloud? Were they satisfied with whatever he chose to give them until they reached the land to which he was leading them? No! They complained that there was no meat for them to eat. "We remember the fish we had in Egypt," they said. "We remember the cucumbers, the melons, and the onions. Now we have nothing at all but this manna."

The Lord was very angry with them, and Moses was upset. Then he complained to the Lord too. He asked why the Lord had given him the care of all these wicked people. It was too much for him, he said.

God had always helped Moses when he was in trouble, and he was willing to help again. Moses should not have complained—he should have trusted God.

God told Moses to tell the people that he would give them meat, for he had heard their complaining. They would have meat not only for one day or five days, but for a whole month, until they couldn't stand the taste or sight of it.

Moses could hardly believe it. He said, "Here are 600,000 soldiers, and yet you say you will give them meat to eat for a whole month? Even if we killed all our sheep and cows, we wouldn't have enough. If we caught all the fish of the sea, we still wouldn't have enough."

The Lord answered, "Have I grown weak? Is that why you think I can't do it? Wait, and you will see whether my words will come true or not."

So Moses told the people what the Lord had said.

Then the Lord sent a wind that brought quail from the sea, and they flew down all around the camp. There were so many that the ground was covered with them. The people went out and gathered them all that day, all that night, and all the next day. But as soon as they began eating the meat, many of the people died.

Then the cloud lifted again, and the people followed it until it stopped. The people also stopped and made their camp.

Moses was the leader of the Israelites because the Lord had chosen him. He didn't try to act important. But Miriam, his sister, and Aaron, his brother, were jealous. They found fault with him for marrying a woman who was not an Israelite. They said God had chosen them also, and that they, too, should be rulers over the people.

The Lord was angry. He told Aaron and Miriam to go with Moses to the Tabernacle. While they were there, the cloud pillar came down and stood by the entrance. Then the Lord called to Aaron and Miriam from the cloud, so they stepped forward. God told them he had chosen Moses. And he asked them, "Shouldn't you be afraid to speak against him?"

As soon as the cloud pillar rose again, Miriam's skin was as white as snow. God had sent a disease called leprosy as punishment for Miriam's and Aaron's wickedness. When Aaron saw it, he was terribly frightened and said to Moses, "We have sinned." He begged for Miriam to be healed.

So Moses prayed to the Lord, "Heal her now, O God, I ask." The Lord listened to his prayer and healed Miriam from her leprosy.

Then the people traveled back to the wilderness of Paran.

Good Fruit and Strong Giants
Numbers 13–14

The people of Israel had almost reached the Promised Land of Canaan. Moses told them to go in and check out the land that God had promised to give them. He sent twelve men, one from each tribe. He told them, "Look at the land to see whether it is good or bad. Find out what sort of people live there and how many there are. What are their towns like? Do they have walls around them?"

Moses told the men not to be afraid. He said to bring back samples of the fruit that grew in the Promised Land.

So the twelve men walked through the land from one end to the other, and the Lord kept the people who lived there from hurting them. At one place they cut a branch of grapes with a single cluster so large that it took two men to carry it! They hung the cluster on a pole with a man at each end, carrying it between them! They also brought back to Moses some samples of the wonderful pomegranates and figs that grew in the Promised Land.

The men were away for forty days before returning with their report and with the samples of fruit they had found. They said the crops grew tall and strong in the fields, and there was plenty to eat and drink. But there were a couple of problems to deal with. The cities were big, with walls all around them. And the people were strong and powerful. Ten of the men who had looked over the land were afraid. They didn't think Moses and the people would be able to win over people like that.

But two of the spies, Caleb and Joshua, remembered God's promise that he would give the land to his people. They knew he would keep his promise, for they had faith in him. Caleb begged the Israelites to enter the land at once. He said, "We can do it. We can win!"

But the other men talked the people out of it. They said, "We saw giants in the land. They were so large that we felt no bigger than grasshoppers!"

So the Israelites refused to enter the Promised Land.

Moses and Aaron felt terrible about this. So did Joshua and Caleb, who once more told the people what a wonderful country the Promised Land was. They begged the Israelites not to be afraid, but God's people became angry and wanted to kill Caleb and Joshua.

Then God became very angry with the people of Israel. He told Moses that he would send a terrible sickness. He said they could no longer be his people. Instead he would give many children to Moses, and they would become a greater nation than the people of Israel were.

But Moses begged the Lord not to kill the Israelites. Moses said that if God didn't bring his people into the Promised Land, other nations would say it was because God couldn't do it!

The Lord listened to Moses' prayer and promised not to destroy the people after all. But the people had disobeyed God too often, and they wouldn't believe his promises. So God said they couldn't enter the Promised Land for forty years. They would have to wander around in the wilderness all that time until they grew old and died. At the end of the forty years, God said he would bring their children into the land. And he promised that Caleb and Joshua would live and enter Canaan with them.

The Israelites returned to their camp and stayed there several days. Then the Lord led them back into the wilderness.

STORY 47

Moses Doesn't Believe God

Numbers 20–21

Some time later all the Israelites moved their camp again, this time to the Zin Desert. Moses' sister, Miriam, died and was buried there.

Once again the people ran out of water, and they were upset with Moses. "Why did you make us leave Egypt?" they shouted. "We're going to die of thirst."

Then Moses and Aaron went to the Tabernacle

*The Israelites wanted water. God had told Moses
to speak to the rock. But Moses disobeyed God
and hit the rock instead.*

and bowed down with their faces to the ground.
They knew that God was there with them.

The Lord told them to get the shepherd's staff
and to gather all the people by a rock. "As the
people watch, speak to the rock," God told Moses.
"Then water will gush out before their eyes."

So Moses took his shepherd's staff from its place

in the Tabernacle and called the people together. But instead of just speaking to the rock as the Lord had told him to, Moses yelled angrily at the people. "Listen, all of you who are upset with me. Must we get water for you from the rock?" Then he hit the rock twice, even though God had not even mentioned hitting it. He had only told Moses to speak to it.

Suddenly water began flowing from the rock. Then all the people and their cattle drank and drank until they had enough. But God said to Moses, "You didn't believe me, did you? You didn't think it would work just to speak to the rock as I told you to. So you hit it twice. The people would have respected me more if the water had started flowing from the rock when you only spoke a word. Now I will not let you lead my people into the Promised Land."

How sad that Moses did wrong and had to be punished! How he had looked forward to going into the Promised Land! But now he would never get there.

The people arrived at a mountain named Mount Hor almost forty years after they left Egypt. At Mount Hor the Lord told Moses and Aaron that the time had come for Aaron to die. "Take Aaron's son Eleazar with you to the top of Mount Hor," God told them. "When you arrive, take the high priest's garments off Aaron and put them on his son Eleazar. Aaron will die while you are up there, and Eleazar will be the new high priest."

Moses did as the Lord commanded. While all the people watched, he and Aaron and Eleazar went up on the mountain. When they got to the top, Moses took the high priest's clothes from Aaron and put them on Eleazar. Then Aaron died, and Eleazar became the high priest in place of his father.

Moses and Eleazar came down from the mountain and told the Israelites that Aaron was dead. The people had a time of mourning for him to show how sad they were. It lasted thirty days.

The Israelites were very tired of traveling, and again they sinned by being angry with God and Moses. "We have no bread and no water, and how we hate this manna," they complained.

The Lord was angry and sent snakes into the camp. The snakes bit the people, and many of them died.

The rest of the people were afraid. They ran to Moses, screaming, "We have sinned, for we have complained against the Lord and against you. Please pray that the snakes will go away."

So Moses prayed for them. Then the Lord told Moses to make a bronze snake that would look like the real snakes that were biting people.

"Put the bronze snake on a pole," God said. "People who get a snakebite will live if they just look at that snake."

So Moses made the bronze snake and put it on top of a pole. Many people looked at it and lived instead of dying from their snakebites.

But it wasn't the bronze snake that made them

well. It was the Lord who did it. The bronze snake on the pole reminds us of Jesus, our Savior. He was lifted up on a pole too. It was a wooden cross. There he died for our sins. If we look up to the Savior on the cross and realize that he died to take away our sins, God will give us eternal life. That's even better than the life he gave to the people in Moses' time who looked up at the bronze snake.

STORY 48

Balaam's Donkey Speaks!

Numbers 22–24

As the Israelites went on, they came to Moab, where Balak was the king.

When Balak saw them coming, he was afraid. He thought they wanted to fight with him, and he knew there were too many of them for his soldiers to win. So he sent for a man named Balaam to curse the people of Israel. To curse people means to ask God to make bad things happen to them.

The king told Balaam he would make him rich and do anything he asked if he would curse the people of Israel. Balaam loved money, but he said he could not do anything that God did not want him to do.

God told Balaam he could go with the men who were sent by the king. "But," said God, "do only what I tell you to do." So Balaam got up early in the

God gave this donkey a special message for Balaam because Balaam did not see the angel in the road. Balaam paid attention when he heard the donkey speak.

morning, saddled his donkey, and started off with the men whom the king had sent.

But God was angry with Balaam for wanting to

go with the men. So God sent an angel with a sword to stand in front of Balaam on the road. Balaam couldn't see the angel, but his donkey did. She ran into the field by the side of the road to get away. Balaam beat his donkey and told her to behave!

The angel went ahead and stood at a place where there was a wall on each side of the road. When the donkey came to that place, she pressed up very close to the wall to get by the angel. Balaam's foot was crushed against the wall, so he hit his donkey again.

Then the angel went still farther ahead and stood in a narrow place where there was no room at all to get by. The donkey saw the angel with the sword and was so afraid that she lay down with Balaam on top of her. This made Balaam very angry, and he beat her as hard as he could.

Then the Lord had the donkey speak like a person! She said, "What have I done to deserve getting hit by you three times?"

Balaam said she had disobeyed him and had made him look like a fool. "If I had a sword with me, I'd kill you," Balaam said.

Then the donkey asked, "Don't you always ride on me? Have I ever done anything like this before?"

"No," Balaam said, "you haven't."

Then the Lord helped Balaam see the angel standing in front of him. The angel had a sword and was ready to kill him. Balaam was afraid and threw himself flat on the ground in front of the angel.

Then the angel said to him, "Why did you hit your donkey three times? I came here to stop you from doing wrong. The donkey saw me and got out of the way. If she hadn't, I would have killed you and saved her life." Then the angel told Balaam to go on with the men. But he was to say to King Balak only what God would tell him to say.

So Balaam went with the king's men. The king came out to meet him and welcome him. But the next day King Balak was disappointed and angry when Balaam blessed the Israelites three times instead of cursing them. "I sent for you to curse my enemies, and instead you have blessed them three times," he growled. Then he told Balaam to go home. So Balaam didn't get any of the silver and gold he wanted so much.

STORY 49

Almost There

Numbers 26; 32–33

The people of Israel had been wandering around in the wilderness for forty years. God wouldn't let them go into the Promised Land of Canaan during all that time. Do you remember why? It was because they had refused to go in when God had told them to. They had been afraid of the powerful giants who lived there.

These forty years finally ended, and God brought

them back again to the edge of the Promised Land. He told Moses and Eleazar to count the men who were old enough to be soldiers. The two men discovered that everyone who had refused to enter Canaan the first time had died as the Lord had said they would. Only Caleb and Joshua were still alive, for God had promised they could go into the Promised Land.

Now the Lord led the Israelites to the Jordan River, where they waited for him to tell them when to cross. On the other side was the Promised Land of Canaan. Every Israelite family was to be given enough land for a home and a farm over there.

But two of the tribes of Israel came to Moses and requested permission to live on the east side where they were, instead of on the west side. They asked to stay because on this side there was land on which their cows and sheep would have good grass to eat. The two tribes were the tribes of Reuben and Gad. Some of the people from Joseph's family also asked to live east of the Jordan.

At first Moses was angry with them. He thought they wanted to stay behind because they were afraid of the wicked people in Canaan on the other side of the river.

"Do you want to stay here while your brothers go over to fight?" he demanded.

"No, no," they replied. "We don't mean that. We'll cross over with the others to fight, but we want to leave our families and animals here. Then afterwards, when the war is over, we will come back here and live on this side of the river."

So Moses agreed. He spoke to the rest of the people and told them to let the two tribes have the land they asked for. So everyone agreed to do this.

The Lord told Moses that the Israelites were to drive out all the wicked people living across the river. All their idols were to be destroyed. God wanted the Israelites to do this so they wouldn't be tempted to sin by worshiping the idols.

STORY 50

Moses' Last Words

Numbers 27; Deuteronomy 1; 3–4; 8–9

While the people of Israel were camped beside the Jordan River, waiting to go across, Moses spoke to them for the last time. He knew he couldn't go into Canaan with them. That's because he had angrily hit a rock with his staff instead of just speaking to it as God had told him to.

He was afraid the people would forget God's laws when he was gone. In this last talk, Moses told the people again how kind the Lord had been. He reminded them of the time forty years before when they were so close to Canaan, but they had refused to go in. They had listened to the ten men who told them that the people in Canaan were too strong to fight against. Moses reminded the Israelites how angry the Lord had been with them and how God had sent them back into the wilderness for forty years.

Then Moses told the people that he had begged the Lord to let him cross the river with them, to enter the good land of Canaan. But the Lord had said no. He had said he would only let Moses see the Promised Land from a high mountain.

Moses asked the Lord to give the people of Israel another leader to take his place. Otherwise, he said, the people would have no one to guide them and care for them. They would be scattered and lost, like sheep without a shepherd. The Lord announced that he had chosen Joshua as the new leader, so all the people were to obey him just as they had obeyed Moses.

Moses told the people to teach God's commandments to their children. They were to talk about these laws when they were in their homes or out for walks. They were to do this before going to sleep at night and after waking up in the morning. Everyone was to talk about God's laws many times each day and remind one another about how great and good God is.

Moses said, "You must never forget how God led you through the wilderness for forty years and fed you with manna. In all that time your clothes did not wear out, and your feet never became sore from traveling. God led you through a lonely wilderness.

"But now he is bringing you to a better land. That land has streams that run through fields and springs of water that pour down from the hills. In that good land across the river the grain grows tall, and there are huge crops of juicy grapes. There are fig trees and pomegranates and olive trees—food enough to spare. And there is iron and copper in the hills." The people could dig out the iron and copper to make many wonderful things.

"You must never become proud," said Moses. "Don't say that you got these things by yourselves, for it was the Lord alone who gave everything to you. Don't forget about God and worship idols. If you do, you will be treated like the wicked people who are now living in the land."

Then Moses said, "When the Lord gives you victory over the people living in Canaan, never say God did this for you because you were so good! No, God will give you victory because the people living in Canaan are so wicked. And he will do it because he promised Abraham, Isaac, and Jacob that he would give the land of Canaan to their family—to you, the people of Israel."

THE
BOOK
about
a New
Land

The Cities of Safety

Deuteronomy 19; 27–28; 30–32; 34

Moses told the people of Israel that they were to set aside some of their cities as safety zones. God's rule was that a person could run to one of those cities and be safe if he had accidentally killed someone. For instance, if he was cutting down a tree, the head of the ax might fly off the handle and kill someone. Then the man with the ax could run to a city of safety. Otherwise a relative of the dead man might purposely try to kill the one who had accidentally killed the man.

Moses told the people that as soon as they crossed the river and entered the Promised Land, they should set up some large stones. On these stones they were to write the laws of God for everyone to read.

Moses said that if the people of Israel obeyed God's laws, God would make them the greatest nation on earth. He would bless them and their children, their land, and their sheep and cows. Their enemies would be afraid of them and would stay far away.

But if the people of Israel didn't obey God, they would always have trouble. The seeds they planted in their fields wouldn't grow, locusts would come and eat up their growing grain, and worms would eat their grapevines. The people would be weak and sickly, and the Lord would send fierce enemies to fight against them. The enemies would take the old and the young away to other countries as slaves.

Moses told the people that they must choose between good and evil ways. He begged them to choose the good ways. If they did, they and their children would live long and well.

Then he presented Joshua to them as their new leader.

The Lord now called Moses and Joshua to the Tabernacle. He came to them there in the cloud pillar, and he set Joshua apart as the new leader of Israel.

Moses wrote down God's laws. Then he ordered that every seven years the priests, leaders, and all the people, including the children, must be called together. They were to listen as these laws were read aloud to them, for they needed to hear them again and again. Then they could remember to obey them. Moses gave the book of laws to the Levites and told them to keep it with the gold box called the Ark.

After this the Lord told Moses to climb to the top of Mount Nebo so he could look across the Jordan River into the Promised Land. Then he would die on the mountain, just as Aaron had died on Mount Hor.

Moses said a last good-bye to his people and climbed to the top of the mountain. There he looked across the Jordan at the Promised Land of Canaan. This was the land God had promised long before to Abraham, Isaac, Jacob, and all the people who would be in their family.

Then Moses died on top of the mountain. The Lord buried him in a valley in the land of Moab, but no one knows where. Moses was 120 years old when he died, but he was well and strong until the day of his death.

Since that time there has never been another leader just like Moses. It was through Moses that God showed his great power.

STORY 52

A New Leader

Joshua 1–5

After Moses died God said to Joshua, "Now you must lead my people. Take them across the Jordan River into the land I promised them. Be strong and brave, and be sure to obey all of my laws. Then you will always be successful. Don't be afraid, for I will be with you and help you wherever you go."

Then Joshua spoke to the Israelite leaders. "Go through the camp," he said. "Tell all the people that in three days we will cross the Jordan River and go into Canaan, the Promised Land!"

Meanwhile, Joshua had already sent two men to check out the land around Jericho. They came to the city of Jericho and went into the house of a woman named Rahab. Someone told the king of Jericho that two Israelites had come to the city and were at Rahab's house. So the king sent messengers to Rahab's home. They told her to bring out the two men.

Rahab had taken the Israelite men up to the flat roof of her house and had hidden them there. But she told the king's messengers that the two men had left the city. So the messengers went away.

That evening Rahab talked with the two Israelite men on the roof. She said, "I know that the Lord has given this country to your people. Everyone here in Canaan has already heard how the God of Israel made a dry path for you through the Red Sea. We have heard how he helped you fight against your enemies."

Rahab said that her people were very much afraid of the people of Israel. Then she asked the two men, "Will you remember my kindness to you? Promise that you won't let any of my family be killed when Israel takes over this city."

The men said that she must keep it a secret that they had been in Jericho. Then they would protect her.

The city of Jericho had a high, thick wall around it, and Rahab's house was built on the wall. The king had ordered the gates of the city to be closed to keep the two Israelites from getting away. So Rahab used a red rope to let the two men down on the outside of the wall. She warned them to hide in the nearby hills for three days until the soldiers stopped looking for them.

The men told Rahab to leave the red rope hanging from the window of her house. When the Israelite army came to take the city, no one inside her house would be hurt.

The two Israelites stayed in the hills for three days. Then they crossed the river to tell Joshua all that had happened.

Early the next morning Joshua and all the people got up and traveled to the Jordan River. They stayed beside it for three days. Then Joshua said, "Get ready! Tomorrow we will cross the river, and the Lord will do wonderful things among you.
The priests will go first, carrying the Ark. As soon as their feet touch the water, the river will stop flowing, and they will walk through on dry ground!"

Everything happened just as Joshua had said. The next morning the priests carried the Ark toward the river, and all the people followed them. When the priests stepped into the water, it opened up in front of them. So they walked on dry ground into the middle of the river! The priests waited there with the Ark while all the people walked past them to the other side, into the Promised Land of Canaan.

After all the people had crossed, the priests carrying the Ark followed. As soon as they stepped out of the river onto the shore, the river began flowing again!

The Israelites camped at a place called Gilgal. There they found some grain in the fields, which they roasted and ate. It was the first time they had eaten anything but manna for forty years! The next day the manna stopped coming. God knew that in Canaan there was plenty of food.

STORY 53

Jericho's Walls Fall Down

Joshua 5–6

Joshua left the camp and walked to Jericho to check out the city with its high walls. Looking up, he saw a man with a sword in his hand. Joshua went right up to him. "Are you a friend or an enemy?" he asked.

"I am in charge of the Lord's army," the man said. Joshua realized that this was not an ordinary man. This was the Lord, who had come to help his people. So Joshua fell to the ground and worshiped him.

The people of Jericho had shut the city gates to stop the Israelites from coming in. But the Lord said he would help Joshua win anyway. He even told Joshua how to plan his attack.

The Lord said, "Have all the Israelite soldiers march around the city once every day for six days. Seven priests will walk ahead of the Ark, each

Joshua led the Israelites around Jericho for six days. On the seventh day they marched around the city seven times. Then the priests blew their horns and the people shouted. The walls tumbled down!

carrying a ram's horn." (Horns from rams—male sheep—were often used as musical horns, like trumpets.)

"On the seventh day," said the Lord, "march around Jericho, not once, but seven times. Do this while the priests blow their horns. After the seventh time around, the priests must blow a loud, long blast. When you hear this, have everyone give a mighty shout. Then the walls of the city will fall down flat, and all of my people can walk right in!"

Joshua told the people what God had said. They did as the Lord commanded.

The first day they all marched around the city once, the priests following behind the soldiers and blowing the horns. Then came the priests who carried the Ark.

On the second day they marched around the city again. They did this for six days.

But on the seventh day the Israelites got up early, before it was light, and marched around the city seven times. The last time around, the priests blew a great blast on their horns. And Joshua called out to his people, "Shout, for the Lord has given you the city!" Joshua said that only Rahab and those with her in her house would be able to live. The Lord had commanded that all the rest of the people of Jericho must die for their sins. All the silver, gold, brass, and iron in the city belonged to the Lord and must be put into the place where gifts to the Lord were kept.

The people gave a mighty shout, and at that moment the walls of the city tumbled down. So they rushed into Jericho and took it. Joshua told the men who had been at Rahab's house to keep Rahab and everyone with her safe, just as they had promised her. So they did. Afterwards the army of Israel burned the city; but they saved the silver, gold, iron, and bronze for God's house.

STORY 54

Joshua Gets Fooled

Joshua 7–10

After the Israelites took Jericho, they tried to take the city of Ai. They did not win at first because of sin among them. But they got rid of the sin, and then God helped them win against Ai. When the other kings in Canaan heard what Israel was doing, they brought all their armies together to fight against Joshua and his people.

But the people from the city of Gibeon didn't want to fight. They knew that the Lord was helping the Israelites. So they sent men to Joshua who were wearing very old clothes and worn-out shoes. They even carried dry and moldy bread, pretending that they had come from far away.

They told Joshua, "We have come from a faraway country, for we have heard of your God and all the great things he has done for you. Our people have sent us to ask you to make peace with us and be our friends."

Joshua and the men of Israel didn't ask the Lord what to do, as they should have done. Instead they agreed to be friends with the people of Gibeon.

Three days later the Israelites learned the truth. These men had not come from a country far away. They lived close by in Canaan and were among the wicked people that Israel had been told to destroy.

So Joshua called for the men of Gibeon and asked why they had lied to him. They said it was because they were afraid. They had heard that God was going to destroy the people living in Canaan. Now Joshua couldn't hurt them because only three days before he had promised not to. But he said they would have to cut wood and carry water for the people of Israel.

When the king of Jerusalem heard that the people of Gibeon had given themselves over to the Israelites, he was very angry. He and four other kings put their armies together and went to Gibeon to fight against it.

Then the men of Gibeon sent a messenger to Joshua. "Quick! Come and help us," they said. "The kings who live in the hills have come to fight us."

So Joshua and his army went to help Gibeon by fighting against the five kings and their armies. The Lord made the other armies afraid of the Israelites, so they ran away. But as they ran, the Lord sent big hailstones. More of the enemies were killed by hail than by Israelites.

The sun began to set, and Joshua was afraid that God's enemies would escape in the darkness. So he prayed that God would not let the sun go down, and that he would make the moon stay where it was.

The Lord did what Joshua asked. He made the sun and moon stand still in the sky so that the Israelites could keep on fighting their enemies and winning. There was no day like it either before or afterwards.

STORY 55
The People Choose God
Joshua 22–24

The men from the tribes living across the Jordan River had stayed with the Israelite army ever since crossing the river. They had helped to fight against the wicked people in Canaan. They received a full share of the cows, gold, silver, and anything else taken from the enemy.

Joshua called these men to him and thanked them for their help. "You have obeyed me," he said. "You have helped your brothers fight. You have done what God wanted you to do. Now go back to your homes on the other side of the Jordan. But be very careful, after you get there, to obey all the commandments Moses gave us. Be sure to love and serve the Lord your God with all your heart."

The priests and Levites had brought the Tabernacle to Shiloh, a city near the center of their new country, and had set it up permanently as the Lord had told them to.

So the men started back home. When they came to the Jordan River, they stopped and built a big altar. It was like the one at the Tabernacle, which was now in Shiloh, where God had said it should stay. God had told the Israelites not to sacrifice gifts to him on any other altar except the one at the Tabernacle. When the people from the other tribes of Israel heard about the new altar, they were angry. They sent their armies to fight the men who built that altar.

The son of one of the priests and ten Israelite leaders arrived ahead of the army. "We want to know," they said, "why you have built another altar to offer sacrifices on. The Lord said we should have only the one altar at Shiloh."

The tribes from across the river were surprised. They said they did not plan to use the altar for sacrifices. It was just a monument to prove that they were truly people of Israel. "We want your families to remember that we worship God just like all of you who live in the Promised Land of Canaan. We know that gifts to God can be sacrificed only on the altar at the Tabernacle."

So then everyone was happy again.

As the years went by, Joshua became an old man. One day he called the leaders of Israel together. He reminded them of all the Lord had done for them and told them to always honor God in everything they did. Then, he said, the Lord would bless them and give them everything they needed.

"The Lord has driven out your enemies and given you cities, fields, and a land of your own to live in," Joshua reminded them. "Love the Lord and worship him with all your heart. Would you rather worship idols? As for me and my family, we will worship the Lord."

The people answered, "We will never leave the Lord to worship idols. It was the Lord who brought us out of Egypt and gave us this land. We will worship the Lord, for he is our God. He is the one we will obey."

Then Joshua put a great stone beneath an oak tree. The tree was beside the Tabernacle in Shiloh. That stone, he said, would remind them of the promise they had made to worship only the Lord.

Soon after that Joshua died. He was 110 years old.

STORY 56

Gideon and His Wool

Judges 2–4; 6–8

A long time after Joshua died the people of Israel began worshiping idols. The Lord was very angry about this and sent enemies to fight against his people.

But when God's people turned away from the idols and asked the Lord for his help, he gave them leaders called judges. These men helped them fight against their enemies and win. Yet, as soon as the Lord set the people free, they would forget him. They would sin again by worshiping idols. This sinning and coming back to God went on for more than three hundred years! During that time fifteen judges were their leaders. One of them was a woman named Deborah. Another was a man named Gideon. This is Gideon's story.

After forty years of freedom, the people of Israel began worshiping idols again. Then the Midianites came to fight them and make slaves of them. As they had done before, the Israelites cried to the Lord to help them. So the Lord sent Gideon to be their judge.

Gideon was threshing wheat one day and trying to hide it from the Midianites. As he worked, the Lord came to him in the form of an angel. Gideon told the Lord about the troubles the people of Israel were having because of the Midianites.

"You will free the people of Israel from the Midianites!" the Lord told him.

"But, Lord, how can I do that?" Gideon asked.

"That's easy!" the Lord replied. "I will be with you, and you will destroy their whole army as if it were only one man!"

Soon a large army of Midianites came with some friends from other countries and camped nearby.

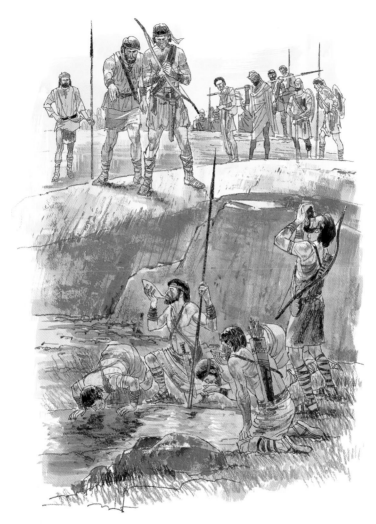

God told Gideon to send his soldiers home except for three hundred of them who drank from their hands. God promised to use these men to win over an enemy army.

Gideon blew a horn and called the men of Israel to go with him and fight them.

Then Gideon asked God to do a miracle. He wanted God to prove that he really was going to help fight against the Midianites. Gideon said he would leave some wool out on the ground all night. If the wool was wet with dew and the ground all around it was dry in the morning, this would be a miracle. And he would know that the Lord was going to help him.

So Gideon left the wool on the ground all night. Early the next morning he found it full of water. He wrung the dew out with his hands and filled a bowl with the water, but the ground around was dry. It was a miracle!

Then Gideon asked the Lord if he could try it again. This time he asked God to make the ground wet with dew and to let the wool stay dry. God agreed, so Gideon left the wool out another night. In the morning the wool was dry, but the ground all around was wet. It was another miracle!

Gideon knew now that the Lord would certainly help him fight against the Midianites. Gideon's little army got up early in the morning and started toward the big army of Midian. But the Lord told Gideon that his little army was too big!

"Send some of your men home," God said. "Anyone who is afraid may leave."

When Gideon told his men this, twenty-two thousand of them went home, while ten thousand stayed.

"There are still too many!" the Lord said. "Bring them down to the river, and I will choose the ones I want in the battle."

So Gideon brought them to the river. All the men were thirsty and began to drink. Some lifted the water to their mouths in their hands, and some stooped down and put their mouths into the water. The Lord said that only the three hundred men who drank from their hands could go with him to the battle!

Gideon told those men to come with him, for the Lord would help them win. He put them in three groups and gave each man a horn and a clay jar with a flame inside. He told them that when they came to the camp of the Midianites, they must all blow their horns. And they must shout, "For the Lord and for Gideon!" So that's what they did in the middle of the night.

When the Midianites heard the noise and saw the flames that had been hidden in the jars, they yelled in fear and ran for their lives. The Lord made them afraid both of the men of Israel and of each other, too. They were soon fighting one another all over the valley.

Gideon and his men chased them across the Jordan River. So the Midianites were driven out of Canaan, and the people of Israel were no longer their slaves.

Gideon was the judge of Israel for forty years. God gave him many sons and helped him live to be an old man.

STORY **57**
A Visit from an Angel

Judges 13

The people of Israel sinned again by worshiping idols. Again they became slaves, this time to the Philistines for forty years.

A man named Manoah and his wife were among those who still worshiped the Lord. But they were sad because they had no children. One day the angel of the Lord came to tell Manoah's wife that she and her husband would have a son. The angel said their son was to be set apart for God. He was never to drink wine or any other drink like it. And he was never to have his hair cut. The angel also said that when their son was grown, he would free Israel from the Philistines.

The woman ran and told her husband that a prophet had spoken to her, for she did not realize he was an angel. Then Manoah prayed, "Lord, let the prophet come again and teach us how to raise the child you are going to give us."

So the Lord heard and sent the angel again to the woman as she was out in the field. She ran to her husband and told him the man had come again. Manoah went with his wife and asked the angel, "Are you the man of God who was talking to my wife?"

"I am," he said.

Then Manoah asked him, "How shall we raise the child you have promised us?"

The angel answered, "Be sure to do everything I told your wife before."

Manoah begged the angel to stay and eat. (He still didn't know it was an angel.) But the angel said, "Even if I stay, I will not eat your food."

Then Manoah said, "Tell us your name so that we can honor you when the child you have promised us is born."

The angel answered, "Why do you ask my name? You wouldn't understand it."

Then Manoah put a young goat and some grain on a rock and offered it to God. The angel did a wonderful thing as a fire burned on the rock. The angel of the Lord went up toward heaven in the flames and disappeared! When Manoah and his wife saw this, they fell to the ground in worship.

Manoah was afraid. "We have seen God," he said. "We are going to die!"

But his wife told him, "If the Lord was going to kill us, he would not have accepted our offering or promised us a son."

A few months later God gave Manoah and his wife the son he had promised them, and they named him Samson. As the child grew, the Lord was kind to him and blessed him.

Samson, the Strong Man

Judges 16

When Samson grew up he fell in love with a Philistine woman named Delilah. The leaders of the Philistines told Delilah they would give her eleven hundred pieces of silver. All she had to do was find out what made Samson strong. So Delilah begged Samson to tell her how he became strong and how he could be made as weak as other men.

Samson told her a lie. He said that if he were tied with seven wet strings from a bow, he would be as helpless as any other man.

Delilah told this to the Philistine leaders. They brought her wet strings and hid in the room. She tied Samson up while he was asleep. Then she cried out, "The Philistines are here to get you, Samson!" He woke up and broke the wet strings as easily as if they were tiny, dried-up threads.

Delilah said he had told her a lie and begged him to tell her the truth. How could he be tied up so that he couldn't get away? This time Samson said that if he were tied with two new ropes that had never been used before, he would not be able to break them. So she tied him with two new ropes while men hid in the room again. Then she called out to him as before that the Philistines were coming to get him. But he broke the new ropes, too.

Samson is standing against two pillars. He has pushed them apart and the building is falling down on everyone.

Delilah scolded him for lying to her again, and once more she begged him to tell her how to tie him so he couldn't get away. Samson said that if she would weave his long hair into a loom, his strength would leave him and he would be helpless. So she did this. But when she told him the Philistines were coming, he was as strong as ever.

"How can you say that you love me when all you do is make fun of me and lie to me?" she asked. Day after day she begged him to tell her what made him strong. She gave him no rest. At last he told her the truth. He said that his hair had never been cut. If it were, he would no longer be strong, but as weak as other men.

Delilah realized that Samson was finally telling the truth. She sent this message to the Philistines: "Come once more. This time he has told me the truth!" So they came again and brought her the money they had promised.

Then, while Samson was asleep, a man came and cut his hair.

Delilah woke Samson up and told him that the Philistines were coming to get him. He thought he could get away as he always had before, for he didn't realize that the Lord had let his strength go away. But he could no longer fight against the Philistines. So they tied him with bronze chains. They poked out his eyes, making him blind, and put him in prison. There they made him work very hard grinding their corn.

But while he was in prison, his hair began to

grow longer again, and the Lord gave him back his strength.

One day the Philistine leaders called the people together to offer a sacrifice to their god, Dagon. Everyone praised Dagon at his temple because they thought he had helped them catch Samson.

"Send for Samson so we can tease him," someone said. So a young man led blind Samson out of prison and set him between the two pillars that held up the temple roof. Samson told the young man he wanted his hands on the pillars so he could lean against them. So the young man placed Samson's hands on the pillars.

The temple was filled with people, including all the Philistine leaders. Many of the people were having a party on the roof, laughing at Samson.

Then Samson prayed, "O Lord, help me, and make me strong one more time." He pushed hard against the two pillars he was leaning against and said, "Let me die with the Philistines." As he pushed, the pillars moved apart. Then the roof fell on the Philistine leaders, and all the people were killed.

Samson died too. But as he died he killed more of the enemies of Israel than he had while he was alive. His family came to get his body so they could bury it in a grave.

A Beautiful Love Story

Ruth

During the time judges ruled Israel, a man moved his family from Israel to the land of Moab so they could have food to eat. His sons married girls from Moab, and they all lived together for about ten years. Then the man and his two sons died, leaving his wife, Naomi, alone with her two daughters-in-law.

Naomi decided to go back home to the city of Bethlehem in Israel. Her daughters-in-law started the trip with her. When she told them they should go back to their homes, they cried. One of them, Orpah, went back to Moab. But Ruth didn't want to leave Naomi.

"I'll go with you," she said, "and live wherever you live. Your friends will be my friends, and your God will be my God."

When Naomi saw how much Ruth loved her, she didn't try to make her stay in the land of Moab. She agreed to let Ruth come with her to Bethlehem.

One day when it was time to gather grain, Ruth said to Naomi, "Let me go out to the fields. I will pick up grain dropped by the workers." She knew that one of God's laws said that poor people must always be allowed to pick up any grain that the field workers left. They could take this home to make food.

Naomi let Ruth go to the fields. So Ruth found a

field belonging to a man named Boaz and began picking up the grain that his workers left. When Boaz came out to the field later that morning, he asked the man in charge, "Who is that girl over there?"

Ruth came to Israel with Naomi, her mother-in-law. Ruth worked hard, and God helped her. Her son was Obed, her grandson was Jesse, and her great-grandson was King David.

"She is the one who came with Naomi from the land of Moab," the man replied.

Boaz went over and talked to Ruth. He was kind and told her to stay with his workers. When she was thirsty, he said she should help herself to as much water as she wished. And he told her to sit with his workers and eat the lunch he put out for them.

Ruth thanked him very much and asked him why he was so kind to her since she was from another land. Boaz said it was because he knew about her kindness to her mother-in-law. He knew that she had left her family and the land where she was born. She had come to live among the people of Israel to worship God. He said he hoped God would bless her and be good to her because she had done these things.

Ruth stayed in his field until evening. Then she took the grain she had gathered and carried it home to her mother-in-law. Naomi was happy to see how much Ruth brought. She asked the Lord to bless the man who had been so kind. Then she asked her daughter-in-law, "Who was it?"

Ruth said, "The man's name is Boaz." Naomi was surprised and told her he was from their own family!

Ruth said he had asked her to keep coming back to his field until the workers were done. Naomi told her, "Yes, do as he said." So Ruth went back day after day until the grain was all gathered.

One day Naomi said to Ruth, "Boaz will be working with the grain tonight." She told Ruth to go and find Boaz.

Ruth did as her mother-in-law said. Boaz worked hard that night. After a big supper, he lay down for the night beside a pile of grain. When it was dark, Ruth went over and lay at his feet! Around midnight he woke up, surprised that someone was there. "Who is it?" he asked.

"It's only me, sir," Ruth replied. Then she said what Naomi had told her to say. Because he was from her husband's family, she wanted him to take care of her and marry her.

The idea pleased him very much. "May the Lord bless you, my child," he replied. He said he would gladly marry her if he could, because everyone in Bethlehem knew what a fine person she was.

The next day Boaz called together ten city leaders and told them that he wanted to marry Ruth. All the city officials prayed that the Lord would bless Ruth and do great things for Boaz.

Naomi was happy when Boaz married Ruth, and Naomi was happy when the Lord gave them a son. They named the baby Obed, and they loved him very much. So did his grandmother, Naomi!

STORY 60

Job's Terrible Troubles Job

There was a man in the land of Uz named Job who worshiped God and was careful to do good at all times. God gave him seven sons and three

daughters. He also had a
lot of money. And he had three
thousand camels, seven thousand sheep,
one thousand oxen, five hundred donkeys,
and many servants. In fact, he was the richest
man in that part of the world.

After Job had enjoyed this good life for many
years, God sent him some terrible troubles. He let
all of Job's money and children be taken from him.
God did this to see if Job would still love and
worship him.

Job tore his clothes and bowed down to worship
God. He said, "I had nothing of my own when I was
born, and I will have nothing when I die. It was God
who gave me my children and everything else I
had. And now it is God who has taken them all
away. He knows what is best, and I thank him for
being the great God that he is."

After this, to test Job even more, God let him be
covered with sores from head to foot. Job's wife
became angry when she saw him sitting on the
ground in pain. She said, "Why do you still trust

Job worshiped God. And God blessed him with many children, along with many sheep, camels, donkeys, and oxen. For a while Job had terrible troubles, but then God blessed him again.

God? Speak against him for treating you like this even if he kills you for doing it."

Job answered her, "You are talking like a foolish woman. After we have had so many good things from God, should we not accept bad things too?"

So Job still said nothing that was wrong.

Three friends came to talk with Job and comfort him. He had changed so much that at first they didn't know him. Then they tore their clothes and cried and sat beside him on the ground. They said nothing for many days because they could see how much he was suffering.

These friends thought Job's troubles had been sent to him because he had done something bad. After a while they said, "You must have sinned. But if you will be sorry for your sins, God will forgive you and make you well again."

Job knew he had not done any bad things. He said to them, "You came to help me feel better, but what you say doesn't help me at all. I would rather you hadn't come."

Then Job talked about his troubles. "The Lord has sent me terrible troubles," he cried out. "Oh, that he would put me to death so that I wouldn't need to suffer anymore! Oh, that I had someone to speak to God for me, for he doesn't listen to my prayers anymore. Yet I know that my Savior is alive, and that after many years he will come to earth. And I shall rise from the grave and see God for myself."

But when Job could neither die nor get well, he became upset. He accepted his troubles for a little while, but he did not want to wait any longer for God to take them away.

Then Job began to say that his troubles were too great and that God was being unkind to him. And his three friends, instead of trying to cheer him up, still told him he had made God angry. They said Job must have been very, very bad to have so much pain.

Job became angry with his friends. That made them angry with him. They kept on talking back and forth for a long time, and all of them said things they shouldn't have.

Then God spoke through the wind. He reminded Job that he had made the earth, the sea, and the sky. God made it clear that he is the one who gives the wild animals their food and feeds the young birds when they are hungry. It is God who gives the beautiful tail to the peacock and the feathers to the ostrich. He makes the horse fast and strong and unafraid. He teaches the eagle to build her nest on the high rocks and to find food for her young ones.

Then Job knew he had sinned when he said that God was unkind. "I have spoken of things that I don't understand. I am sorry for my sin and sit here in the dust to show how sorry I am."

After this the Lord made Job well again. God blessed Job twice as much as before and made him twice as rich. Now Job had fourteen thousand sheep, six thousand camels, two thousand oxen, and one thousand donkeys. He also had seven more sons and three more daughters. So now, counting those in heaven also, he had twice as many children as before.

Job lived 140 years more after all these things happened to him. And he died when he was a very old man.

STORY 61

Jonah and the Giant Fish

Jonah

Long ago Nineveh was one of the greatest cities in the world, but it was also a very wicked city.

One day God said to the prophet Jonah, "Go to Nineveh. Tell the people that I am going to punish them because of their sins."

But Jonah didn't want to go. Instead, he ran away to Joppa, a city by the sea. There he found a ship headed in the opposite direction from Nineveh. So Jonah bought a ticket and got on board to try to get away from God.

After the ship sailed out to sea, the Lord sent a strong wind. The storm put the ship in danger of sinking. But Jonah didn't know about the danger, for he had gone to sleep at the bottom of the ship. The captain found him and woke him up.

"How can you sleep like this?" the captain

shouted. "Get up and pray to your God. Perhaps he will help us so we won't die."

Then the sailors said to one another, "This storm has been sent because someone on the ship has been bad. Let's draw straws to find out who it is."

While he was inside a giant fish, Jonah told God he was sorry about trying to run away. So God told the fish to spit him out onto the shore.

They did, and Jonah drew the short one. They said to him, "Tell us, what wicked thing have you done? What country do you come from?"

Jonah replied, "I am from Israel, and I am running away from the God who made the sea and the land."

Then the men were very much afraid and asked, "Why have you done this? What should we do so that the storm will stop?"

Jonah told them, "If you throw me into the ocean, it will become still again. I know that the storm is my fault."

The sailors didn't want to do it. But they knew they had to. As soon as they threw Jonah into the water, the wind stopped and the ocean was still. The men were amazed. They offered a sacrifice to the Lord and promised to worship him.

The Lord sent a huge fish to swallow Jonah as soon as he fell into the water! Jonah stayed alive in the fish three days and three nights. He prayed and told the Lord he was sorry about his sin. God heard his prayer and told the fish to spit him out on the shore.

Then the Lord spoke to Jonah a second time. "Go to Nineveh," he said, "and give the people there my message."

So Jonah went to Nineveh. It took a long time to walk through the big city. Finally he shouted out God's message, "Forty days from now Nineveh will be destroyed because of the sins of its people."

When the king of Nineveh and the people heard this, they believed God had sent Jonah. And they knew what he said would come true.

God saw that the people were sorry and that they had stopped being bad. So he did not destroy the city after all.

Jonah was very angry about this because the people of Nineveh were enemies of Israel. Also Jonah was afraid that people would laugh at him and say he didn't know what he was talking about.

He said to the Lord, "I knew you wouldn't destroy the city. That's why I ran away. Now please kill me, for I would rather die than live."

Then Jonah went to a place outside the city and waited to see if the city would be destroyed. That night the Lord caused a vine to grow, and the next day its thick leaves shaded Jonah's head from the hot sun. He was very glad it was there. But soon God sent a worm that ate through the stem of the vine, and the vine died. Then God sent a hot wind, and the sun beat down on Jonah. He grew tired and sick from the heat. Again he became angry.

Then God said, "You are angry because I have destroyed the vine, but you want me to destroy Nineveh. That's a city with more than 120,000 people who don't know the right way to live! Shouldn't I care about them?"

So God taught Jonah how wrong he was to wish that Nineveh would be destroyed.

Samuel Hears a Voice

1 Samuel 1–3

There was a man from Israel named Elkanah. Every year he and his family took a trip to the Tabernacle in Shiloh to worship God.

His wife Hannah was unhappy because she had no children. So one day while Hannah was at the Tabernacle, she prayed for a son. She promised the Lord that if he would give her a son, she would give that child back to him again. Her son would be set apart to serve the Lord all his life at the Tabernacle.

Hannah was crying as she prayed. Eli the priest was sitting there and saw her lips moving. But he couldn't hear her speaking. For some reason he thought she was drunk and scolded her for it.

But Hannah told him, "Oh, no, sir, I am not drunk. I am praying with all my heart to the Lord."

Then Eli told her he hoped God would give her what she prayed for. Hannah thanked him and didn't feel sad anymore.

The Lord answered Hannah's prayer and gave her a son. She named him Samuel, which means "I asked the Lord for him."

Soon after Samuel was born, the time came for his father to go to the Tabernacle at Shiloh again. But Hannah didn't go this time. She wanted

One night Samuel heard a voice. God was speaking to him. "Samuel, Samuel," God called. Then God told him what was going to happen to Eli and his sons.

to wait until her little boy was older. Then she would take him with her and let him stay at the Tabernacle to help God and his priests with their work.

Finally the time came when Samuel was old enough to live at the Tabernacle. So Hannah and her husband took him there.

"Do you remember me?" she asked Eli. "I am the woman who stood here praying to the Lord several years ago. You thought I was drunk, but I was praying for this child. The Lord has given me what I asked for. Now I am giving him back to the Lord again. As long as he lives, he will belong to the Lord." So Hannah and her husband let Samuel stay at the Tabernacle to help Eli the priest.

Eli had two sons who were also priests at the Tabernacle. The Lord had said that all his priests must be holy and good. But Eli's sons were very bad.

Eli, who was an old man, heard about the bad things his sons were doing. He scolded them, but he didn't make them stop being priests as he should have done.

Samuel, even though he was only a child, did what was right and pleasing to the Lord. His mother made him a coat each year and brought it to him when she and her husband came to the Tabernacle to worship God.

Samuel stayed at the Tabernacle and helped Eli in any way he could.

One night when Samuel had gone to bed, he heard a voice calling him. "I'm here," he answered. He jumped up and ran to ask Eli what he wanted.

But Eli said, "I didn't call you. Go back to bed."

After Samuel went to lie down, he heard the

voice again. He ran to Eli and asked again, "Why are you calling me, Eli? What do you want?"

"I didn't call you, my son," Eli said. "Go and lie down."

So Samuel went to lie down again. But he heard the voice a third time. He went to Eli and said, "I'm sure I heard you calling me. What do you want me to do?"

Then Eli knew it was the Lord who had called the child. He said to Samuel, "Go lie down. If you hear a voice again, say, 'Speak, Lord, I am listening.'"

So Samuel went back to bed. And the Lord came and called as before, "Samuel, Samuel."

Samuel answered, "Yes, Lord, speak, for I am listening." Then the Lord told him he was going to punish Eli and his sons. God said that Eli's sons were wicked, and Eli hadn't punished them.

The next day Samuel told Eli what God had said. As Samuel grew up, he kept on listening to God. And he told the people of Israel what God wanted them to know.

THE BOOK

about
One
Kingdom

God wanted to lead his people and be their king. But they wanted a man to be their king. They wanted to be like the wicked nations around them. So God let them have their own way.

The People Want a King

1 Samuel 7–9

Eli and his two sons were killed in a battle with the Philistines. Some time after that the Lord chose Samuel to be the judge of Israel.

Samuel said to his people, "If you will destroy your idols and obey the Lord, he will save you from the Philistines." So the people knocked down their idols. Then Samuel told them, "Come, all of you, to the city of Mizpah, and I will pray for you there."

So they came to Mizpah and said, "We have sinned against the Lord."

But when the Philistines heard that the people were at Mizpah, they went to fight them there. The Israelites were afraid and said to Samuel, "Pray hard that God will save us." Samuel took a young lamb and sacrificed it as an offering to the Lord. Then Samuel prayed, and the Lord listened to him. As Samuel was offering the lamb, the Philistine army came closer and closer. But God spoke with the sound of thunder, and they ran away in fear. So the Lord helped the men of Israel win.

When he was old, Samuel let his two sons help him rule. But they weren't fair like their father. So the leaders of Israel came to Samuel. They told him they wanted a king so that they would be like the other nations around them. Samuel was upset and asked the Lord what he should do.

God said, "The people don't want me to be their king any longer. You may do what they ask, but warn them what it will be like to have a king." So Samuel told them, "The king will make your sons serve in his army and work in his fields. Your daughters will be cooks and bakers in his kitchen. He will steal the best of your fields and gardens, and he will take your cattle and sheep. You will cry out because of the trouble your king will bring to you, but the Lord won't listen."

But the people still wanted a king.

A young man named Saul was good looking and taller than anyone else in Israel. One day some donkeys that belonged to Saul's father ran away and got lost. Saul's father said to him, "Take a servant with you, and look for the donkeys."

Saul and the servant went a long way but couldn't find the donkeys. Finally Saul said, "Let's go back. By now my father has probably stopped worrying about the donkeys and is worrying about us!"

By this time they were near the city where Samuel lived. The servant told Saul that a prophet lived there whose words always came true. "Let's go and ask him where to find the donkeys," he suggested.

"That's a good idea," Saul replied. "Come on, let's try it."

The Lord had already told Samuel, "Today I will send you the man who will be king of Israel." When Samuel saw Saul, the Lord said to him, "This is the man I told you about."

Saul didn't know Samuel. So he went up to him and asked, "Can you tell us where the prophet's house is?"

"I am the prophet," Samuel answered. Then he told Saul to bring his servant and come to a special dinner. As for the donkeys, Samuel said to stop worrying about them. Saul's father had already found them!

Samuel brought Saul and his servant to the dinner and gave them the best places to sit among the guests. Samuel told the cook to bring in the food that had been saved for an important guest. So the cook brought it and set it before Saul. Samuel told Saul to enjoy it because it had been chosen just for him. So Saul stayed with Samuel all that day. How surprised he was to receive all this special attention!

Samuel Says That Saul Is the One

1 Samuel 9–12

Early the next morning as soon as they got up, Samuel had a talk with Saul. Afterward he went with him to the gate of the city. As they were walking together, he said to Saul, "Tell the servant to go on ahead, but you stay here so I can show you what the Lord has commanded me to do."

When the servant was gone, Samuel took a bottle of olive oil and poured it on Saul's head. (Many years before, Moses had done this to Aaron to make him the high priest. Kings were anointed in the same way.) When Samuel poured the oil on Saul's head, it meant that God had chosen Saul to be the king of Israel. But no one except Saul and Samuel knew that God had done this, for the Lord was not yet ready to tell it to the people.

One day not long afterward Samuel made a speech to the people at Mizpah. He reminded them of the way God had brought them out of Egypt. But they were not satisfied with God's care. Now they were asking for a king to rule them instead. Samuel said that Saul was the one. Everyone wanted to see him, but they couldn't find him anywhere. So they asked the Lord where he was, and the Lord answered, "He is hiding," and told them where to look for him!

Then the people brought him out of his hiding place. He was a big, handsome fellow, taller than any of the rest of them. Samuel said, "See, here is the man the Lord has chosen for you. There is no one like him among all the people of Israel."

And they all shouted, "God save the king!"

After this the Ammonites came up to fight against an Israelite city. The Ammonites said they would punch out the right eye of each person there.

Then the leaders of the city sent messengers to Gibeah, where Saul lived, and told the people what the Ammonites had said. The people cried out in fear. Just then Saul came in from the field with some cows and asked what the trouble was.

When he found out, he took two oxen, cut them in pieces, and sent a piece to each part of the land of Israel. He also sent this message: "I will do this to the oxen of anyone who doesn't come to fight against the Ammonites."

Three hundred thousand came to Saul right away. He led them out against the Ammonites and won the battle.

Then Samuel made another speech to Israel. He told them that they had done wrong to ask for a king. The Lord was their king, and they shouldn't have wanted another. "Now see what the Lord is going to do," he said. "This is the time to bring the crops in from the fields. It never rains this time of the year. But I will ask the Lord to send thunder and rain. Then you will realize how wrong you were to ask for a king."

So the Lord sent a terrible storm. Then all the people were afraid of God and Samuel. "Pray for us," they said to Samuel.

"I will never stop praying for you," Samuel said. "You have sinned. But now if you obey the Lord, he will forgive you and take care of you. He will do it because he has chosen you to be his people. But if, instead of obeying him, you keep on doing what's wrong, you and your king will be destroyed."

STORY 65

Two Men against an Army

1 Samuel 13–14

Two years after Saul became king, he formed an army of three thousand soldiers. He led two thousand of them himself, and one thousand were led by Saul's son, Jonathan.

One day Saul gathered the whole army to fight some Philistines, who had come with thousands of chariots and horses. And they had so many soldiers that they couldn't be counted. When Saul's army saw the large number of soldiers coming to attack them, they went to hide. They hid in caves and bushes, among rocks on the mountains, and in holes in the ground. Some of them even went across the Jordan River, where the other tribes of

Israel lived. Only a few soldiers stayed with Saul, their king, and they were shaking with fear.

King Saul was waiting for Samuel, who had promised to meet him at Gilgal. Samuel was a priest, so he could offer gifts to God and ask God's directions for Israel's battle plans. Saul waited seven days for Samuel. When he still didn't come, Saul was upset and didn't know what to do. "Bring an offering," he commanded. Then he sacrificed an offering himself. This was a terrible thing for him to do, for God let no one sacrifice offerings except priests.

Just then Samuel arrived, and King Saul went to meet him. Samuel said at once, "You have done a terrible thing." Saul said he had been afraid to wait any longer. He thought the Philistines would come. But Samuel said it was wrong to disobey the Lord no matter what. He said that now the Lord would not let Saul keep on being the king. God would soon make someone else king.

One day King Saul's son, Jonathan, asked his helper to go with him to the camp of the Philistines. Jonathan thought the Lord might let the two of them win against the huge army of Philistines. He told his helper they should go and stand where the Philistines could see them. If the Philistines called out to them and told them to wait, they would go no farther. They would know that the Lord was not going to help them win. But they would know that God was going to help them if the Philistines said, "Come on up and fight!"

So Jonathan and his helper climbed up to where the Philistines were and stood where they could be seen. The Philistines made fun of them and said, "Look, the Israelites are coming up out of the holes where they were hiding!" Then they called out, "Come on up, and we will show you how to fight!"

When Jonathan heard them say this, he told the young man who was with him, "The Lord will help us win!" Then Jonathan climbed up the rocks to the camp of the Philistines. He used his hands as well as his feet to climb the steep hill, and his helper followed him. When they got to the top, they began to fight their enemies. And God helped them.

Then God sent an earthquake. The ground shook, and everyone in the Philistine army was afraid. They all ran away!

Saul and his men saw what was happening, so they went up to join the battle. Many of Saul's soldiers had been afraid. But now they came out of their hiding places and joined him again.

The Israelite soldiers were very hungry that night, for Saul had ordered them to eat nothing until evening. He wanted them to keep on chasing their enemies, who were running away. So none of them ate any food all day.

They came to a place where there was honey on the ground. But the hungry men were afraid to eat the honey. They were afraid King Saul would kill them for disobeying him. But Jonathan didn't know what his father had said. So he took the end of a stick he was carrying, dipped it into the honey, and ate some. When Saul heard about this, he was angry. "You must die, Jonathan," he said.

But the people said, "Jonathan is the one who has helped us win against our enemies!" So the king let Jonathan live.

STORY 66

A New King

1 Samuel 15–17

Sometimes King Saul obeyed God. But he did not always do everything God told him.

One day God told Samuel, "I am sorry that I made Saul king. He has not obeyed me."

When Samuel heard that, he felt sad and talked to God about it all night. But the next morning he knew he had to find King Saul and give him some bad news. When he found the king, Samuel told him, "You have not obeyed God. So now God will not let you keep on being the king."

King Saul knew he had sinned. He asked Samuel to go with him to worship God, so Samuel did. Later each of them went home, and they never saw each other again.

Then God told Samuel to go to Bethlehem and find a man there named Jesse. God said to anoint one of Jesse's sons by pouring oil on his head. That would set him apart as the next king.

But Samuel answered, "How can I? If Saul hears about it, he will kill me."

The Lord told Samuel to take a sacrifice to offer as a gift to him. "Ask Jesse to come and watch you," said God. "Then I will show you which son to anoint."

Samuel did as God commanded. He went to Bethlehem and got his sacrifice ready. Then he invited Jesse and his sons to come and watch.

When they came, Samuel saw that Jesse's oldest son was a fine-looking young man. Samuel thought God would want him to be the next king. But the Lord said no. He said, "Don't choose a person by the way he looks. I don't choose people that way. I see their thoughts and know what is in their heart."

Then Jesse called his second son, but the Lord said no. Jesse brought out his third, fourth, fifth, sixth, and seventh sons. But Samuel said, "The Lord has not chosen any of these. Are these all the sons you have?"

"No," Jesse answered, "there is one other. My youngest son is out taking care of the sheep."

"Send for him," Samuel said. So they brought in David.

The Lord said to Samuel, "Anoint him, for this is the one." So Samuel poured oil on David's head. Then the Lord sent his Holy Spirit into David's heart to make him wise and good. But the Lord took his Spirit away from Saul.

While angels are good spirits who serve God, there are also evil spirits who serve Satan. One of

David was a shepherd before he became the king of Israel. One time he killed a lion to keep his sheep safe.

these evil spirits went into Saul and troubled him by making him afraid and angry. Saul's helpers suggested that harp music might chase out the evil spirit whenever it troubled him.

One of Saul's men knew David and knew that besides being a shepherd, he could play the harp well. So Saul sent messengers to Jesse and told him to send his son David to him. Jesse got a young goat and loaded a donkey with bread and wine. He sent these with David as a present to King Saul. But he didn't let Saul know that Samuel had anointed David to be the new king! David stayed with Saul and helped him. Whenever the evil spirit troubled Saul, David played sweet music on a harp to quiet him. Then the evil spirit would go away. When David was no longer needed, he would return home. He would take care of his father's sheep until the next time the king needed him.

STORY 67
David Kills a Giant
1 Samuel 17–18

Once again the Philistine army came to fight Israel. So King Saul and the Israelites got ready for the battle.

One of the Philistine soldiers was a giant named

Goliath. He wore a lot of armor. He had a bronze helmet to protect his head. He wore a metal coat. And sheets of bronze covered his legs so that no sword or spear could hurt him.

Goliath stood in the valley between the two armies. From there he yelled to the army of Israel, "I'll fight the best man in your army. If he can kill

Goliath laughed at David's sling. But David used it to shoot a stone that hit Goliath in the forehead. And Goliath fell to the ground.

me, we Philistines will be your slaves. But if I kill him, then you must be our slaves!"

Saul and the men of Israel were afraid. No one in Saul's army would go out and fight with the giant. For forty days he came out every morning and evening to dare the men of Israel to fight him.

During this time David was taking care of his father's sheep at Bethlehem. But his three oldest brothers were in Saul's army. One day David's father said to him, "Take this food to your brothers, and take all this cheese to their captain. See how they are getting along."

David found his brothers. As he was talking to them, the giant, Goliath, came out and shouted at the Israelites the way he always did.

"How dare this giant talk like that to the army of the living God?" David asked. When some of the men realized that David wanted to fight Goliath, they told Saul. So the king sent for him.

"You can't fight that giant," Saul said. "Why, you're only a boy, while Goliath has been a soldier for many years."

"But I can!" David answered. "One day while I was watching my father's sheep, a lion grabbed a lamb. I went after the lion and hit it. Then he dropped the lamb. The lion came after me, but I caught him by his beard and killed him. Another time I killed a bear with my hands. And I'll do the same to this wicked giant, for he has dared the army of the living God to fight him. The Lord who saved me from the lion and the bear will save me from the giant."

"All right," Saul said. "Go and fight him, and the Lord be with you."

Then Saul gave David his own armor—his bronze helmet and his metal coat. But David said, "I'm not used to these." And he took them off again.

The young shepherd took only a sling and the stick that he used to keep the sheep safe. Choosing five smooth stones from a stream of water, he put them into his shepherd's bag. Then he walked toward Goliath.

The giant didn't think David was worth fighting. David wasn't a soldier. He was just a shepherd boy. "Come over here so I can kill you," Goliath yelled.

David answered, "You come to me trusting in your sword, your shield, and your spear. But I come to you trusting in the God of Israel. Today he will give you to me!"

As Goliath came closer, David ran toward him. Putting his hand into his shepherd's bag, he took out a stone, put it into his sling, and sent it sailing toward Goliath. It hit him right in the forehead, and he fell to the ground.

The Philistines started to run away. Then the army of Israel gave a great shout and started after them. The Israelites won against their enemy.

Abner, the captain of the army of Israel, took David to Saul.

"Who are you, young man?" Saul asked.

David answered, "I am the son of Jesse from Bethlehem." For some reason Saul didn't realize that this was the same boy who used to play the harp for him.

STORY 68
Saul Is Jealous of David
1 Samuel 18

After the battle with the Philistines, Saul made David a captain in his army.

One day King Saul and David were traveling together through some of the cities of the land. The women came out with songs and dances to praise them for winning. But they praised David more than they did Saul! They said that Saul had killed thousands of Philistines, but David had killed tens of thousands! Saul was very upset about this, and from then on he was very angry with David.

The next day an evil spirit came into Saul's heart and troubled him. So David played for him on the harp. But Saul had a spear in his hand, and he threw it at David, trying to kill him. David saw it coming and jumped out of the way just in time.

Saul was afraid of David because he saw that the Lord was with him. The Lord helped David do everything well, and all the people loved him.

One day Saul said to him, "I will let you marry my older daughter if you will go out and fight against the Philistines." Saul said this because he hoped the Philistines would kill David.

So David went out to fight with the Philistines. He won the battle, but Saul didn't keep his promise, for he made his daughter marry someone else instead.

One day Saul heard that his younger daughter, Michal, loved David. He said David could marry her if he would kill one hundred Philistines. Saul hoped that this time David would really be killed.

So David went with his soldiers to fight the Philistines. They killed two hundred of them. This time King Saul let his daughter marry David.

Saul became more and more angry with David and afraid of him. He hated David and became his enemy.

STORY 69

David's Best Friend

1 Samuel 19–20

Saul was so angry that he told his helpers and his son Jonathan that they should try to kill David. But Jonathan, who was David's best friend, told him what the king had said. "Go and hide for a while until I talk with my father," Jonathan said, "and I will tell you what he says." So David went to hide in a field.

Jonathan begged his father not to hurt David. He

said, "David has always helped you. He killed Goliath, the giant. Then our men of Israel won against the Philistines. You were happy then, so why are you trying to kill David now?"

Saul promised not to hurt David. Then Jonathan got David from his hiding place. He brought David to Saul, and David stayed at Saul's house as before.

But once again the evil spirit came into Saul's heart. While David was playing the harp, Saul threw the spear at David again. Once more David jumped away just in time, and the spear went into the wall. Then David ran for his life.

Jonathan hadn't heard that his father was after David again. When David found him, he promised to do everything he could to help.

The next day was a special religious holiday, and Saul would expect David to eat at his table. But David was afraid to go. He said to Jonathan, "Tell your father that I asked to go home to Bethlehem. Say that I want to be with my family when they offer a special gift to God. If Saul is angry when he hears this, we'll know that he wants to kill me. But if he isn't angry, we'll know everything is all right." Jonathan agreed to this plan.

"But how will I find out what your father says?" David asked Jonathan.

"Come out into the field with me and I'll show you what to do," Jonathan said.

Jonathan showed David a large rock and told him to hide behind it until the next day. "I will come out into the field and shoot three arrows,"

David and Jonathan were good friends. They helped each other and enjoyed being together.

said Jonathan. "And I'll send a boy to pick them up. If I tell him that the arrows are on this side, you will know that my father is not angry. But if I say that the arrows are beyond you, then you must leave so my father can't hurt you."

When David's seat at Saul's table was empty for two days, Saul asked Jonathan, "Where is David? He hasn't been here either yesterday or today."

Jonathan answered, "David asked if he could go to Bethlehem, for his family is offering a special gift to God. His brother told him to be there."

Saul was very angry with Jonathan for letting David go. He said, "You'll never get to be king as long as David is alive. Bring David to me so I can kill him."

The next day Jonathan went to the field where David was hiding. He took a boy with him. Then he shot an arrow over the boy's head.

"The arrow is beyond you. Go find it. Hurry, hurry," Jonathan shouted to him. David heard him and knew he must go away.

The boy found the arrows and brought them to Jonathan. Then Jonathan gave his bow and arrows to the boy and told him to take them back to the city.

As soon as he was gone, David came out from his hiding place. The two friends cried together over what was happening. Jonathan told David to go in peace. He said they would always be friends. So David had to run away and keep hiding as if he had done something wrong.

A Piece of Saul's Robe

1 Samuel 22–24

David went from one place to another to hide from King Saul. Other men came with him. Soon about four hundred men were traveling with David.

One day King Saul learned where David was. The king said, "Now I will catch him. I'll gather my soldiers all around the city, and he won't be able to escape."

Saul called his whole army to go down and get David. So David asked the Lord if the people in the city would fight against Saul.

The Lord answered, "No, they will let Saul get you!"

So David and his men went to hide in the woods. There were about six hundred of them now. Saul searched for him everywhere, but God kept him safe.

One day Prince Jonathan, King Saul's son, came to see David. "Don't worry," Jonathan said. "My father will never find you. You are going to be the next king of Israel." And again they promised to always be friends. Then Jonathan went back home, but David stayed in the woods.

Some people from Ziph went to King Saul and said, "We will show you where David is hiding." So Saul and his men went looking for David again. But just as they were closing in on him, a messenger came to Saul. He said, "Hurry back, for the Philistines have invaded your land." So Saul had to return home. The Lord had saved David again! Now he went to a new place to hide.

Saul came back after fighting the Philistines. He chose three thousand of his soldiers and took them out to hunt for David among the rocks where the wild goats lived.

Saul went into the same cave where David and his men were hiding! Saul didn't know they were there, of course, so he walked into the cave alone. David's men wanted to kill Saul, but David wouldn't let them. Instead, he quietly crawled up behind Saul and cut off a piece of his robe. Then he hid again.

After Saul left the cave, David shouted to him. Saul looked around to see who was calling. Then David asked Saul, "Why do you listen to the wicked people who say that I want to hurt you? I could easily have killed you. Some of my men said that I should. But I told them I would never kill the man chosen by the Lord to be king."

Then David held up the piece of Saul's robe he had cut off. "Look at this piece of your robe!" he said. "I cut it off, but I didn't kill you. Now you know that I'm not trying to hurt you. So why are you trying to kill me? Let the Lord decide which one of us is doing wrong. Perhaps he will punish you for what you are doing to me, but I will never harm you in any way."

When Saul heard David speaking like this, he started crying. He said to David, "You are a better man than I am, for you have done good to me, while I have done wrong to you. Even today you have shown me how kind you are, for you could have killed me but you didn't. May the Lord be good to you because of the good you have done. I know for sure now that someday you will be the king of Israel. Promise me that when you become the new king, you won't hurt anyone in my family." David promised.

Then Saul went back home, but David and his men stayed where they were.

STORY 71

A Cruel Man with a Kind Wife

1 Samuel 25

David went to a place where a very rich farmer lived. The man owned three thousand sheep and one thousand goats. His name was Nabal, and his wife's name was Abigail. She was a kind and beautiful woman, but he was mean and not truthful.

David and his men had been camping near the place where Nabal kept his sheep and goats. David needed a lot of food for his men, but he never took one sheep or goat from Nabal.

Then the time came for Nabal's workers to cut the wool off his sheep. David told ten of his young men to go and talk with Nabal. He said to ask the farmer if he would share some of the food that had been fixed for his workers.

But when the young men talked to Nabal, he laughed. "Who is David?" he asked. "There are plenty of men like him who run away from their masters!"

So David's ten men came back and told him what Nabal had said. Then David told his men, "Get your swords." So they did. Then they started out for Nabal's place.

Before the men got there, one of Nabal's servants went to Abigail. He told her how mean Nabal had been to David's messengers. "Yet David's men have always been very good to us," the young man said. "They kept us safe night and day when they were camping near us."

Quickly Abigail took two hundred loaves of bread, two bags of wine, five sheep, five sacks of grain, one hundred raisin cakes, and two hundred fig cakes. She loaded them on donkeys and went out to find David. But she didn't tell her husband.

Abigail met David and his men as they were coming toward her house, ready to fight. She got down from her donkey and bowed low before David. She said, "Here is a present I have brought for you and your men." She told David she knew that the Lord would bless him and save him from King Saul. She knew that David would become the king of Israel. Then she said, "Please don't do something you'll be sorry about later on."

David listened to her and thanked the Lord for sending her. He was glad for the things she had said, because her words kept him from going in anger to kill Nabal. He took the food Abigail brought and told her he would not hurt her husband. After he sent her home, he and his men went back to their camp.

When Abigail came home, Nabal was having a big party and was drunk. So she said nothing to him about David until the next morning. Then she told him everything, and all his strength left him. He couldn't move—he lay as still as a stone for about ten days. Then he died.

When David heard that Nabal was dead, he sent messengers to Abigail to ask her to come and be his wife. She said yes!

STORY 72
David Steals the King's Spear
1 Samuel 26–27

Some enemies of David came to King Saul and told him where David was hiding. Saul hadn't really changed. He still wanted to kill David. So when he learned where David was hiding, he took three thousand men to look for him.

David heard about it and sent some men to see

what Saul was doing. They soon brought back word that Saul had come. Then David and another man quietly went into Saul's camp one night. Saul was sleeping, with his spear stuck in the ground by his head. Abner, the general of Saul's army, and the rest of his soldiers were sleeping around the king.

The man with David wanted to kill Saul. But David said no. "Don't do it," he said. "It would be a sin to kill the king God gave us. Perhaps the Lord will kill him, or he may die in a battle. But I won't kill him."

Then David had an idea. "Let's steal his spear and bottle of water!" David said. So they crawled up close to Saul's head and took them. They got away before anyone woke up, because the Lord had put Saul and his men into a deep sleep.

Then David stood on top of a hill where he was safe and shouted to Abner. The general woke up suddenly and jumped to his feet. "Who is it?" he called.

David shouted back, "Why haven't you kept better watch over the king, so that no one could come and kill him? Where is the king's spear and the bottle of water that were beside his head?"

Saul knew David's voice. He asked, "Is that you, David?"

David said, "Yes, my king. Why are you still chasing me and trying to kill me?"

Saul said, "I have sinned. I have been wrong. Come back, my son, for I won't try to hurt you anymore."

King Saul has been trying to catch David and kill him. Now David is taking the king's spear, but he doesn't try to hurt him.

David answered, "Here is your spear. Let one of the young men come over and get it."

Then David went away again, and Saul went back home.

David didn't believe that Saul would stop trying to kill him. The king had cried and called David his son before. But then he had come out with three thousand men to get David.

"Someday he will finally find me and kill me," David said to himself. "I must go and live in the land of the Philistines. Then Saul will give up looking for me."

So David took his six hundred men and their families to a Philistine city. The king there welcomed David and all the others, letting them stay in his land. Then he gave them the city of Ziklag to live in. He hoped David and his men would help his people in times of war.

When Saul heard that David had fled to the Philistines, he stopped looking for him.

STORY 73

David Becomes the King

1 Samuel 31; 2 Samuel 1–2; 4–5

While David was living in the land of the Philistines, those people began fighting King Saul. One day Saul's army lost the battle with the Philistines. Then his enemies began moving in on him. They killed

Many years before David became king, God had told Samuel to anoint the shepherd boy as the next king of Israel.

Jonathan and two of Saul's other sons. Then Saul fell on his own sword and died.

David was still at his home in Ziklag. He didn't know that the Philistines had won over the Israelites in the battle. But soon a messenger arrived to tell David about it. "The Israelites have lost the battle and many are dead. Saul and Jonathan are dead too."

"How do you know?" David asked.

The young man said, "I was with Saul when the Philistines surrounded him and were ready to kill him. When he saw me he shouted, 'Quick! Come and kill me before they take me and hurt me.' So I did."

But the young man was lying, for Saul had fallen on his own spear. The young man thought that Saul's death would please David and that David would give him a reward. But David wasn't pleased at all. He was so sad that he tore his clothes. All the men who were with him tore theirs, too. They cried for Saul and his son Jonathan, and for all the men of Israel who had died.

David asked the young man why he wasn't afraid to kill the king God had chosen. "You must die for this," David told him. And so he was killed instead of getting a reward.

Afterward, David asked the Lord if he should go to the land of Israel. And the Lord said yes. Then David asked him what part of Israel he should go to. And the Lord told him, "Go to the city of Hebron."

David was now thirty years old. When he came to Hebron, the leaders of the tribe of Judah asked him to be their king, and he agreed.

But the other tribes of Israel didn't come to David, for they already had a king. He was a son of Saul. One day when that king was taking a nap, two of his army captains came into his house. They pretended they wanted to bring him a gift. But when they came into his room, they killed him.

David was angry. He reminded them that he once had a man killed for saying he had killed Saul. Now these two army captains must die too, for they had killed another king.

When the other tribes saw that their king was dead, they asked David to be their king. So at last David was king over all twelve of the tribes of Israel.

David now took over the city of Jerusalem and lived there in a strong fort. He became a very great man, for the Lord helped him in everything he did.

King Hiram of Tyre and King David were good friends. King Hiram's people were very good builders. So Hiram sent men to build a palace for David in Jerusalem.

King David Wants to Build a Temple

2 Samuel 7; 1 Kings 1–2; 1 Chronicles 22; 28–29

One day as David was sitting in his beautiful palace in Jerusalem, he started thinking about the Ark of God. This important gold-covered box had God's commandments inside it. The box was out in the Tabernacle, which was like a great big tent. David felt in his heart that he should build a Temple for the Ark, and it should be more beautiful than his palace.

At that time, there was a prophet named Nathan. The Lord said to Nathan, "Tell David not to build the Temple." The Lord was glad David wanted to build it, but he said one of David's sons would be the next king. He was the one who should build the temple. So David stopped his building plans and left it for his son to do, as the Lord had told him to.

The years went by and King David fought many battles. God was with him and helped him win over his enemies. He was a good ruler over his people.

David remembered what God had said about the beautiful Temple for the Ark. His son was to build it. So David collected stones and timber and iron— everything his son would need to build the Temple when he became the new king.

Then David talked to his son Solomon. David said

to Solomon that God wanted him to be the next king. David explained that many years before, he himself had wanted to build God's Temple. But God told him not to, because he was a soldier and had killed many people. God wanted a man of peace to build his Temple. He promised that Solomon would rule in peace and could build God's Temple.

King David called together all the leaders of his kingdom and told them that the Lord had chosen Solomon to build the Temple. Then David said to these princes and great men, "You must be very careful to do whatever the Lord tells you to do. Then you will always have this good land that God has given us. And you can leave it to your children when you die."

Then, as the leaders of the kingdom listened, David said to Solomon, "My son, obey God and worship him with all your heart. If you do, he will be your friend. But if you turn away from him, he will destroy you."

Then David gave Solomon the plans and drawings of the Temple and of all the furniture inside. The Lord had given David these plans, and now he was passing them on to Solomon. And David gave Solomon all the gold and silver he had collected. "It is a big job," David said to his son. "But don't be afraid to begin building, for the Lord God will keep on helping you until the Temple is finally built."

David prayed a beautiful prayer for the people, and for Solomon his son. He asked the Lord to help them keep on loving him and obeying his laws.

Now David was getting old, and he knew he soon would die. He commanded his government officials to take his own mule and let Solomon ride on it to a fountain just outside Jerusalem. There they were to anoint him as king over all the land. "Blow the trumpet," he said. "And shout that Solomon is the new king! Then bring him back here to the palace and let him sit on my throne, and he will be the new king of Israel."

So that is what they did, and that is how Solomon became the new king.

David finally died after being king for forty years. All the people loved him, and they buried him in the city of Jerusalem.

God's Beautiful Temple

1 Kings 3; 5–7; 2 Chronicles 2–4

Solomon loved God. He was careful to do what was right, just like David, his father.

One night God spoke to King Solomon in a dream, telling him he could have anything he wanted! Solomon asked for wisdom. He wanted to always know what was the best way to help his people.

God was pleased with what Solomon asked for. God was pleased that he had not asked to have money, or a long life, or to win over his enemies. Because he hadn't done that, God would give him

It took seven years to build this beautiful Temple for the Lord. The people of Israel brought lambs, goats, and cattle to be sacrificed as gifts to God.

the wisdom he asked for and all these other things too! So God made Solomon very rich as well as very wise.

Solomon now got ready to build the Temple. He asked David's friend, King Hiram of Tyre, to send men into the forests to cut down trees for the building. He knew Hiram's men were good at cutting down trees. Hiram agreed and sent his men to the Lebanon mountains, where cedar trees grew. They worked together, cutting down the trees and then bringing them to the sea, which was not far away. There they made them into rafts, and floated them along the shore toward Jerusalem.

Solomon sent many thousands of his own people to Lebanon too. Some of them helped get the cedar logs ready for the Temple. Some cut stones for it. And some were in charge of the work.

Now Solomon began to build, carefully following the pattern his father, David, had given him. The Temple was to be 90 feet long, 30 feet wide, and 45 feet high.

No noise was heard all the time the Temple was being built. The bottom of the Temple was built of stone. And each stone was cut into the right shape before it was brought to the place where the Temple was being built.

When the walls were up, Solomon had them covered on the inside with cedar boards. These boards were carved with the shapes of flowers, then covered with gold. Even the floor of the Temple was covered with pure gold.

Across the middle of the Temple he hung a blue, purple, and red curtain. This made two rooms just as there had been in the Tabernacle. The room way at the back was for the Ark and was called the Most Holy Place. The inside walls of this room were covered with wood carved into the shapes of angels, palm trees, and flowers. These walls and the floor were then covered with gold. In this special room he made two figures of angels with their wings spread out. The figures were fifteen feet high. They were carved out of the wood of olive trees, then covered with gold. They stood with their faces turned toward the main room of the Temple. And their wings reached from one side of the little room to the other.

Solomon asked for one of Hiram's best workers to come and make the Temple as beautiful and perfect as possible. This man made beautiful things from gold, silver, bronze, and iron. He also made things from wood and from costly linen cloth.

He made two great bronze pillars to stand in front of the Temple, one on the right side and the other on the left. And he made a bronze altar, which was four times as large as the one Moses had made for the Tabernacle. There was also a great tank of water that rested on the backs of twelve bronze oxen.

He made ten huge brass tubs. They were set on wheels so they could be moved from one place to another. These were to hold water for washing the sacrifices that would be offered to God.

And he made ten gold lampstands to give light inside the Temple.

It took seven years to finish all this work.

Solomon Forgets God

1 Kings 8–11

Now Solomon called all the leaders of Israel to Jerusalem. He wanted them to take the Ark of God from the Tabernacle to the Temple.

The priests carried the Ark into the Most Holy Place and set it under the figures of the angels. When the priests came out, leaving the Ark inside, a bright cloud filled the Temple—God was there!

The king stood in front of the people and thanked God for helping him build the Temple. Then he knelt down, spreading out his hands toward heaven. He asked the Lord to hear and answer all the prayers the people of Israel would ever pray there. Maybe their enemies would win over them because of their sins. If that happened, Solomon asked that the Lord would forgive his people and help them when they came to the Temple and prayed. Maybe the Lord would need to punish his people by not sending rain on their fields and keeping their crops from growing. Or sickness might come into the land. Or swarms of locusts and caterpillars might come and eat their grain. Whatever trouble might come,

Solomon asked that the Lord would always forgive his people and help them. The king asked God to do this when the people came to the Temple and prayed.

Then King Solomon gave many animals to the people to sacrifice. He gave them 22,000 oxen and 120,000 sheep! So the king and all the people set the Temple apart as a house for the Lord. It would be a special place for his Ark and a place where sacrifices would always be offered to him.

One night soon afterward, the Lord told King Solomon that he had heard the king's prayer. God said he would accept the Temple as his home. He promised that when the Israelites sinned against him, he would forgive them and stop punishing them. But they would need to be sorry and come to the Temple to pray. God promised again that if Solomon would obey him, Solomon would be the king as long as he lived. And his children and children's children would be kings after him.

But if Solomon and his people turned away from God and worshiped other gods, God would no longer bless them. Instead he would drive them out of the good land he had given them. And he would no longer stay in the beautiful Temple but would destroy it. Then all who passed by would ask, "Why has the Lord done such terrible things to this land and to his Temple?" And the answer would be, "Because the people disobeyed the Lord God of their fathers, who brought them out of Egypt."

Many people learned to know about Solomon and

his wisdom. The queen of Sheba, a country far away, heard about Solomon, so she came to visit him. She brought many servants with her, along with camels carrying spices, gold, and precious stones. She asked Solomon hard questions about many things. Solomon answered them all and explained everything. She saw his beautiful palace, all the food on his table, and the many servants he had. She saw the Temple and all that went on there. She said, "I heard of your riches when I was in my own land. But you are far richer and wiser than I was told!"

Solomon became wiser than all other kings. People from all over the world came to learn from him.

But Solomon had married many young women from other countries. The Lord had told him never to do this, but he did it anyway. Instead of loving God, Solomon's wives worshiped other gods. And when the king grew old, his wives talked him into worshiping their gods too. So he didn't keep on obeying God as his father, David, had done. Solomon even built beautiful places where his wives could worship their gods.

The Lord was very angry. He said that because Solomon had done these things, his son could not be king of all the land. But because of David, the Lord didn't take away all the kingdom from Solomon's son. God let him be the king of just a small part of Israel, giving the rest to someone else. And the Lord brought enemies to make trouble for Solomon because of this great sin.

THE
BOOK
about
Two
Kingdoms

Two Kings and
Two Kingdoms

1 Kings 11–12; 2 Chronicles 10–11

One day as a young man named Jeroboam was leaving Jerusalem, a prophet came up to him with a message from God. The prophet grabbed Jeroboam's new coat and tore it into twelve pieces! Then he gave Jeroboam ten of the pieces. The prophet explained why he did this. It was because the Lord was going to let Jeroboam be king over ten of the tribes of Israel.

When King Solomon heard about this, he tried to kill Jeroboam. But Jeroboam ran away into the land of Egypt where Solomon couldn't hurt him.

Solomon was the king of Israel for forty years. Then he died and was buried in Jerusalem.

After that, Jeroboam's friends sent a message to him in Egypt. They told him to come home, so he did. Then he and all the people went to Solomon's son to make him their king. The son's name was Rehoboam.

The people talked with Rehoboam about how

hard his father, Solomon, was on them when he was their king. They wanted to know if Rehoboam planned to treat them better than his father had. If he would promise, then they would let him be their king.

Rehoboam told them to come back in three days. At that time he would give them his answer.

After they had gone, Rehoboam went to the old men who had been friends of his father. He asked them what he should do. They told him to promise to be kind to the people. They said that if he did this, the people would be happy to let him be their king for as long as he lived.

But Rehoboam did not like what the old men said. So he asked the young men who had grown up with him what they thought. The young men told him to say that he would be even harder on the people than his father had been.

When the people came back for his answer three days later, Rehoboam did what the young men had told him to. He shouted, "If you think my father was hard on you, well, I'll be even harder on you than he was."

The people were very angry when they went home. Only the tribes of Judah and Benjamin let Rehoboam, Solomon's son, be their king. The other ten tribes said that Rehoboam couldn't be their king. They wanted Jeroboam instead. So Jeroboam was king over ten tribes, as the prophet had said, and Rehoboam was king over only two.

When Rehoboam saw that the ten tribes had left

him, he sent a messenger to them, asking them to come back. But they threw stones at the messenger and killed him. Then Rehoboam quickly called together all the soldiers of Judah and Benjamin. There were 180,000 of them. He formed them into an army to go out and fight against the ten tribes. But God sent a prophet to Rehoboam and the

King Jeroboam and the people of Israel did not obey God. They worshiped these gold idols.

people. The prophet said that God did not want his people to fight against their family in the other ten tribes. He wanted them to go back home. So they did.

Now there were two kings ruling over the people of Israel. Until this time, one king had ruled over all of them—first Saul, then David, and then Solomon. But now Rehoboam, Solomon's son, was king over just the tribes of Judah and Benjamin. His kingdom was called Judah. Jeroboam was king over the other ten tribes. His kingdom was called Israel.

One day King Jeroboam said to himself, "My people will go to worship at the Temple. That's in the city of Jerusalem, which is in Judah. There they will see King Rehoboam, the son of the great King Solomon. And they will want him to be their king instead of me."

So King Jeroboam made two gold idols shaped like calves. He put them in different parts of his land—one at Bethel and the other at Dan. And the people went there to worship the idols, for Jeroboam said to the people, "It is too far for you to go to Jerusalem to worship God. These gold idols are your gods; worship them." What a wicked thing for Jeroboam to say!

All the good priests who lived in Israel moved to Jerusalem in Judah. And many other good people who would not worship the gold calves went with them. They chose Rehoboam as their king.

A Little Boy Lives Again!

1 Kings 16–17

Jeroboam was a bad king, but he ruled over the ten tribes of Israel for 22 years. The kings who ruled after he died were bad too. King Ahab was worse than any of the others.

Ahab married the daughter of a king who did not worship God. The woman's name was Jezebel, and she worshiped Baal, a god that was not real. King Ahab built a temple for this idol in the city of Samaria and worshiped Baal too.

The Lord was angry with King Ahab and sent the prophet Elijah to him. Elijah said that as punishment, there would be no more rain in the land of Israel for many years. It would not rain until he asked God to send it.

The Lord told Elijah to hide after he talked to the king. "Go and hide beside a brook east of the Jordan River," the Lord said. "You can get drinking water from the brook, and I have told the birds to feed you there!" So Elijah hid by the brook, and big, black birds called ravens brought him food every morning and evening. But after a while the brook dried up because there had been no rain.

Then the Lord said to Elijah, "Go to the city of Zarephath. I have told a woman whose husband died to feed you there."

When Elijah came to the gate of the city, he saw a woman gathering sticks. He called to her and said, "Please bring me a cup of water to drink." As she was going to get it, he called to her again, "And bring a piece of bread, too!"

But she answered, "God knows I have no bread. I have only a handful of flour in a jar and a little olive oil in a bottle. Now I am gathering sticks to bake a small loaf of bread for my son and me. After we eat it, we will have no more food and we will die."

But Elijah said, "No, you won't! Go and bake the bread, but make a small loaf for me first. Then there will be plenty left for you and your son! That's because the Lord says the little flour and olive oil you have will last until he sends rain and the crops grow again!"

The woman did as Elijah said. And sure enough, there was always olive oil left in the bottle and flour in the jar, no matter how much she used! It was a wonderful miracle that went on for a long time!

One day the woman's son became sick and died. Elijah took him from her arms and carried him upstairs. Elijah went to his own room and put the boy on his bed. Elijah prayed, "Lord, why have you let this terrible thing happen to the woman who lets me stay in her home? Please, Lord, let the child live again!"

God heard Elijah's prayer, and the boy came back to life. What a wonderful miracle! Then Elijah took him down to his mother. She was very happy and said, "Now I know for sure that God sent you and that your words are from him."

God sent Elijah away to hide. He camped beside a brook and ate the food the ravens brought him.

STORY 79

Elijah Faces Baal's Prophets

1 Kings 18

Many other prophets of the Lord besides Elijah brought messages from God to the land of Israel. But Queen Jezebel, the wicked wife of King Ahab, hated them all and tried to kill them.

Obadiah, who was in charge of Ahab's palace, loved God. So he hid a hundred of the Lord's prophets in caves where Jezebel couldn't find them. He sent food and water to them there.

For more than three years there had been no rain. Then the Lord said to Elijah, "Go to King Ahab and tell him I will soon send rain."

King Ahab and Obadiah were out looking everywhere to find grass for the king's horses and mules to eat so they wouldn't die. The men went in different directions so they could finish their work faster.

As Obadiah was walking along, Elijah came toward him. Obadiah asked, "Is it really you, Elijah, sir?"

"Yes," Elijah answered. "Now go and tell King Ahab that I am here."

So Obadiah found the king, and he came to

meet Elijah. When King Ahab saw Elijah, the king blamed the prophet for all the trouble in the land.

But Elijah answered, "I have not made trouble, but you and your family have. That's because you worship Baal instead of the Lord."

Then Elijah told King Ahab to have all the people come to Mount Carmel. He said to bring all 450 prophets of Baal. So everyone came.

Elijah asked the people, "How long will it be before you decide whether you will serve God or Baal?" No one answered.

"Bring two young bulls as an offering," Elijah said. "Let Baal's prophets kill one of them and lay it on Baal's altar, without any fire under it. And I will take the other young bull and kill it and lay it on the Lord's altar, without any flame under it. Then let them pray to Baal to send down fire from heaven to burn up their young bull. And I will pray to the Lord for fire to come from heaven to burn up the young bull on the altar of the Lord. The god that sends fire from heaven to burn up his offering is the real God."

So Baal's prophets put a young bull on Baal's altar. They cried out to Baal from morning till noon.

"Hear us, Baal!" they shouted. But no fire came down from heaven to burn up their offering.

About noon, Elijah made fun of them. He said, "Call louder, for perhaps your god is talking to someone and isn't listening. Or maybe he is away. Or he might be asleep!"

So Baal's prophets yelled and shouted to Baal until evening. But no fire came.

Then Elijah gathered all the people around him. He used twelve stones to once again build the altar of the Lord that had been torn down. He dug all around the altar. Then he placed wood on it and put a bull on top of the wood as an offering.

Elijah said to the people, "Pour four large jars of water over the bull and the wood." He had them do this three times. Water filled the place he had dug around the altar.

That evening Elijah went over to the altar and prayed, "Lord, show that you are the true God. Answer me, Lord."

Then the fire of the Lord fell from heaven upon the altar. It burned up the offering and the wood, and even the stones of the altar and the water all around it.

When the people saw it, they all bowed down with their faces to the ground. They shouted, "The Lord is God! The Lord is God!"

STORY 80

Elijah's Strange Picnic

1 Kings 18–19

Elijah told King Ahab to go and have something good to eat, for the rain was coming and soon there would be plenty of food. Then Elijah went up to the top of Mount Carmel and prayed that God would send the rain. After he had prayed he said to his servant, "Go and look out toward the sea. Are there any clouds yet?"

The servant went to look but came back and said, "I couldn't see any."

"Go and look," Elijah told him again. He said this seven times.

So the servant kept going to look. Finally on the seventh time he said, "There is one tiny cloud."

Then Elijah knew the Lord was going to send the rain. So he said to his servant, "Go and tell Ahab to get into his chariot right away. Tell him to get down off the mountain before the rain stops him!"

Soon the sky was black with clouds. The wind began to blow, and there was a very heavy rain. Ahab rode home in his chariot. And the Lord gave Elijah strength to run ahead of the chariot until he came to the gate of the city.

When he got home, King Ahab told his wife, Queen Jezebel, all that had happened. Jezebel was very angry and sent this message to Elijah: "By tomorrow at this time you will be dead, for I will kill you."

When Elijah heard this, he ran for his life. He ran to a desert, where he found one little tree. He sat under the tree and asked the Lord to let him die. "Take away my life," he said, for he was very tired of running away from his enemies. But asking to die was wrong.

Finally he fell asleep under the tree. And as he

lay there, an angel came and touched him and said, "Get up and eat." Elijah looked around and saw a loaf of bread that had been baked on hot stones. And there was a bottle of water, too! So he ate and drank, and then he lay down and slept again.

The angel of the Lord came a second time and touched him. The angel told him to eat so that he would be strong enough for the long trip ahead. So he got up and ate again. Then he was strong enough to live without eating again for forty days and forty nights. Finally he came to Mount Sinai, and he went into a cave in the mountain.

Then God asked him, "What are you doing here, Elijah?"

"The people of Israel have broken their promise to obey your laws," Elijah said. "They have torn down your altars, and killed your prophets. Now I am the only one left, and they are trying to kill me, too."

The Lord told him to go out and stand on the mountain. Then the Lord passed by. A terrible wind hit the mountain and even moved the rocks, but the Lord was not in the wind. And after the wind there was an earthquake, but the Lord was not in the earthquake. And after the earthquake there was a fire, but the Lord was not in the fire. After the fire there was a quiet, small voice. When Elijah heard the voice, he knew that God was there. He covered his face with his coat, for he was afraid to look at God. Then he went out and stood by the opening to the cave.

The Lord told Elijah to leave the cave and return

to the land of Israel. When he got there he was to anoint a man named Elisha to take his place. Elisha would be the next prophet of the Lord, for soon Elijah would leave the world behind and go to heaven.

So Elijah returned to Israel as the Lord had told him to. As he was walking along, he saw Elisha plowing a field. Elijah went over to him and threw his coat over Elisha's shoulders. Elisha knew that when a prophet did this to someone, it meant that the person should leave his home and become a prophet too. So he left the plowing and ran after Elijah.

STORY 81
Ahab Steals a Grape Garden

1 Kings 20–22

Ben-hadad, an enemy king, now called his army to fight against the city of Samaria. That was where King Ahab of Israel lived. The enemy king sent messengers to Ahab to tell him, "All your silver and gold and all your wives and children are mine."

But the Lord sent a prophet to Ahab who told him not to be afraid. He told Ahab to fight the enemy army.

Ben-hadad and his leaders were having a drinking party in their tents when Ahab and his little army arrived. The huge enemy army was taken by surprise and ran away in fear. When Ben-hadad saw what was happening, he jumped on a horse and got away.

The next year Ben-hadad gathered another army. And the Lord helped Israel win again, for they destroyed 100,000 soldiers in one day. But Ben-hadad ran into a city and hid.

Ben-hadad's men came to him and said, "We will dress in sackcloth to show that we are sorry, and we will ask the king of Israel to save your life. Perhaps he will let you live." So the men went to Ahab and said, "Your servant Ben-hadad begs you to let him live."

"Wasn't he killed in the battle?" Ahab asked. Then he told the men to bring the enemy king to him. When Ben-hadad arrived, Ahab let him ride with him in his chariot as though they were friends. Then Ben-hadad promised to give Ahab some of his cities, so Ahab let him go home to his own land.

But God was angry with Ahab for doing this. Now God sent a prophet to Ahab who said, "Because you have let this man go, you must die instead."

Soon afterward King Ahab wanted to buy a grape garden from a man named Naboth. The king liked it because it was near his palace and he could use it as a vegetable garden. "I'll give you a better grape garden for it," he said. "Or I'll pay you for it."

But Naboth didn't want to sell his grape garden. It had belonged to his family for many years, and he wanted to keep it.

Ahab returned home angry and unhappy. He lay

down and wouldn't look at anyone. He even refused to eat! When Queen Jezebel saw him she asked, "What's the trouble? Why are you so sad?"

"Because Naboth won't sell me his grape garden," Ahab answered.

"Are you the king of Israel or not?" Jezebel wanted to know. "Get up and eat. Don't worry— I'll get the grape garden for you!"

Then Jezebel wrote letters and signed them with Ahab's name. She sealed them with his seal and sent them to the city leaders. In the letters she said to find some bad men who would tell lies about Naboth. They were to say that they had heard him speak evil of God and the king.

The city leaders did as Queen Jezebel said. They found two men who lied about Naboth.

Now the Lord had commanded that anyone who spoke against him should be stoned. Naboth had not done that, but the bad men lied and said that he had. So the people took Naboth out of the city and killed him. Then they sent a message to Jezebel: "Naboth is dead."

When Jezebel heard it she said to Ahab, "Go and take Naboth's grape garden, for he is dead." So Ahab went down to the grape garden and let everyone know it belonged to him now.

But the Lord told Elijah to go out and meet Ahab in the grape garden. Elijah said that God knew Ahab had killed Naboth and was taking his grape garden. Because of this, Ahab was going to die also.

Some time later King Ahab went out to fight King

Ben-hadad again. He went with Jehoshaphat, the king of Judah. But Ahab would not wear his king's robe because he didn't want anyone to know him.

No one was aiming at Ahab, for no one knew who he was. But an arrow hit Ahab anyway. That evening he died.

STORY 82

A Chariot Ride to Heaven

2 Kings 2

The day soon arrived when the Lord was ready to take Elijah up to heaven. Elijah wanted to be alone when the Lord took him. So he said to Elisha, "Stay here, please, for the Lord has told me to go to Bethel."

But Elisha said, "I'll never leave you." So they went to Bethel together.

The prophets from Bethel came over to Elisha and asked him, "Do you know that the Lord will take Elijah away from you today?"

"Yes," he said, "I know."

Then Elijah said to Elisha, "Stay here at Bethel, please, for the Lord has told me to go to Jericho."

But Elisha said, "I'll never leave you." So they went to Jericho.

The prophets from Jericho came to Elisha and asked him, "Do you know that the Lord will take Elijah away from you today?"

God took Elijah to heaven in a chariot of fire.
As he left, he gave his coat to Elisha. This
showed that Elisha was to be the new prophet.

"Yes, I know," he answered.

Then Elijah said to Elisha, "Stay here at Jericho, for the Lord has told me to go to the Jordan River."

But again Elisha answered, "I'll never leave you." So they went on together. Fifty prophets followed them to watch and see what would happen.

Elijah and Elisha stood beside the river, and Elijah hit the water with his coat. Then the river divided into two parts so they could walk across on dry ground!

When they were on the other side, Elijah turned to Elisha. He said, "Tell me what you want me to do for you before I am taken away."

Elisha asked to have even more of God's Spirit upon him than Elijah had.

"You have asked a hard thing," Elijah said. "But if you see me when I am taken from you, you will have what you are asking for. If not, you will not get it."

As they walked along and talked together, suddenly they saw a chariot of fire pulled by horses of fire. It came between them and took Elijah away from Elisha. Then a wind came, turning around and around. It took Elijah up to heaven in the chariot. Elisha saw it and cried out, "My father, my father, the chariot and drivers of Israel!"

Elisha never saw Elijah again on earth. He picked up Elijah's coat that had fallen on the ground and hit the river with it. Then the water divided before him as it had for Elijah, and Elisha went across on dry ground!

The leaders of Jericho came to Elisha. They told him, "Our city is a beautiful place to live, but the water is no good. Nothing will grow here."

"Bring me a new bowl with salt in it," Elisha told them. So they brought it to him. He went to the spring where the city got its water and threw the salt into it. And he said, "The Lord wants you to know that he has made the water good. It will never hurt anyone or keep the crops from growing." And sure enough! The water was always good after that.

STORY 83

The Oil That Kept Coming

2 Kings 3–4

Joram was now the king of Israel. He gathered his army to fight against Moab and asked King Jehoshaphat of Judah to help him.

"All right," Jehoshaphat said. "I'll go with you."

The king of Edom went with them too. So these three kings took their armies and marched for seven days. In all that time they found no water to drink.

King Joram of Israel was afraid, for he knew that his soldiers were so thirsty they couldn't fight. King Joram worshiped idols, but King Jehoshaphat worshiped the Lord. So Jehoshaphat asked, "Isn't there a prophet who can find out from the Lord what we should do?"

One of King Joram's men said, "Elisha is here. He was Elijah's helper."

"Let's ask him," Jehoshaphat said. So the three kings went to visit Elisha.

When Elisha saw the king of Israel, he asked, "Why have you come to me? Why don't you go to the false prophets of Ahab, your father, and Jezebel, your mother? If King Jehoshaphat of Judah were not with you, I wouldn't even listen to you."

The Lord told Elisha what to say to the kings. The Lord said there would be no wind or rain in the valley where the kings and their soldiers were. But the valley would be filled with water! Then all the soldiers could drink as much as they wanted.

"You will win over the cities of Moab," Elisha said. "You will cut down their trees, and stop up their water, and throw stones in their fields."

Elisha's words all came true the next morning. After the three kings won over Moab, they went home.

One day a woman who had been married to a prophet came to Elisha with a big problem: "My husband is dead," she said. "You know that he loved the Lord. But he owed some money, and I can't pay it back. Now the man I owe it to has come to take away my two sons and make them his slaves."

Elisha asked her, "What do you have in your house?"

"Nothing," she answered, "except one jar of olive oil!"

"Well," he said, "I'll tell you what to do. Go and borrow empty jars from all your neighbors. Take the jars into your house and shut the door. Then begin pouring oil from your jar into the jars you borrow."

So the woman borrowed empty jars and took them into her house and shut the door. Then, as her sons brought the empty jars to her, she poured olive oil into them from her one jar. And the oil kept coming until all the jars were full! Finally, when she told one of her sons to bring her another jar, he answered, "There is not another empty one left!"

The woman went to see Elisha again. He said, "Go and sell the olive oil. Then you can pay the man what your husband owed him. And take the money that is left to buy food for yourself and the children."

STORY 84

Elisha Does Great Miracles

2 Kings 4

As Elisha was traveling around the land, he came to the city of Shunem. A rich woman who lived there asked him to stop at her house for dinner. From then on, whenever he came that way, he stopped for a meal.

One day the woman said to her husband, "I'm sure this man is a prophet of the Lord. Let's make a little room for him. Whenever he comes to visit us, it will be ready for him." So that is what they did.

Once when Elisha was there with his servant, Gehazi, he said to him, "Call this woman."

When she came, Elisha had Gehazi say, "You have been very kind to us. What shall we do for you? Is there anything you want Elisha to ask the king to give you?" But she said she didn't need anything.

Later Elisha said to Gehazi, "Can you think of anything we can do for her?"

Gehazi said, "She has no child."

"Call her again," Elisha said. So Gehazi called her. She came again and stood at the door. Then Elisha told her that the Lord would give her a son. And Elisha's words came true the following year.

When the child was old enough, he went out one day to the field with his father. While he was there, he cried out to his father, "My head! Oh, my head!"

His father said to one of the servants, "Carry him to his mother." The child sat in his mother's lap until noon, and then he died.

The sad woman took her son up to Elisha's room and laid him on the bed. She shut the door and left him there. Then she sent a message to her husband in the field, asking him to send one of the servants and a donkey. She said she wanted to hurry to the prophet and come right back again. But she didn't tell her husband that their boy was dead. So he asked, "Why today? There isn't any special meeting today!"

This mother had waited many years to have a little boy. When he suddenly died, she was very sad. But the prophet Elisha brought him back to life.

"I need to go today," was all she would say.

"Drive hard," the woman said to the servant. "Hurry, and don't stop for anything."

When she came to Mount Carmel, Elisha saw her in the distance. He said to Gehazi, "Run to meet the woman from Shunem. Ask her if everything is all right. Find out if her husband and her child are well."

Gehazi ran to ask her. And she said, "Everything is fine." But when she came to Elisha, she got down and took hold of his feet. Gehazi came to push her away, but Elisha said, "Let her alone. She is in some sort of trouble, and the Lord hasn't told me what it is."

Then the woman said to Elisha, "You said I would have a son. But didn't I tell you not to get my hopes up?" So then Elisha knew that her boy was dead.

When Elisha came into the house, the boy's body was on the prophet's bed. So Elisha went in and shut the door and prayed. Then he lay down on the child's body and put his mouth on the child's mouth. He put his eyes on the child's eyes and his hands on the child's hands. And the child's body became warm again!

Elisha walked around the room for a while. Then he lay down on the child's body again. This time the child sneezed seven times, opened his eyes, and came to life again!

Then Elisha said to Gehazi, "Call the child's mother!" So Gehazi did.

"Take your son!" Elisha said to the woman as she came into the room.

Oh, how thankful that mother was!

A Little Girl Helps Naaman

2 Kings 5

Naaman was an army leader in Aram, a land that was an enemy of Israel. The king of Aram liked his army leader because he had won so many battles. But Naaman had leprosy. His skin had sores that would not go away.

Now it so happened that when the people of Aram won over Israel, they brought back with them an Israelite girl. She became a maid for Naaman's wife.

One day the girl said to the woman, "I wish Naaman could go see God's prophet in Samaria, for he would take away Naaman's leprosy."

Naaman told the king what the little girl had said. So the king said Naaman should go to see the prophet.

Naaman took silver and gold with him, and ten sets of new clothes. All this would be a present for the prophet if he could take away the leprosy. Naaman came in his chariot and stood at the door of Elisha's house. Instead of going out to meet Naaman, Elisha just sent a message. The message said, "Go and wash yourself seven times in the Jordan River. Then you will be healed of your leprosy."

Naaman was angry. "Do you mean to tell me the prophet isn't even going to come out here? I thought he would pray to the Lord his God for me and put his hand on me to make me well," he said. "Aren't the rivers in my own country better than all the rivers in the land of Israel?" He turned around and went away very angry.

But then some of his men came to him and said, "Sir, if the prophet had told you to do some hard thing to make you well, wouldn't you have done it? But he has told you just to go and wash, and you will be healed. So why don't you at least try it and see?"

So Naaman went down to the Jordan River and dipped seven times. Suddenly his skin became new like a little child's, and the leprosy was gone. He went back to Elisha's house and said, "Now I know that there is no other God in all the earth except the God of Israel."

Naaman wanted to give Elisha a present. But Elisha said, "No, I won't accept it." Naaman begged him, but Elisha wouldn't take it.

Then Naaman asked for two loads of dirt from the land of Israel to take home with him. He would make an altar from the dirt. And he never again would give an offering to any other god but the Lord.

Naaman started the trip home to his own country. But back at Elisha's house, Elisha's servant Gehazi thought about something. He said to himself, "It's a shame my master wouldn't accept the present Naaman wanted to give him. I'll run after him and get something for myself."

Naaman had leprosy. His wife's maid was a girl from Israel. She told Naaman that God's prophet Elisha could make him well.

When Naaman saw Gehazi running after him, he stopped his chariot and stepped down to meet him. He asked, "Is everything all right?"

"Yes," Gehazi answered, "but my master has changed his mind. He sent me to tell you that after you left, two young sons of prophets came to visit him. He asks you to give them a big piece of silver and two sets of clothes."

"I'll give two pieces of silver!" Naaman replied.

So Naaman gave Gehazi two pieces of silver and two sets of clothes, and he sent two servants to help Gehazi carry the gifts, for the silver was very heavy. But when they were near Elisha's house, Gehazi took the gifts and sent the servants back to Naaman again. Then Gehazi hid the silver and clothes, for he didn't want Elisha to know about them. But the Lord had already told Elisha. So when Gehazi came to him, Elisha asked, "Where have you been, Gehazi?"

"Nowhere," Gehazi said.

Elisha replied, "I know that Naaman got out of his chariot to meet you. This was not the time for us to take money and clothes. And now, because you have done this, you and your family will have the leprosy that Naaman had." As Elisha spoke, leprosy covered Gehazi, and he went out with white spots all over his body.

Four Men Find Food for a City

2 Kings 6–7

Not long after this, King Ben-hadad and his army came again to fight Samaria. His soldiers were all around the city, so no one could get in or out. There was no food in the city, and no one could bring food to the people inside.

King Joram was as wicked a man as his father, Ahab. That is why God sent these terrible troubles to him and his people. Joram should have been sorry and asked God to help him. Instead, he blamed the troubles on Elisha and said the prophet would be put to death that very day.

Elisha knew the king was planning to kill him. So when a man sent by the king came to his house, Elisha told those with him to lock the door.

Then the king himself came to Elisha's house with one of his helpers. Elisha told them that the next day there would be plenty of food, for the Lord had told him this.

The king's helper wouldn't believe what Elisha said. So Elisha told him that because he didn't believe the words of the Lord, he would only see the food. He wouldn't get to eat it.

That night four men with leprosy were sitting

outside the city walls. They said to each other, "Why sit here with nothing to eat? If we go into the city we'll die because there is no food. If we sit here with no food we will die. Come on, let's go out to the enemy army. If they don't kill us, we will live. If they kill us, we will only die like we're going to anyway."

So they went across the field to where the enemy army was camped. But no one was there! The Lord had made the soldiers from Aram hear the sound of a large army coming out against them. So they ran away in the night, leaving their tents and horses and everything else. But there really was no one coming to fight them at all!

When the four men with leprosy found no one in the camp, they went into a tent and ate the food there. They took money and clothes and hid it. Then they went into another tent. They carried away more silver and gold and hid it, too. But then they stopped and looked at each other. "This isn't right," they said. "We have good news for our people, and yet we aren't telling them."

So they went back to the city that night. They shouted to the people watching the gates, "We have been to the enemy camp, and no one is there! The horses are tied and the tents are standing there, but no one is around!"

The people at the gates hurried to tell the king. But he said, "It's a trick. The enemy soldiers are hiding outside the camp. When we go over, they will hurry back and take us."

One of the king's helpers said, "We still have a

God scared the enemy army away. Four lepers found food left behind in the camp. The lepers shared the food with all the other Israelites.

few horses. Let's ride over and see." So the king sent a few of his men to the enemy camp, and they found no one. They looked as far as the Jordan River. And all along the road there were clothes and tools thrown away by the soldiers as they ran. Then the men returned to Samaria and told the king what they saw.

When the people heard about it, everyone ran out to the enemy camp. The Israelites brought back huge supplies of flour and grain left by the soldiers when they ran away. So now there was plenty of food. The king sent his helper to stand at the gate and keep the people in order. He was the man who wouldn't believe Elisha. This man fell and was run over by the crowd of people, and he died. So it happened to him as Elisha had said: He saw the food but never tasted it.

STORY 87

The End of the Kingdom of Israel

2 Kings 13–15; 17; Amos 4–7; Hosea 14

After King Joram died, more bad kings ruled over Israel.

One day the prophet Elisha became sick and died. Jehoash was the king of Israel at that time. After the death of Elisha, King Jehoash took his army out against the army of Aram. Israel won three times, just as Elisha had said. Jehoash was king for sixteen years, then died and was buried in the city of Samaria. His son Jeroboam the Second became the next king.

The Lord was kind to Jeroboam and the people of Israel. He felt sorry for them because of all they had suffered from their enemies. So he helped Jeroboam win against their enemies.

But the people of Israel didn't thank God for his kindness. He helped them in their trouble and saved them from their enemies, but they still worshiped idols at Dan and Bethel. They worshiped gold calves instead of worshiping God.

The Lord sent Amos the prophet to talk to them about this. The Lord had seen all of their sins, Amos told them. So he had kept back the rain from their fields. He had kept their crops from growing and had not given them enough food or water. But still they hadn't turned from their evil ways. So now even more bad things were going to happen. There would be crying in their streets and on their farms, for an enemy would come and win over them. They would be taken away as slaves to other lands, and their king would be killed. But Amos told them that if they would be sorry and obey the Lord their God, the Lord would even now forgive them. Then these terrible things wouldn't happen to them.

Amaziah, a priest from the idol temple at Bethel, was very upset when he heard Amos tell the people these things. He told King Jeroboam that Amos was saying the king would be killed and the people of Israel would be taken away as slaves. The priest told Amos to get out of the country.

The prophet Hosea, too, warned the people

about the bad things the Lord would send to them. He also begged the people to be sorry for their sins so that the Lord could forgive them. But they wouldn't listen.

Finally, after being king of Israel forty-one years, Jeroboam the Second died, and his son became the new king. More evil kings ruled over Israel during the next few years. They kept on worshiping the gold calves.

Instead of doing as God had taught them, the people of Israel worshiped idols, just as the people around them did.

God was very angry with his people for doing such things. Yet he waited and waited for them to stop doing wrong. He sent his prophets to warn them again and again. These prophets preached to the people, telling them of the terrible things that would happen if they didn't stop doing wrong. The prophets said that if the people would be sorry, God would forgive them and keep them as his children. But they wouldn't listen. So at last God did as the prophets had warned. He sent an enemy to win over them and take them far away to another country to live as slaves. They never saw their own country again.

So the kingdom of Israel came to an end. It had lasted just a little over two hundred years, ever since the ten tribes asked Jeroboam to be their king. Twenty wicked kings had ruled over them during that time. Now the king of Assyria took the Israelites to his land. And he sent his people to live in the cities of Israel.

That is the end of the story of the kingdom of Israel. Now we will go back two hundred years and begin the story of the kingdom of Judah.

The Little Kingdom of Judah Grows

1 Kings 14–15; 2 Chronicles 12–14; 16

After King Solomon died, his son Rehoboam became the king of the two tribes of Judah and Benjamin. Rehoboam lived at Jerusalem near the Temple built by his father, King Solomon.

Rehoboam was forty-one years old when he became king of Judah, and he ruled seventeen years. Then he died and was buried in Jerusalem, and his son Abijam became king instead.

Soon there was war between the armies of Judah and Israel. The army of Judah had four hundred thousand men in it, but the army of Israel had eight hundred thousand. Before the battle began, King Abijam of Judah stood on a mountain and called down to King Jeroboam and the men of Israel. Abijam shouted, "Don't you know that God promised King David that only people from his family should be kings of our land? Jeroboam isn't a son of David, but he has made himself to be Israel's king. This is wrong.

You have twice as large an army as we do, but you worship the gold calves made for you by Jeroboam. He says they are your gods. We worship only the Lord, and he is with us. He is our leader. Men of Israel, do not fight against the Lord, for you can never win against him."

But while Abijam was speaking, Jeroboam led the army of Israel against him and his army of Judah. The men of Judah cried to the Lord for help, and the priests who were with them blew their trumpets. Then the men of Judah gave a great shout. As they did, God helped them win. Jeroboam and his army ran away, and the men of Judah won the fight because they trusted in God.

King Abijam ruled for three years. Then he died, and his son Asa became the new king of Judah.

Asa was a good king who tried to please God. So God gave his people rest from war. Then King Asa said to them, "Let us build more cities in our land. We'll build them with walls, towers, and gates so that our enemies can't win over us." So the kingdom of Judah grew strong, and the people had everything they needed.

Thirty-five years after Asa became the king of Judah, King Baasha of Israel went to war against him. But instead of praying to the Lord for help, King Asa took the silver and gold from the Temple and from his palace. He sent it to the king of Aram and asked him to come and help fight the king of Israel. The king of Aram did as Asa asked and sent his army against some of the cities of Israel. So King

Baasha went back home to fight for his country, ending the war against Asa.

But the Lord sent a prophet to tell Asa he should have asked for help from God instead of from the king of Aram. "The Lord is looking everywhere around the world to find those who love him, so that he can help them. You were foolish to trust the king of Aram instead of trusting God. From now on your enemies will keep fighting you."

Asa was angry with the prophet for saying this and put him in jail.

Three years later Asa got a sickness. It had to do with his feet. The trouble grew worse and worse, but he didn't ask the Lord to make him well. He trusted only in his doctors. Finally he died. The leaders of Judah laid him in a bed of sweet-smelling spices. Then they buried him in Jerusalem. And his son Jehoshaphat became the new king.

STORY 89

God Helps a Good King

1 Kings 22; 2 Chronicles 17–20

The Lord was with King Jehoshaphat because the king did what was right. All his people brought him gifts. He became rich, and people thought well of him. In the third year that he ruled, he sent teachers to all the cities of Judah. They used the Book of God's Laws to teach the people how to obey the Lord.

One day Jehoshaphat went to the city of Samaria to visit King Ahab of Israel. King Ahab had a big party for him. Then Ahab talked him into going with him to fight against the king of Aram. That's the fight where Ahab wouldn't put on his king's robe because he was afraid he would be killed. Jehoshaphat did put on his king's robe. The enemy army tried to kill him. But he asked God to save him, and God did. He stopped the enemies from following the king. When the battle was over, Ahab was dead but Jehoshaphat came back to Jerusalem.

The Lord sent a prophet to ask him, "Was it right for you to help a wicked man like Ahab? The Lord is angry with you. But you have done well in other things. You have taken away the altars where the people worshiped idols. And you have worked hard to serve God."

Some time later three enemy armies came to fight against King Jehoshaphat. When he heard that they were coming, he sent a message to all his people. He asked them not to eat for a few days. Instead they were to pray hard, asking for God's help. People came from all over Judah to the Temple at Jerusalem to pray.

Then King Jehoshaphat stood up in front of the people and prayed, "Lord, you are our God. You drove out the wicked people from this land and gave it to your people. But now three enemy armies are coming to drive us from the land you have given us. Will you let them do this? We are not strong enough to fight against this great army they are bringing. We don't know what to do. But we are looking up to you for help."

Then the Lord sent a prophet to tell King Jehoshaphat and the people, "Don't be afraid of this huge army. Go out and face them tomorrow. Just stand still when you get there, and you'll see how the Lord will help you. People of Judah and Jerusalem, don't be afraid, for the Lord will help you."

Then King Jehoshaphat bowed down with his face to the ground, worshiping God. All the people of Judah and Jerusalem did the same.

Early the next morning the army of Judah went out to fight. As they were going, King Jehoshaphat said to his soldiers, "Trust in the Lord and believe what his prophet has said. Then you will win."

Jehoshaphat placed singers in front of the army to lead the way and sing praises to God! As they began to sing, God helped the men of Judah by having the three enemy armies begin fighting each other! When the men of Judah arrived, there were no enemies left to fight. The people gathered in a valley to bless the Lord and thank him for giving them the victory. After that the valley was always called the Valley of Blessing.

Then King Jehoshaphat and his army went back to Jerusalem, playing harps and trumpets. They went right to the Temple, where they praised God with their music and prayers of thanks.

Other people were afraid to fight Jehoshaphat after that. So God gave him and his people rest from war.

But later King Jehoshaphat did wrong again, for he and his people worked with the wicked king of Israel to send ships to another land. A prophet came and told him that because he had done this, his ships would be destroyed. And what the prophet said came true.

King Jehoshaphat was king for twenty-five years. For the most part he did what was right and pleasing to the Lord. Then he died and was buried in Jerusalem.

STORY 90

A Little Boy Becomes a King

2 Kings 11–12; 2 Chronicles 21–24

Jehoshaphat's son was a bad king. He married Athaliah, an evil daughter of King Ahab. Sometime after her husband died, her son died too. When Athaliah heard that her son was dead, she wanted to be the queen. But she had a grandson, a baby boy named Joash. The baby's aunt and her husband, Jehoiada the priest, hid the baby at the Temple. They took care of him there until he was seven years old. Then Jehoiada said that it was time to put a crown on the prince and make him king of Judah. So he did. And he gave little King Joash a copy of God's laws. Then Joash was the ruler instead of his wicked grandmother. Everyone clapped and shouted, "Long live the king!"

When little Prince Joash was seven years old, he became King Joash. He took the place of wicked Queen Athaliah.

Afterward, the priest and King Joash and all the people said that they would obey the Lord. They all began worshiping God at the Temple again.

When Joash grew older he decided to fix up the Temple of the Lord, for no one had taken care of it for a long time. He told all the priests, "Go into the cities of Judah and collect money from the people to fix up the Temple of the Lord. And see that you hurry." But the priests didn't hurry.

Finally the king sent for Jehoiada the priest and asked him, "Why don't all the priests collect the money and fix up the Lord's Temple?" Then the king said to make a hole in the top of a big wooden box. He said to set it at the door of the Temple. A message was sent to everyone in Judah. The people were told to come to the Temple and bring some money as an offering to the Lord. Everyone was happy to come and drop their money into the box. Whenever it was full, Jehoiada and one of the king's helpers counted it and put it in bags. They gave it to the men who were in charge of the builders.

As long as the priest Jehoiada lived, he helped King Joash know how to do what was right. But Jehoiada finally died at the age of 130. He was buried in Jerusalem in the graves of the kings because he had done so much good for the people of Judah. He had not only obeyed the Lord himself, but had taught the people to obey him too.

After Jehoiada died, the wicked leaders of Judah told the king they didn't want to worship God anymore. King Joash said it was all right to worship idols instead. He let the wicked leaders talk him into letting them do what was very wrong.

Isaiah Tells the Future
2 Chronicles 25–27; Isaiah 5; 11; 44; 53

King Joash had a son named Amaziah. He became the next king. Amaziah led his army against an enemy army, and the Lord helped him win. But when he came back from the battle, he brought idols from the enemy army with him. He set them up to be his gods.

Then Amaziah began to fight Israel. The king of Israel broke down the walls of Jerusalem. Then he went into the Temple and took the gold and silver bowls that were there. He also took things from the king's palace and took some of the people to his own city of Samaria.

After King Amaziah died, his sixteen-year-old son, Uzziah, became the new king. As long as he did right, the Lord helped him. He had many cows and fields and grape gardens. Many farmers worked in his fields for him.

There were more than three hundred thousand men in Uzziah's army. They all had spears and helmets and bows and slings. The king built war machines to shoot arrows and stones. These machines were placed on the walls around the city of Jerusalem. God helped him fight against his enemies, and he took over many of their cities.

But that made him proud, and sometimes he did not obey the Lord. He went into the Temple where only the priests were to go. He went to offer a gift to God on the golden altar. Then eighty priests went in after him and told him, "Get out! Only the priests are to do this work. Leave at once, for you have sinned! The Lord is not happy with you for doing this."

But instead of hurrying outside, Uzziah became angry with the priests for talking to him like that. Then suddenly the white spots of leprosy came out on his forehead. The priests saw it, so they pushed him out of the Temple.

The king never got well. He had to live in a house by himself because God had said that no one with leprosy could live with other people. His son Jotham ruled the land in his place. When King Uzziah died, Jotham became the king.

Jotham built towns in the hills of Judah. He built castles and towers in the forests. He won over his enemies and made them his servants. Each year they gave him money, wheat, and barley. And he became very great because he always tried to please the Lord.

But his people were wicked. So God sent Isaiah the prophet to warn them. The Lord was very angry with them because of their sins, Isaiah said. So he would call their enemies from far-off countries to come and win over them. These enemies would be as mean as lions, and no one could stop them. The people of Judah would be taken away to distant lands. Their land would be left with no one to take care of the fields. Their cities would be empty and everything in them would be destroyed. But after many years, Isaiah said, the cities would be built again. The Lord would raise up Cyrus, a great king who would command that the city and the Temple should be built again.

Isaiah told the people many other things about the future. He said that Jesus would be born in the family line of King David. He said that when Jesus grew up he would be sad and people would hurt him. Then he would be put to death for everyone's sins. Isaiah told about these things seven hundred years before they happened, for he was a prophet. God told him about things to come.

But the people of Judah wouldn't listen to the preaching of Isaiah. Then their good king, Jotham, died. And his son Ahaz became their king instead.

STORY 92
King Ahaz Closes the Temple
2 Kings 16; 2 Chronicles 28–29

King Ahaz didn't obey God as his father had done. He worshiped idols instead. So the Lord sent the king of Aram against him. The enemy army took many people away from Jerusalem to the city of Damascus.

Israel also came to fight against Judah and won. They took many women and children with them to Israel.

Other enemy armies began to fight against Judah too. Then the king of Judah took some of the silver and gold from the Temple and some nice things from his own palace. He sent them to the king of Assyria and asked him to fight against the enemies of Judah. The king of Assyria did as King Ahaz asked him to. He took the city of Damascus from the people of Aram. But it did Ahaz little good, for he was wicked and the Lord was against him.

After this, Ahaz became even more wicked. For he broke up the beautiful furniture at the Temple and closed the doors so that no one could go there to worship. But he placed idols all over Jerusalem and in every city throughout the land. The Lord was very angry with Ahaz and the people of Judah because they were so wicked.

Ahaz was king for sixteen years. When he died, his son Hezekiah became king.

Hezekiah did what was right and obeyed the Lord. As soon as he became king he opened the Temple again. He called the priests back and told them to put everything in order. Then the people could come and worship God again.

After working hard for sixteen days, the priests told the king, "It's all finished! All the cleaning has been done, the altar is ready for use, and we have

King Ahaz led the people of Judah away from God. He even closed up the Temple so that no one would worship God.

brought back the gold and silver bowls taken away by Ahaz. Everything is ready."

King Hezekiah got up early the next morning and went up to the Temple with the leaders of Jerusalem. They took with them seven young bulls, seven rams, seven lambs, and seven goats as an offering. Hezekiah commanded the priests to put the animals on the altar. He said to give them to God as a sacrifice for the sins of the people of Judah. He also gathered priests to sing praises to the Lord. He gathered more priests to play cymbals, harps, and trumpets. As the offering started to burn on the altar, the music began and everyone worshiped God.

Afterward the people brought their own offerings. And the priests offered these gifts for the people's sins. The king and all the people were glad that everyone wanted to bring offerings to God. They were glad that the Temple was open again so they could worship the Lord.

STORY 93

A Holiday in Judah

2 Chronicles 30–31

King Hezekiah now wrote a letter to all of his people in Judah, and also to the people in Israel. He asked them to come together in Jerusalem to remember the Passover of the Lord. It had been many years since the people had done this as the Lord wanted them to.

Messengers carried the king's letters throughout Judah. But when they came to the land of Israel, the people from the ten tribes wouldn't listen to them. Most of the Israelites just laughed. However, a few were sorry for their sins and came to Jerusalem.

In the land of Judah, the Lord made all the people want to come. So there was a great crowd in Jerusalem for the Passover festival. Before beginning it, they went through the city and knocked down all the idol altars and threw them away.

Then the Passover time began. The priests worshiped God at the Temple. And each family roasted a lamb to eat that night. This was what the people of Israel had done on the night they left Egypt hundreds of years before. The Lord wanted his people to remember that night in Egypt, and how he had saved them from Pharaoh. That is why he had commanded them to celebrate the Passover festival each year. But they had stopped doing it. Now Hezekiah had called them together to begin to obey the Lord again, so that he would be pleased with them and bless them.

They had seven happy days together. The priests sang praises to God every day, playing on harps and trumpets. And the people told God they were sorry for their sins.

At the end of the seven days, the people agreed to stay seven more days to praise God and worship him. King Hezekiah and the leaders gave them many young bulls and sheep to offer as gifts to God. So all the people of Judah and those who came from Israel were filled with joy. Since the days of Solomon there had never been such a wonderful time in Jerusalem.

When the festival finally ended, the people went everywhere to break up the idols. And they tore down the altars where the idols had been worshiped.

Then King Hezekiah set up times for the different groups of priests to lead the worship of the Lord at the Temple. He made plans for morning and evening sacrifices, and for special sacrifices. The king told the people to bring to the Temple a tenth of all their crops so that the priests would have enough to eat. God had commanded this, but the people had not done it for a long time. Now the people of Judah obeyed the king. So did many who had moved from Israel to Judah.

King Hezekiah and the leaders came to the Temple and saw the great heaps of food brought in by the people. And they thanked the Lord for making the people want to bring so much.

STORY 94
The Savior Will Come!
2 Kings 20; 2 Chronicles 32; Micah 1; 5–6

One day King Hezekiah became very sick from a large sore that wouldn't go away. The prophet

King Hezekiah showed off his nice things to visitors from Babylon. Years later these things were stolen and carried away to Babylon.

Isaiah told him, "The Lord says to get ready to die."

Then Hezekiah turned his face sadly to the wall. He prayed, "Lord, remember how I have tried to please you in all I do." Then he broke down and cried.

So the Lord told Isaiah to go back to Hezekiah and give him this answer: "I have heard your prayer and seen your tears, and I will make you well again. Three days from now you will be well enough to go to the Temple. And I will add fifteen years to your life!" So Isaiah gave the Lord's message to the king.

Hezekiah wanted to know for sure that this was going to happen. So Isaiah prayed for a sign from God. He prayed for the shadow on the palace steps to move backward ten steps. God answered his prayer!

Then Isaiah said to the king's helpers, "Take a lump of figs and lay it on the big sore." So they did, and King Hezekiah was soon well again!

The king became very rich and well known. He had many cows, sheep, and goats. That's because God helped him in everything he did.

But strange as it seems, Hezekiah did not stay thankful to God for his blessings. He grew proud of his riches and power. He acted as if he had gotten these things by himself.

Then the king of Babylon sent messengers with letters and a present for him. Hezekiah was proud to have them visit him because they represented a great king. He showed them everything that belonged to him.

Then Isaiah the prophet came to Hezekiah and asked, "What did these men want? And where did they come from?"

"They came from Babylon," Hezekiah replied.

"What have they seen in your palace?" Isaiah asked.

And Hezekiah answered, "Everything!"

Then Isaiah gave him this message from the Lord: "After you die, all your nice things will be carried to Babylon. Nothing will be left."

Hezekiah answered, "Whatever God does is right. At least there will be peace while I'm alive."

King Hezekiah had talked the people into putting away their idols and worshiping the Lord. But soon they began praying to idols again. God sent the prophet Micah to speak to them about this.

"This is all that God requires," Micah said. "He wants the people of Israel to do what is right, to be kind and merciful to each other, and to be humble and obedient to the Lord!"

Like Isaiah, Micah talked about the Savior. Micah said that the Savior would be born in the city of Bethlehem. (Many other prophets also told about the Savior hundreds of years before he was born. Because they did this, everyone can know that the Savior is the Son of God and that he was sent by God.)

King Josiah and the Lost Book

Deuteronomy 31; 2 Kings 22–23; 2 Chronicles 34–35

Josiah was eight years old when he became king of Judah. While he was still a boy he began to serve the Lord. When he was a young man he went all through the land of Judah. He tore down the altars of Baal wherever he found them and destroyed the idols. He also traveled through the land of Israel and did the same thing there. (The people of Israel were no longer living there, for they had been taken to Assyria.)

Then Josiah returned to Jerusalem and had his men start fixing up the Temple, for there was a lot of work to do again. The people brought gifts of money to pay the workers.

One day when the high priest was counting the money the people brought, he found a very special book. He said to one of the king's helpers, "I've found the Book of the Law! It was here in the Temple!"

Hundreds of years before this, Moses had written down the laws God had given him. God had commanded that these laws must be read out loud to all the people every seven years. But the wicked kings and people of Judah hadn't cared to hear God's laws, so the book had been lost and forgotten. Now the high priest had found it again. He gave it to King Josiah's helper, who took it to the king and read it to him.

When King Josiah heard the words of God's laws, he learned that he and the people had not been obeying God. So he tore his clothes and

When King Josiah heard the Book of the Law, he knew that he and his people had not been obeying God.

cried. Then he asked several of his helpers to go to the Temple. He wanted them to learn more about the Book of the Law.

At the Temple the king's helpers talked to the prophet Huldah. She told them these words from the Lord: "I will destroy this city, for the people have worshiped idols, and I am angry with them. But King Josiah, you were sorry when you learned you had not obeyed me. I heard you cry, so nothing bad will happen to the city as long as you live."

The men took God's message back to King Josiah. Then the king called all the people to come to the Temple. There he read the book to them. Then Josiah promised to obey God's commandments. The people promised to obey God's laws too.

Many years before this, King Hezekiah had called the people together for the Passover festival. But after he died, the Passover was forgotten again for a long, long time. Now Josiah called everyone to Jerusalem for this special festival. He gave the people many lambs, goats, and bulls so that everyone would have a sacrifice to offer. But even though the people obeyed the king and came to the Passover, they didn't really love God. They didn't really worship him, for in their hearts they still trusted in their idols.

Jeremiah Writes a Sad Letter

2 Kings 23–24; 2 Chronicles 36; Jeremiah 15; 29; 36

After Josiah, the next king ruled for only three months. He didn't do right as his father had, and the people did not obey God. So the king of Egypt came to fight against him and took him in chains to Egypt.

Jehoiakim, the new king of Judah, had to give a lot of silver and gold to the king of Egypt. Afterward the people of Judah faced a new danger. King Nebuchadnezzar of Babylon came to fight them. Nebuchadnezzar took some of the beautiful things from the Temple and carried them to Babylon.

In the fourth year that Jehoiakim ruled, the Lord told the prophet Jeremiah to write down all the terrible things that were still going to happen to God's people. The Lord said that when the people saw those things written down, perhaps they would be sorry and turn back to him. Then he could forgive them. Jeremiah spoke the words of God's message to Baruch, a good man who wrote the message on a scroll. Then Baruch read it to the people at the Temple, and to the king's helpers.

The king's helpers told him what they had heard. He asked one of his helpers to get the scroll and read it to him. The king was sitting beside a fire. As soon as his helper read part of God's message, the king would use his knife to cut up that part and throw it into the fire. Three of the men with him asked him to please not do this. But he wouldn't listen. He wasn't sorry about any of the bad things he and his people had done. Instead, he was very angry with Jeremiah and Baruch for writing these messages, so he sent some men to find them and put them in jail. But the Lord hid them.

Because the king burned up God's messages, the Lord told Jeremiah he must let Baruch know what to write again. So Jeremiah had Baruch write the same words down once more, and a lot more besides.

The people hated Jeremiah for telling them about their sins, and he complained to the Lord about it. "I have not hurt them," he said, "but they all say bad things against me."

Then the Lord promised that when the enemies of Jerusalem arrived to take the city, they would not hurt Jeremiah. "I will make them treat you well," the Lord said.

Another new king ruled in Judah for only three months. Then King Nebuchadnezzar of Babylon came to fight him. Nebuchadnezzar took away more of the beautiful things from the Temple and from the

When the Babylonian army conquered Judah, Nebuchadnezzar ordered his soldiers to burn the city of Jerusalem and the beautiful Temple of God.

king's palace. He also took the king and his family, the leaders of Judah, the builders, and all the soldiers. He made them go to far-off Babylon.

After they had gone, the prophet Jeremiah wrote a letter to them, telling them that God said to build houses and plant gardens there. God said to be happy in that faraway land of Babylon, because they must stay there seventy years and serve the king of Babylon. But when the seventy years ended and they had asked God to forgive their sins, then he would bring them back again to their own land.

STORY 97

Jerusalem Is Burned

2 Kings 24–25; 2 Chronicles 36; Jeremiah 21; 27; 37–39; 52

Nebuchadnezzar left some people in the land of Judah and appointed Zedekiah as their king. Zedekiah had to promise to obey Nebuchadnezzar. But after Nebuchadnezzar went back to Babylon, Zedekiah didn't do what he promised. So Nebuchadnezzar came back again with all of his army. He made forts around Jerusalem and kept the people from going in or out of the city.

Jeremiah was inside Jerusalem with the rest of the people. King Zedekiah asked him to please pray that God would help them save Jerusalem.

But the Lord had Jeremiah tell the king that
Nebuchadnezzar would take over the city
and burn it. If the people would give in to
Nebuchadnezzar without fighting and be his
slaves, they would not be killed. But if they
would not give in to him, they would die.

The Lord told Jeremiah to act out this message
by wearing a wooden yoke on his shoulders. A
yoke stands for hard work or slavery. So when the
people saw Jeremiah wearing it, they understood

The prophet Jeremiah walked around wearing a heavy wooden yoke. This was God's way of showing his people that they must become slaves.

that God was going to make them work hard as Nebuchadnezzar's slaves.

Then the Lord gave this message to Jeremiah. "Jerusalem will certainly be taken and burned," the Lord said. "This is how I will show my anger to the people for their sins."

Some of the leaders of Judah said to King Zedekiah that Jeremiah must be killed for saying such things. They said he made the people feel sad and afraid.

The king told the leaders to do as they liked with Jeremiah. So they let him down by ropes into a deep well that was filled with mud at the bottom.

But one of the king's helpers said to the king, "Jeremiah may die of hunger in that well."

So the king had thirty men take Jeremiah out of the well, but they didn't set him free. They kept him in the palace prison.

Then King Zedekiah sent for Jeremiah again. They talked secretly at the Temple. The king said, "I want to ask you a question. Don't hide the truth from me."

Jeremiah answered, "If I tell you the truth, will you promise not to have me killed?"

"Yes," the king replied, "I promise."

Then Jeremiah told him what the Lord said: "If you will give in to the king of Babylon and be his slave, you and your family will be safe and Jerusalem won't be burned."

But King Zedekiah wouldn't obey and give in. So King Nebuchadnezzar's army came against

The angry leaders of Judah put Jeremiah into a well because he told the truth about their sins. Later the king decided to save him.

Jerusalem for two and a half years. By the end of that time the food was all gone.

One night Zedekiah tried to get away from the city with his army, but he was caught. The mean king of Babylon and his men put out Zedekiah's eyes. Then they put chains on him and took him to Babylon, where they kept him in jail until he died.

Nebuchadnezzar's army burned the Temple and the palace and all the homes. They broke down the walls all around the city, too. They took all of the people away as slaves, except some of the poorest people. They were left to work in the fields and grape gardens.

So the kingdom of Judah came to an end just as the kingdom of Israel had, because of the sins of the people. It had lasted about 340 years, ever since Rehoboam was made king over the tribes of Judah and Benjamin. Nineteen kings and one queen had ruled over the people during that time. Of these, fifteen were wicked, and five obeyed the Lord. But even when there were good kings, the people often worshiped idols. And even though the Lord gave them time to be sorry and sent his prophets to warn them, they wouldn't obey him. So at last he sent the people of Judah far away to Babylon, just as he had already sent the other ten tribes to Assyria.

THE BOOK
about People Far from Home

The Lord told Ezekiel to say to the winds, "Come and blow on these dead bodies so that they will have breath and live again."

Dead Bones Come to Life

Ezekiel 37

Before Jerusalem was finally destroyed, a Jewish priest named Ezekiel had been taken away to Babylon. God showed Ezekiel many strange things through visions. It was like having dreams when he was awake!

One day the Lord showed Ezekiel this vision. Ezekiel seemed to be in a valley where the ground was covered with the old, dry bones of dead people. The Lord asked him, "Can these bones live again?"

Ezekiel said, "Lord, only you know the answer to that."

Then the Lord told Ezekiel to say to the bones, "Dry bones, listen to what God says. I am going to put muscles on you and cover you with skin. I will put breath into you, and you will come to life. Then you will know that I am the Lord!" As soon as Ezekiel said this, a strange, rattling noise began as the bones came together to form their skeletons. Then muscles grew on them and skin covered them. Soon the bones were bodies again, but they were still dead.

Then the Lord told Ezekiel to say to the winds, "Come and blow on these dead bodies so that they will have breath and live again." When Ezekiel said this, the wind blew and the dead bodies began to breathe. They came to life and stood up like a great army!

Then the Lord explained to Ezekiel what this vision meant. He said that his people, the Israelites, were like bones that were dry and dead. They had lost all hope of ever being happy or seeing their own land again. But the Lord said he would raise them up out of their troubles as he had raised those dry bones to life. "I will put my Spirit into their hearts and bring them back to their own land again. Then my people will know that I am the Lord. They will see that I have done what I promised."

After this the Lord told Ezekiel to get two sticks. He said to name one for the kingdom of Israel and the other for the kingdom of Judah. He told Ezekiel to hold the two sticks close together, and they would grow into one stick in his hand.

Then God said to Ezekiel, "People will ask what this means. Tell them that I will bring my people back to their own land. They will not be divided into the two nations of Israel and Judah anymore, for I will make them one nation again. They will not worship idols anymore either. I will put my Spirit into their hearts and make them holy. They will be my people, and I will be their God. They will live in the land where their fathers lived, and their

children and grandchildren will live there always.
I will be kind to them and give them a good king
who will rule over them forever."

Daniel and the King's Dream
Daniel 1–2

King Nebuchadnezzar of Babylon decided that he
needed some new leaders. So he started a school
to train some of the boys that his people had taken
from Jerusalem. He said that all the students had
to be good looking, quick to learn, and in perfect
health. He wanted them to learn everything there
was to know. After three years they would work for
the king as his leaders.

Among those chosen to go to school were four
Jewish boys named Daniel, Shadrach, Meshach, and
Abednego. These young men loved God and wanted
to obey him, but the king didn't want them to.

The king said that they should eat rich food that
may have been offered to idols. But Daniel asked
one of his teachers for other food. This man liked
Daniel a lot, but he said, "I'm afraid it will make the
king angry. If he notices that you don't look as
strong as the young men who eat his food, he will
kill me."

"Please give us only vegetables and water for just
ten days," Daniel said. "Then see if we don't look as

well as the men who eat the other food. If we don't, we will eat the same as the others do."

The teacher finally agreed. After ten days Daniel and his friends looked stronger than any of the others! So from then on they could eat whatever they wanted to. God helped them become wise, and he helped Daniel understand the meaning of dreams.

One night King Nebuchadnezzar woke up from a dream and couldn't get back to sleep. So he called all his wise men and said, "I had a dream that makes me worry."

"Well," the wise men replied, "tell us the dream, and we will tell you what it means."

But the king said, "If you won't tell me what I was dreaming and what it means, you will be killed and your houses will be torn down and made into piles of ruins. But if you tell me my dream and what it means, you'll be the richest, most honored men in the kingdom."

The wise men said, "No one can tell a person what he dreamed. And no king has ever asked such a thing. Only the gods can tell you, and they don't live on earth."

Then the king was very angry and ordered all of the wise men to be killed!

Daniel and his three friends were wise men, so they were to be killed too. When the captain of the king's soldiers came, Daniel was very wise and asked what it was all about. Right away he went to the king and asked for more time so he could tell the king about his dream.

Then Daniel went home and told his friends to pray that God would show them what the king's dream was. That night, in a vision, God showed the dream to Daniel.

Then Daniel praised God. He said, "I thank you and praise you, God, because you have heard our prayer and have told me what the king wants to know."

Then Daniel went to the captain and said to him, "Don't kill the wise men of Babylon. Take me to the king, and I will tell him the meaning of his dream."

So the captain quickly took Daniel to the king. And the king asked, "Can you tell me my dream and what it means?"

Daniel said, "The wisest man on earth could not tell it to the king; but there is a God in heaven who tells secrets. God has told me your dream so that you will know that he is the true God."

Then Daniel told the king the dream and its meaning. He said the dream was about things that were going to happen in the future.

The king bowed down to the ground in front of Daniel and said, "Your God is the God of gods. He is the King of all other kings. And he knows all secrets."

Then the king gave Daniel gifts and made him ruler over all of Babylon. He put Daniel in charge of the wise men. And the king let Daniel's three friends become rulers too, because that's what Daniel wanted.

Three Men in a Fire

Daniel 3

King Nebuchadnezzar of Babylon now made a huge statue of gold. He sent for all of his leaders to come and worship it. When they came, one of the king's helpers told them, "The king commands that you must fall down and worship his gold statue as soon as the band begins to play. Anyone who won't do it will be thrown into a furnace with hot flames."

The band began to play, and right away everyone bowed down and worshiped the gold statue.

But Daniel's three friends would not do it, because they knew it was wrong to worship a statue. Some of the Babylonians went to the king and said, "Didn't you make a law that everyone must worship the statue when the band begins to play? Doesn't it say that anyone who won't do it will be tossed into a hot furnace? Well, some of your Jewish leaders haven't obeyed you. They don't worship your gods, and they will not bow down to your gold statue. They are Shadrach, Meshach, and Abednego."

Shadrach, Meshach, and Abednego were thrown into a furnace of fire because they would not worship the king's statue. But God was with them, keeping them safe.

King Nebuchadnezzar was very angry. He ordered the three young men to be brought to him. "Is it true, Shadrach, Meshach, and Abednego," he shouted, "that you will not bow down to my gold statue? I'll give you one more chance. When you hear the band begin to play, you must worship the statue. If you don't, you will be thrown at once into a hot furnace. And what god will be able to save you from my anger?"

Then Shadrach, Meshach, and Abednego said to the king, "We won't do it! If you throw us into the furnace, our God is able to save us, and he will. But even if he doesn't, we will not worship your gods, sir, or bow down to your gold statue."

Nebuchadnezzar was even angrier than he had been. "Heat the furnace seven times hotter than ever before!" he told his men. Then he called for the strongest soldiers in his army to tie up Shadrach, Meshach, and Abednego and throw them in the furnace. It was so hot that the flames killed the soldiers. But after Shadrach, Meshach, and Abednego had fallen down into the fire inside the furnace, they got up again and walked around in the flames! The only things that burned were the ropes they were tied with!

King Nebuchadnezzar couldn't believe what he saw! "Didn't we throw three men into the fire, tied tightly with ropes?" he asked. "And now there are four of them, loose and walking around in the fire! And the fourth looks like a son of the gods!"

Nebuchadnezzar got as near as he could to the furnace. He shouted to them, "Shadrach, Meshach, and Abednego, you servants of the Most High God, come out!"

So they came out of the furnace. The leaders crowded around them and saw that the fire hadn't hurt them a bit. They didn't even smell of smoke!

Then Nebuchadnezzar said, "Praise to the God of Shadrach, Meshach, and Abednego, who has sent his angel and saved these young men who trusted in him. I now make a law that anyone who says anything bad about the God of Shadrach, Meshach, and Abednego shall be destroyed, and his house shall be torn down and made into a heap. No other God can save people as their God can!" Then the king made Shadrach, Meshach, and Abednego even greater leaders than they had been before.

STORY 101

The King Who Ate Grass

Daniel 4

Nebuchadnezzar was a mighty king, and soon he forgot about God. So God made something very strange happen to him. After it was all over, he sent a message to his people about it. This is what he said to them.

"I was enjoying life in my palace, with no

worries at all. Then I had a dream that made me afraid. So I called together all the wise men of Babylon, but they couldn't tell me what my dream meant. At last I called for Daniel, who has the spirit of the holy gods with him. I told him my dream. I said to him that I saw a very high tree standing in the center of the earth. The tree grew taller and taller until everyone could see it. Its branches spread out to the ends of the earth. Its leaves were green, and it was covered with fruit. The animals rested beneath its shade, and birds nested in its branches, and everything that lived came to it for food.

"Then I told Daniel that in my dream I saw an angel come down from heaven. The angel said to chop down the tree and cut off its branches. He said to shake off its leaves and scatter its fruit. He said to send the animals and birds away, but leave the stump of the tree in the ground. Then he said to let this stump live like an animal in the field for seven years.

"I asked Daniel what the dream meant. At first he was afraid to tell me, but I said he must, so finally he did. He said that the giant tree was me. He said I had grown powerful and my kingdom reached to the ends of the earth. It was a holy angel that came down from heaven, saying to cut down the tree and let the stump live with the wild animals of the field for seven years. Daniel said this meant I would no longer live in my palace. He said I would eat grass like a cow and sleep on the ground. I would do that until I learned that God rules over all the earth and decides who will be the king of each land.

"Everything came true just as Daniel said it would. One year after this dream I was walking on the roof of my palace. I looked out across the great city of Babylon with its high walls, temples, palaces, and gardens. And I felt proud. I talked about how I had built that city by my own power and for my own honor. As I was speaking, I heard a voice from heaven saying that I was no longer the ruler of my kingdom. I would now have to live with the wild animals and eat grass like a cow for seven years.

"That very hour my mind stopped working the way it should. I was no longer fit to rule my kingdom. I was chased out into the fields to live, I ate grass like a cow, and I slept on the ground. My hair grew long like eagles' feathers, and my nails were like birds' claws.

"But at the end of the seven years I looked up to heaven, and my right mind came back to me. So did my honor and my kingdom. My leaders made me the king again, and all my greatness was given back to me. Now I, Nebuchadnezzar, praise and honor God, the King of heaven. He does only what is just and right. And he is able to keep the proud from feeling important."

The Hand That Wrote on the Wall

Daniel 5

A number of years later King Belshazzar was the ruler of Babylon. One day he invited a thousand of his leaders to a special party. They were all drinking wine when the king gave an order to his servants. He told them to bring him the gold and silver cups that had been taken from the Temple in Jerusalem a long time before. Then everyone drank from those cups and praised the king's idols.

Suddenly a hand began writing words on the wall. The king's face grew white with fear, and his knees shook. No one could understand the writing.

The king called for the wise men. He said to them, "If you can read that writing on the wall and tell me what it means, I'll give you the clothes of kings and a gold chain. I'll make you the number three ruler in my kingdom." But none of the wise men could read or understand the writing.

The king was really worried by now, and his leaders didn't know what to do. Then the queen came in and said, "My king, don't be afraid. There is a man in your kingdom named Daniel who has within him the spirit of the holy gods. Nebuchadnezzar put him in charge of all the wise men of Babylon, for he knows and understands many things. He can explain dreams and tell what to do about hard problems. Call for Daniel, and he will tell you what the writing says."

So the leaders had Daniel come to see the king. "Are you the Daniel who was brought here from the land of Judah?" the king asked. "I have heard that the spirit of the gods is in you, and that you are very wise. My wise men can't read the writing over there on the wall, and I must know what it means. If you can tell me what it says, I'll give you the clothes of kings and a gold chain. I'll make you the number three ruler in my kingdom."

"Keep your gifts," Daniel said. "But I will tell you what the writing means. God gave Nebuchadnezzar a kingdom and glory and honor. Because God made him so great, people from other lands were afraid of him.

"But when he became proud and forgot God, God took away his kingdom. He became like an animal. He lived with the wild donkeys and ate grass like the cows. He did that until he learned that God rules over all the earth and decides who will be the king of each land.

"You knew all this, Belshazzar. But still you have been proud and have sinned against God. You have sent for the cups from the Temple of God, and everyone at your party drank wine from them. You did it while praising your idols that can't see, hear, or know anything at all. And you haven't praised the true God, who lets you live and gives you all you have. So God has written these words: MENE, MENE, TEKEL, PARSIN. This is what the words mean: Your kingdom is coming to an end. God has taken it from you. He tried you out as king, but you didn't obey him. He has given your kingdom to the Medes and the Persians."

Then Belshazzar gave Daniel the purple clothes of kings and put a gold chain around his neck. He made Daniel the number three ruler in the kingdom. That same night King Belshazzar was killed. Darius the Mede took over the kingdom.

STORY 103

Daniel in the Lions' Den

Daniel 6; 9

Darius decided to divide the kingdom into 120 parts ruled by 120 princes. Daniel was one of the three leaders who were in charge of the princes. Because Daniel was the best leader, Darius was planning to make him ruler over everyone. When the other leaders and princes heard about it, they were upset and tried to find something bad to say about Daniel to the king. But they couldn't find a thing that he did wrong. Finally they decided what to do. "The only thing we might be able to say against Daniel would have something to do with his belief in God."

So the princes and their leaders went to the king.

Daniel's enemies had the king make a bad law. It said that anyone who didn't pray to the king would be thrown to the lions. Daniel prayed to God anyway. And God closed the mouths of the lions!

They said, "King Darius, may you live forever! We want you to make a new law. Tell people they must pray only to you for the next thirty days. Anyone who doesn't obey will be thrown into a den of lions.

Write this law down and sign it. Then even you can't change it." So King Darius signed the law.

Daniel knew that the law had been signed. But he still went home, opened the windows of his room toward Jerusalem, and got down on his knees. He prayed and gave thanks to God three times a day, just as he always had done. Some of the king's helpers went over to Daniel's house and found him praying to God. So they hurried back to the king. They said, "Didn't you make a law that any person praying to anyone but you for thirty days must be thrown into the den of lions?"

"Yes," the king said, "I certainly did. It is a law of the Medes and Persians, which can never change."

Then they said, "Daniel isn't obeying you. He prays to his God three times a day!"

Now the king was angry with himself for signing that law. He tried to find a way to save Daniel. But that evening the men went to him again. They said, "Our king, you know that no law the king has signed can be changed!"

So at last King Darius gave up and had Daniel thrown into the den of lions. But first the king said to him, "You worship God every day. May he save you."

Then, after Daniel was thrown in, a big stone was rolled across the opening into the lions' den so that no one could get Daniel out.

When the king went home to his palace, he wouldn't eat. And he sent away the people who played and sang for him most evenings. He couldn't sleep that night. So he got up very early the next morning and hurried to the lions' den. He was afraid as he called out: "Daniel, you who worship the living God, was your God able to save you from the lions?"

Daniel called back to the king, "My God sent his angel to shut the lions' mouths so that they wouldn't hurt me!"

The king was so happy that he ordered his helpers to take Daniel out of the lions' den at once. So Daniel was not hurt because he trusted in his God.

Then King Darius sent this message to people all over the world: "I now make a new law that in every part of my kingdom people must worship Daniel's God. He is the living God, and his kingdom will last forever. He is the God who can save people from danger, for he saved Daniel from the lions."

While Daniel was in Babylon he read the book written by Jeremiah the prophet. He learned from it that his people, the Jews, would go back to Jerusalem after seventy years. Well, those seventy years had nearly come to an end! So Daniel prayed that the Jews might return to the city of Jerusalem and build it again. He asked God to forgive them for their sins.

Some time later, as Daniel kept on praying this prayer, the angel Gabriel came from God's presence in heaven. It was in the evening. The angel told Daniel about God's love. He said that God heard Daniel's prayer and would soon send the Jewish people back to their own land. Then they could build up Jerusalem again. The angel also said that God would send a special ruler many years after that. It would be almost five hundred years before this would happen. Gabriel was telling about the time when the Savior would be born!

STORY 104
Beautiful Esther Becomes a Queen

Esther 1–2

A number of years after God saved Daniel, Xerxes was the king. The kingdom was now called Persia. One day the king gave a great party for his princes, army leaders, and helpers at his palace. It was at the palace in Susa, where the kings of Persia lived during the winter.

Queen Vashti held a party at the same time for the women who lived and worked in the palace.

On the seventh day of the king's party, when he was drunk, he sent for Queen Vashti. He wanted to show everyone how beautiful she was. But she wouldn't do it. This made the king very angry. So he called in his wise leaders and asked them, "What shall I do to Queen Vashti for not obeying me?"

One of the men said, "Queen Vashti has done wrong not only to you but to everyone in your kingdom. All the women of Persia will stop obeying their husbands when they hear about this. Let the king make a law. And let it be written among the laws of the Medes and Persians, which cannot be changed. Say that Queen Vashti must never see you again and that you are to choose someone else for your queen. When this becomes known, wives everywhere will be afraid not to obey their husbands."

The king thought this was a good idea. So he sent letters to all the different parts of his kingdom. And he told every husband to be the ruler in his home.

Then the king's wise leaders said to him, "Let's look for the most beautiful young women in Persia. Bring them all here to the palace. And the one you decide you like best will be the new queen instead of Vashti." So that is what they did.

One of the helpers at the palace was a Jewish man named Mordecai. He had a young cousin named Esther. Her father and mother had died, so Mordecai had adopted Esther and brought her up in his house. She was very beautiful and was one of the young women who was brought to the king's palace. But would she be the one selected as his queen?

Everyone liked Esther very much. One of the king's helpers did everything he could for her. He gave her a nice place to stay and seven young girls to wait on her. But Esther didn't tell anyone she was Jewish, for Mordecai had told her not to.

When Esther was brought to the king, he loved

her more than any of the other young women. So he placed the royal crown on her head and made her queen instead of Vashti. Then the king had a big party and gave gifts to all his leaders and helpers.

Haman Makes a Bad Law

Esther 2–4

It so happened that two of the king's helpers were angry with him and wanted to kill him. Mordecai heard them talking about their plans. He sent a message to Esther, telling her about the danger the king was in. So Esther told the king, and the men were killed. Mordecai had saved the king's life, and this was written down in a book about the king.

A man at the palace named Haman was very great because the king had put him in charge of the other leaders. They all bowed to Haman, for the king told them to. But Mordecai wouldn't do it. The men at the king's gate asked Mordecai, "Why don't you obey the king and bow to Haman?" They kept talking to him about this for several days, but he wouldn't listen to them. So they finally told Haman about it.

When Haman learned that Mordecai wasn't bowing to him, he was very angry and decided to punish him. But he didn't think it would be enough to punish Mordecai alone. Since Mordecai was Jewish, he decided to punish all the Jewish people of Persia.

So Haman said to the king, "There are Jewish people living everywhere in your kingdom. Their laws are different from our laws; and they don't obey the king's laws. It is not good to let such people live. If you, my king, will make a law to have them all killed, I will give you 375 tons of silver."

King Xerxes agreed to this. He told Haman to keep the money but to make any law he wanted to against the Jewish people. So Haman wrote a law naming a day when the people of Persia were to kill all the Jewish people in the kingdom.

When Mordecai heard about the law Haman had made, he put on clothes made from rough cloth to show how sad he was. Then he went out into the streets of the city, crying. Wherever the messengers brought the news about the law, the Jewish people cried and went without food.

Queen Esther hadn't heard about this new law. But her maids told her that Mordecai was wearing sackcloth and was crying out in the street. This made Esther sad. She sent new clothes to him, but he wouldn't take them. So Esther sent one of the king's helpers to ask Mordecai what the trouble was. Mordecai told him all that had happened and gave him a copy of Haman's law to show to Esther. Then he said to tell the queen to beg the king to save the lives of the Jewish people.

When the king's helper told Esther what Mordecai said, she sent back this message: "Everyone knows that anyone who goes to the king without being sent for will be killed. That's what will happen unless the king holds out his gold rod. And he hasn't sent for me in the last four weeks. How can I go and speak with him?"

Then Mordecai sent another message to Esther: "Don't think for a minute that you will be safe just because you are the queen, when they kill all the other Jews. If you don't try to save your people now, someone else will do it. But you and your family will die. And who knows? Perhaps God made you queen at this time just so you can help the Jewish people."

Then Esther sent another message to Mordecai: "Gather all the Jews in this city. Tell them to go without food and pray for me. Do not eat or drink for three days and three nights. My maids and I will do the same. Then I will try to go in and speak with the king. And if I die, I die."

So Mordecai called the Jews together, and they did as Esther asked.

STORY 106
The King Honors Mordecai
Esther 5–6

Three days later Queen Esther put on the robes she wore as a queen. She went and stood in front of the king as he sat on his throne. God was with her, for the king held out his gold rod to her. So she came to him and touched the tip of the gold rod.

Queen Esther
was afraid to go to the king because it was against
the law unless he asked her to come. But she went
anyway because she wanted to save her people.

Then the king asked, "What is it you wish,
Queen Esther? I will give you whatever it is, even
if it is half of my kingdom."

Esther answered, "Please come with Haman
today to a big dinner I have made for you!"

Then the king said to his helpers, "Tell Haman to come right away to Esther's dinner."

So the king and Haman came to the dinner. The king knew that Esther wanted to ask some favor from him. So as they sat at the dinner table he asked her again, "What is it you wish? I will give it to you, even if it is half of my kingdom."

Esther answered, "Please come with Haman to another dinner I will make for you tomorrow. Then I will tell you what I want to ask of you."

Haman was very happy to be invited again to a dinner with the king and queen. But as he was leaving the palace, he noticed that Mordecai sat at the gate and would not bow to him. He was very angry but said nothing.

When he came home, he called for his friends and for his wife. He bragged about his money and his family. He told them how the king had made him more important than anyone else.

"And Queen Esther invited no one else but me and the king to come to her dinner. Tomorrow I am invited to dinner with the king and queen again! But I can't really be happy as long as Mordecai sits at the gate and won't bow to me."

Then his wife and all his friends said, "Make a place to hang Mordecai. And tomorrow ask the king to let you do it. Then you can be happy at the queen's dinner."

Haman was pleased with this idea. So he had the work done.

That night King Xerxes couldn't sleep. He told

one of his helpers to bring him the book that told about things that had happened while he was king. As the book was read to him, he heard about the time that Mordecai had saved his life.

The king asked, "What special thing did we do for Mordecai because he did this?"

"Nothing, sir," his helpers answered.

While the king was talking, Haman came to the palace to ask the king to let him hang Mordecai. When the king's helpers told him that Haman wanted to see him, he said, "Yes, tell him to come in."

So Haman came in. But the king spoke before Haman could say what he wanted. The king said to him, "Haman, what is the greatest thing I can do to honor a man who has helped me?"

Haman thought that he was the one the king wanted to honor. So he said, "Bring out one of your robes and your horse. Let one of your most important leaders put your robe on the man and lead him through the streets of the city on your horse. Have the leader shout to all the people, 'See how the king is honoring this man!'"

"Good!" the king said to Haman. "Take these robes of mine and get my horse. Then find Mordecai and do for him all the things you have talked about."

Well, there was nothing Haman could do but obey the king. So he put the king's robes on Mordecai and led him on horseback through the streets of the city. Haman shouted out to all the people, "See how the king is honoring this man!"

Afterward Mordecai returned quietly to his duties at the king's gate. Haman hurried home, feeling sad and hoping that no one would see him.

STORY 107

Brave Esther Saves Her People

Esther 7–9

At Queen Esther's second dinner the king asked Esther again, "What is your wish, Queen Esther? Whatever you want it shall be given to you, even half of my kingdom."

Esther answered, "If the king is pleased with me, this is what I want. I want the king to save my life and the lives of all the Jewish people, for we face death. My people and I are all to be killed."

"Who would dare to do such a thing?" King Xerxes asked.

Esther answered, "This wicked Haman is our enemy."

Haman's face looked white because he was so afraid. The king, who was very angry, left the room and went out to the palace garden. When he came in again, Haman had fallen down beside the queen to beg for his life. But the king had decided to kill him.

"Why not hang him where he was going to hang Mordecai?" someone suggested.

"Yes, hang him there," said the king. So that is the way Haman died.

King Xerxes gave Haman's house and land to Queen Esther. Then Mordecai was called in to see the king. The king knew now that Mordecai was Esther's cousin, for she had told him. So the king made Mordecai his most important leader.

Then Esther went to the king again. She bowed down at his feet, crying. The king held out his gold rod, and she asked him to change the law about killing all the Jewish people. "How can I stand to see my people die?" she cried.

But no law of the Medes and Persians could ever be changed, not even by the king himself. So King Xerxes told Esther and Mordecai to make another law that would help the Jews.

So Mordecai wrote a new law in the king's name. It said that the Jews could fight back against anyone who tried to hurt them!

Mordecai sent copies of this new law everywhere in the kingdom. Messengers rode on fast horses to get the message out quickly.

The day came when all the Jewish people were to be killed, but they were ready. They gathered together in every city, armed to fight for their lives. And they destroyed all their enemies.

So God saved Queen Esther and her people. Then Mordecai sent letters to all the Jews telling them to have a special party every year. He said to remember how God helped them win over their enemies. He said they should give each other presents and give gifts to poor people too.

THE
BOOK
about
Coming
Home
Again

As in the days when Solomon built the first
Temple, wood from cedar trees was brought from
Lebanon to build the Temple again.

Many Jews Return to Israel

Isaiah 44–45; Ezra 1–3

At last the seventy years of having to live far from home came to an end for the people of Judah. In the land of Babylon, which was now called Persia, Cyrus was the king. (This was before the time of Queen Esther.) God made Cyrus want to let the Jews go home again to Jerusalem. The prophet Isaiah had written about Cyrus nearly two hundred years before this! Cyrus had not even been born then! And God's people were still living in their own land. But God had told his prophet Isaiah to tell about these things long before they happened.

King Cyrus made a law and sent this message to everyone in his kingdom: "The Lord has told me to build his Temple in Jerusalem again. All of you who are God's people may go back to the city of Jerusalem in the land of Judah. You may go now and build the Temple of the Lord again. And let those who don't go back home help those who do by giving them silver and gold and cows. Also give them food and clothes to take with them."

Then God made the Jewish priests and other

leaders want to go home. So they got ready for their trip to Jerusalem. Those who didn't want to go with them gave them gifts. King Cyrus gave them beautiful things made of gold that Nebuchadnezzar had taken from the Temple long before. In all, there were 5,400 of these gold and silver bowls.

There were 42,360 people who returned to Jerusalem at that time. Their leader was Zerubbabel, and they took with them their 7,337 servants. They also took 736 horses, 245 mules, 435 camels, and 6,720 donkeys.

When they came to Jerusalem, they found that the Temple, along with the houses and the city walls, had been broken down or burned.

The first thing the people did was to build again the altar of the Lord. They built it at the place where the Temple used to be so that they could worship God. They offered gifts to God on the altar every day. They offered one lamb in the morning and another lamb in the evening, just as God's people did before they were taken away to Babylon.

Then they got ready to build the Temple again. They hired workers from Tyre, just as King Solomon had done hundreds of years before. The workers cut down cedar trees on the Lebanon mountains. Then they made rafts from them and floated them in the sea to the shore near Jerusalem.

When the very first stones for the bottom part of the new Temple were laid, the priests were so happy that they played on trumpets and cymbals and sang songs of praise to the Lord. The other people were glad too and shouted their praises to God. But many of the older priests and other leaders remembered the Temple that had stood there before. They couldn't keep back their tears as they thought about what had happened to it. So the shouting and the crying were both heard far away.

STORY 109

The People Build God's Temple Again

2 Kings 17; Ezra 4–6; Haggai 1

It was more than 250 years since the king of Assyria had taken away the ten tribes of Israel. At that time he sent people from his own land to live in Israelite cities. These people, the Samaritans, worshiped idols. But they talked as if they worshiped God. Now that the Jewish people from Judah were back in Jerusalem, the Samaritans said that they would help build the Temple.

But the Samaritans were really enemies of God's people, the Jews. The Samaritans did all they could to stop the Jewish people from building the Temple. They even paid some men to work against Zerubbabel and the others.

A long time later Xerxes became the king of Persia. (He was the king who made Esther his queen.) The enemies of God's people wrote this letter to him: "We want you to know, our king, that the Jews who came from the city of Babylon are building the wicked city of Jerusalem again. You should know that once they get the wall built up, they will stop paying taxes to you. They will not do what you ask them to. We don't want this to happen, so we suggest that you read up on the history of the city of Jerusalem. See for yourself that it has always given much trouble to the kings who tried to take charge of it. In fact, that is why Jerusalem was destroyed."

The king sent this reply: "Thank you for your letter. I have checked into the matter and find that what you said is true. Jerusalem has always made trouble. So tell the men of Judah to stop building the city until I tell them it's all right to do it."

Then the Samaritans hurried to Jerusalem and made the people stop building. So the work came to an end.

Then Darius the Second became king. But even though the Jews knew there was another king, they didn't ask him to let them start building the Temple again. Ever since the Samaritans had stopped them from building God's house, they had become more interested in building houses for themselves.

The Lord was not happy with them. He sent Haggai the prophet to tell them, "You say that it isn't yet time to build the Temple. Well, is it time for you to be living in beautiful houses while my Temple is broken down? You have all hurried to build your own houses instead of building the Temple. That is why I have not made the crops grow in your fields. That is why I have not let you have all the food and clothes you need. Go up to the mountains and cut down trees to make logs. Build the Temple, and I will be pleased."

Then the people obeyed the command of the Lord and began to build the Temple. And Haggai gave them this message from God: "I am with you!"

When the Samaritans heard about this, they came to Zerubbabel and the high priest, trying to stop them again. The Samaritans asked, "Who has told you to build the Temple?"

Zerubbabel and the priest answered them, "King Cyrus did. He sent us here. And he gave us the gold and silver bowls Nebuchadnezzar had taken out of the Temple."

So God was with his people and helped them keep building.

Then the Samaritans wrote a letter to King Darius. They asked him to find out if Cyrus had really told the Jews to build the Temple. When Darius read the letter, he told his servants to look in the old books where all the writings of the kings of Babylon were. And sure enough, one of the books had this note. "In the first year that Cyrus was king, he said to let the people of the Lord build the Temple at Jerusalem again."

As soon as King Darius learned what Cyrus had said many years before, he sent a letter to the Samaritans. He said to let the men of Judah keep building the Temple of the Lord. He said, "Stay away from there, and do not try to stop them!"

STORY **110**

The King Helps Ezra

Ezra 7–8

Many more years went by. Artaxerxes was now the king of Persia, and a Jewish man named Ezra still lived there in the city of Babylon. Other people from Jerusalem still lived there too. Ezra was a good man who loved his people and wanted them to know how to obey God. He asked King Artaxerxes to let him go to Jerusalem. There he would teach God's laws to the Jews so they could obey God.

Artaxerxes let Ezra go. And the king gave Ezra a letter. This is what it said:

I make a law that all Jews who are still in Persia but want to go to the city of Jerusalem may go with you. I want you to check on what is happening in the land of Judah. Take silver and gold as gifts to your God.

If you need more money, Ezra, just ask. And I, Artaxerxes the king, give this command to all those who take care of my money in the places where Ezra is going: Give him whatever he asks for. He may have up to 7,500 pounds of silver, 500 bushels of wheat, 550 gallons of wine, and 550 gallons of olive oil. And give him as much salt as he wants. Help in every way possible to get God's Temple built so that God won't be angry with me and send some trouble to my kingdom.

And when you get to Jerusalem, Ezra, choose leaders to rule the people. Be sure that the leaders you choose know the laws of God. Teach the people who don't. Those who will not obey God's laws or mine will be killed or sent to another land. Or their things may be taken from them. Or they may be put in jail.

Ezra thanked God for helping the king be kind to him and care about the Temple. Then he called together some of the leaders of the Jews in Babylon for a meeting near a river. They camped there three days. They ate nothing during that time, for they spent their time praying to the Lord. They asked him to direct their trip to Jerusalem and to keep them and their children and their money safe.

Then Ezra called twelve of the priests and counted out the gold and the silver and the gold bowls the king had given for the Temple. "This silver and gold is an offering to the Lord," he told the priests. "So guard it carefully. Be sure you have it all so that you can give it to the priests and other leaders at the Temple."

So Ezra and all those going back to Jerusalem with him began the long trip. It was the middle of

April when they left. They had to go through wild desert country, full of enemies and robbers. But the Lord watched over them and helped them reach Jerusalem safely. It took them about four months. There they rested for three days before going up to the Temple.

They counted the silver and gold and the gold bowls again to see that none had been lost. Then they gave them to the priests and other leaders at the Temple. And they worshiped God.

Ezra gave the letters from the king to those who ruled over that part of the kingdom. The rulers obeyed the king by helping Ezra and the people with him and by helping with the Temple.

STORY 111
Building a Wall around a City

Nehemiah 1–4

Artaxerxes was still the Persian king. Zerubbabel had taken some Jewish people back to Jerusalem many years before. And Ezra had taken more Jewish people back to Jerusalem several years ago. Now Nehemiah, a Jew, was living in the city of Susa in Persia.

One day Nehemiah met some men from Judah. He asked them how things were going in Jerusalem.

"Not very well," the men told him. They said the wall around Jerusalem was still broken down, and the gates to the city had burned up in a fire.

Nehemiah cried when he heard this. Then he began going without food as he prayed for his people, the Jews. He asked God to forgive their sins and to forgive him, too. He prayed that God would make the king want to help them.

One day Nehemiah was sitting in the palace with King Artaxerxes. "Why are you so sad today?" the king asked him. "Are you sick?"

"No," Nehemiah said. "But how can I help but be sad? The city of Jerusalem, where my family once lived, is broken down. It has no wall standing around it."

"Well, what do you want me to do about it?" the king asked.

Nehemiah prayed quietly in his heart. Finally he said, "Would you send me to Jerusalem to build the city and the wall around it again?"

"How long will it take?" the king asked. "How soon could you return?"

After they had talked about it for a while, the king told him to go!

Nehemiah then asked the king to write some letters. Nehemiah wanted to take these letters to the leaders of the different places he would pass through. Then the leaders would help him have a safe trip. He also wanted a letter to give to the man in charge of the king's forest. He wanted the king to ask that man for wood for the city wall and gates.

So the king gave him letters and also sent soldiers with him to guard him.

But there were two wicked men named Sanballat and Tobiah living near Jerusalem. They were enemies of the Jewish people. When they heard that the king had sent someone to help the Jews in Jerusalem, they didn't like it at all.

Nehemiah had a safe trip to Jerusalem. After he had been there three days, he went out alone at night so that his enemies wouldn't see him. He checked out the broken-down wall around the city.

The next morning he called a meeting of the city leaders. He told them, "You see the danger we are in, with no wall to keep us safe from our enemies. We must build our wall again."

"Yes, let's get started. Let's build the wall," they said to one another.

Everyone helped to build part of the wall. The priests helped, and some of the women helped too.

But Sanballat was angry when he heard about it. He made fun of the Jewish people. He said to his friends and army leaders, "What are these weak people trying to do? Can they build a wall around Jerusalem in a day? Where will they find enough stones?"

Tobiah, who was with him, said, "If a fox walked on their wall it would fall down!"

Nehemiah prayed. And the Jews kept working until they had built the wall half as high as it had been.

Then Sanballat and Tobiah and all the enemies

of the Jews made plans to fight them. But the Jews heard about the plans. After they prayed, Nehemiah put guards by all of the families. "Don't be afraid," he said. "Remember, the Lord will help us. Fight for your wives, your children, and your homes."

The enemies didn't come when they heard the Jews were ready to fight. So Nehemiah and his people went back to work on the wall. But only half of the men worked. The other half were guards. Even the workers carried their swords with them. Nehemiah kept a man with a trumpet near him so he could let people know if the enemies came.

All the people worked hard from morning till evening.

STORY 112
Finishing the City Wall
Nehemiah 6–7; 12

Sanballat and Tobiah heard that Nehemiah and the Jewish people were almost done building the wall. Only the gates still needed to be fixed. So they sent a message to Nehemiah to meet them in one of the towns. But Nehemiah knew they wanted to hurt him. So he sent messengers to tell them, "I am doing a great work, and I cannot come down. Should I stop the work just so I can talk with you?"

They sent him the same message four times, but each time he gave them the same answer.

Then Sanballat sent a messenger to Nehemiah with this letter: "I am told that you Jewish people in Jerusalem are going to fight against the king of Persia. I am told you are building the wall around the city because you want to be the king. Come and talk with me, or I will tell the king."

But Nehemiah sent back this reply: "It isn't true, and you know it."

Then Nehemiah prayed for God to make him strong so that he and his people could keep on working. In 52 days the wall was finished.

Nehemiah now chose leaders throughout the city. He told them, "Shut the gates at night, and don't open them in the morning until the sun is high up in the sky. And each of you must take his turn at guard duty on the wall, to watch for our enemies."

Then the Jewish people gathered together to thank God for the wall around the city. They walked along the top of the wall in two groups. One group led by Ezra the priest walked in one direction, and the other group walked in the other direction with Nehemiah. There was music, with singers, harps, and clashing cymbals. The singers sang praises to God as they walked around the city until the two groups met. Then they came down from the wall and marched together to the Temple, where they offered gifts to God. All of the men, women, and children were so happy that people far away could hear how happy they were!

A Time to Remember

Nehemiah 8–10; 13

One day after the Jewish people had built the wall around Jerusalem, they met together near one of the gates in the wall. They asked Ezra the priest to bring from the Temple the book of God's laws that Moses had written down. So Ezra brought out the Book of the Law and stood up high where all the people could see him. Then he opened the book and read from morning until noon. Everyone listened—the men, the women, and the children, too. And the Levites explained what he read.

When the people heard God's laws and remembered how often they had disobeyed them, they began crying. But Nehemiah and Ezra and the Levites said to them, "Don't cry, for this is a day to be happy and worship God. Don't be sad, for the joy of the Lord makes you strong. Go and enjoy some good food and sweet drinks. Share your food with those who don't have any." So all the people went to have a big dinner and to share their food. They were happy because they had God's words and understood them.

The next day they came to Ezra again so that he could read more of God's laws to them. This time he read from the part of the book telling them to have a special festival each year. They were to live in little houses made from tree branches. "Go up to the mountains," the book said, "and cut down branches from different trees. Then make little houses and live in them all week." So they moved out of their houses and lived in the little houses for the seven days of the celebration. And there was a great joy among them. There hadn't been such a happy festival in Jerusalem for hundreds of years.

Then the people remembered again how often they had disobeyed God. So they met once more. This time they were sad and went without food as they told God about their sins

Their leaders then wrote out their promise to obey all of God's commands. Then Nehemiah and some of the priests and many other leaders signed the promise.

But several years later the people forgot their promise to obey God's laws. They did not care about the priests or the Temple anymore. And the men married women who did not love God.

Nehemiah asked the people how they could be so wicked. Then he did what he could at the Temple to please God. He prayed that God would remember what he did and be kind to him.

THIS CHAPTER completes the story of the Old Testament. The Bible tells us nothing more about the Jewish people until Jesus came more than four hundred years later.

In the New Testament we will see how God kept his promises about sending the Savior.

The Temple of God was built again by the Jews who returned from Babylon. A few years before Jesus, the Savior, was born, King Herod made the Temple even nicer because he wanted to please the Jews.

THE BOOK
about
Jesus

*An angel told Mary that she would have a baby.
The baby would be Jesus, God's Son.*

Three Visits from an Angel

Matthew 1; Luke 1

Now it was time for the Savior to come to earth. Everyone needed him very much, for no one was pleasing God. All the people in the world were sinners, just as Adam and Eve had been. When Adam and Eve sinned in the Garden of Eden, God promised them that a Savior would come someday to take away their sins. The prophets, too, had often told God's people that this wonderful Savior was going to come.

The prophets said that someone else would come before the Savior did. This person would tell the people to get ready for the Savior by turning away from their sins. We begin the New Testament with the story of this man's family.

Herod was king of Judea, which had been called Judah before. An old priest named Zechariah worked at the Temple, helping the people to worship God. His wife's name was Elizabeth. They were both careful to obey all of God's commands, but God had never given them a child.

One day at the hour of prayer it was Zechariah's turn to go into the Holy Place where the gold altar was. Suddenly he saw an angel standing beside the altar! Zechariah was so afraid.

But the angel said, "Don't be afraid, Zechariah. I have come to tell you that God will give you and Elizabeth a son. You are to name him John. He will bring you great joy. But he must never drink wine or anything else that could get him drunk. He will be filled with God's Holy Spirit from the time he is born. He will tell the Israelites about the Savior who is coming, and he will help many of them turn from their sins and obey God."

Zechariah didn't know what to think. "How can I be sure you are telling the truth?" he asked the angel.

"I am the angel Gabriel," he replied. "I live in heaven and stand close to God, doing whatever he commands me. He has sent me to tell you this good news. And because you haven't believed me, you will not be able to speak until all that I have told you comes true."

Zechariah's wife, Elizabeth, had a young cousin named Mary. Six months after the angel talked to Zechariah in the Temple, God sent his angel to Mary. She was afraid, for she had never seen an angel before. But Gabriel said, "Don't be afraid, Mary! God has decided to bless you. This is how he will do it. You are going to have a baby boy, and you are to name him Jesus. And God is giving a baby to Zechariah and your cousin Elizabeth."

Mary didn't understand how she could have a baby, for she wasn't married and had never slept with a man. But the angel explained that baby Jesus would have no human father, for he would be the Son of God. Mary still didn't understand everything the angel told her. But she said, "I will do whatever God wants."

She was engaged to be married to a kind man named Joseph, who was a carpenter. He was from the family of King David, who had lived hundreds of years before. But when he heard that Mary was going to have a baby, he was sad. He thought she had sinned and some other man was the baby's father. He was going to tell her that now he wouldn't marry her. But while he was sleeping, an angel told him that God was the baby's father. The angel said it was all right for Joseph to marry her after all; so he did. But he didn't sleep with her until after the baby was born.

Meanwhile, God gave Zechariah and Elizabeth the son he had promised them. When the baby was eight days old, their family and friends came to set him apart as God's child and to decide on his name. They wanted to call him Zechariah, because that was his father's name. But his mother said, "No, we will name him John."

"Oh no," they said to her, "no one in your family has that name." Then they talked to Zechariah with motions, asking him what he wanted to name the baby. Because he had not believed the angel, he couldn't speak yet. So he took a sheet of paper and wrote, "His name is John." Everyone was surprised, for they didn't know about the angel giving him this name in the Temple. Suddenly Zechariah could talk again!

Little John grew, and the Lord blessed him. When he was older he lived out in the lonely wilderness away from the rest of the people. He

NO ROOMS, the sign at the Bethlehem inn said. So Joseph took Mary to the stable and made a bed of hay. That is where Jesus, God's Son, was born.

stayed there until the time came for him to preach to God's people and tell them about Jesus. This child God had given to Zechariah and Elizabeth was John the Baptist, the one who came to prepare the way for Jesus, the Savior.

The Birth of God's Son

Luke 2

The Jewish people were now under the rule of the Romans. So they had to do whatever the Roman emperor and his leaders told them to. Now he made a law that the name and address of every person must be written down. He told everyone to go to the city where his family had lived many, many years before. Then the Roman officers could write down their names. So Joseph and Mary went to Bethlehem. That's because Joseph was from the family of King David, who had lived in Bethlehem hundreds of years before.

But when they came to Bethlehem, there was no place for them to stay. So they went out to the stable where the donkeys and camels were sleeping. While they were there, Mary's baby boy was born. He was the baby that the angel Gabriel had told her to name Jesus. Mary wrapped strips of cloth around him and laid him in a manger. That was the place where the animals would eat.

That same night some shepherds were in the fields outside the town. They were watching their sheep, keeping them safe from wild animals. Suddenly an angel came, and the brightness of God was all around them. They were so afraid. But the angel said, "Don't be afraid, for I have good news for you. It's for all the world! Your Savior was born tonight in Bethlehem! His name is Christ the Lord.

"This is how you will know him: You will find him in a manger, all wrapped up in strips of cloth!"

Then suddenly many, many other angels came. They were all praising God and saying, "Glory to God! Peace on earth between God and men!"

After the angels returned to heaven the shepherds talked together. They said, "Let's hurry to Bethlehem and find the baby!" So they ran into the village. Soon they found Mary and Joseph. And the baby was in a manger! Afterward the shepherds returned to their sheep again. As they went back they praised God for what the angels had told them and for the baby they had seen. He was the Savior!

When the baby was eight days old, his parents named him Jesus, just as the angel Gabriel had told them to. And they set him apart as God's child, for he was the Son of God.

Shepherds were taking care of their sheep one night near Bethlehem. Suddenly the sky was filled with angels telling them about Jesus' birth.

Wise Men Visit a Baby King

Matthew 2

It was some time after Jesus had been born. Now several wise men who knew how to study the stars came to Jerusalem from a land in the east. "Where is the child who is king of the Jews?" they asked. "We have seen his star and have come to worship him."

When King Herod heard them asking about a new king, he began to worry. He was the king, and he didn't want anyone else to have his job! He called for some teachers who had spent their lives studying the Scriptures. Then he asked them if the Bible said where the new king would be born.

"Yes," they replied. "One of the prophets wrote that it would be in the city of Bethlehem."

So Herod said to the wise men, "Go to Bethlehem and look for the child. When you have found him, come back and tell me so that I can worship him, too!"

So the wise men went to Bethlehem. On the way, they were very happy when the star they had seen before came to them again. It went ahead of them and stopped right over a house. They went in and saw the young child with Mary, his mother. They bowed low before him, worshiping him. Then they gave presents to the new king—special gifts of gold and spices. Afterward they returned to their own country. But they didn't go through Jerusalem, for in a dream God warned them not to tell Herod where Jesus was. God knew that Herod didn't really want to worship little Jesus. Instead, the king wanted to kill God's Son.

Then an angel of the Lord talked to Joseph in a dream. He told Joseph to hurry to Egypt with little Jesus and Mary, his mother. So Joseph woke them up in the night, and they left for Egypt. That's

Wise men from a land far away learned from the stars that a new king of the Jews had been born. They traveled many weeks to bring their gifts to Jesus.

where they stayed until King Herod died. Then an angel came to Joseph in a dream again and told him, "Go back to the land of Israel. No one who would try to hurt Jesus is living now."

Joseph did as the angel said. He and Mary and the boy Jesus went to a town called Nazareth. And that's where they lived.

STORY 117

Jesus Grows Up

Matthew 3; Luke 2

Joseph and Mary went to Jerusalem every year for the Passover festival. When Jesus was twelve years old, he went with them.

After the special time came to an end, the people started walking back to their homes. They walked with their families and friends and neighbors. Joseph and Mary saw that Jesus wasn't with them, but they thought he was with some of their friends. So they didn't worry. When evening came and they still didn't see him, they began asking everyone if they had seen him. But no one had. By this time they were very worried.

They started going back to Jerusalem to look for him there. It took them a day to return, and it was another day before they finally found him. He was at the Temple, talking with the great teachers there, listening to them, and asking them questions! These

When he was twelve years old, Jesus knew how to talk with these wise teachers. He was God's Son and already knew more about God than they did.

men were very surprised at how much Jesus knew. After all, he was only twelve years old, and they had been teaching for many years.

Mary called to Jesus, "Son! Why have you treated us like this? We have been looking for you everywhere."

Jesus was surprised. "Didn't you know I would be here at my Father's house, the Temple?" he asked.

Joseph and Mary didn't understand what he meant, but his mother always remembered what he had said and often thought about it. Afterward she understood that as God's Son, of course he would call the Temple his Father's house. And of course he would want to be there.

Then Jesus went back home to Nazareth with Mary and Joseph. He did all that they told him to do. And as he grew up, he grew tall and wise. God loved him, and people loved him, too!

The next we are told about Jesus, he was a man thirty years old. But very few knew that he was the Son of God, for John the Baptist hadn't started telling people about him.

At that time John was living alone out in the wilderness. His clothes were made of hair from camels. Around his waist he wore a leather belt. He ate big grasshoppers called locusts. And he ate honey made by wild bees.

But now the time had come for John to preach to the people. He would tell them to get ready for the Savior by turning from their sins. He began preaching beside the Jordan River, where great crowds came to hear him. He told them that the Savior would soon be coming. John said that the people must not think their sins would be forgiven just because they came from a good family like Abraham's! No, they themselves must obey God.

Many who heard John preach were sorry for their sins and turned from them. And John baptized them in the river.

Then Jesus came to John and asked to be baptized. John didn't want to do it. He said, "I need to be baptized by you. Why do you come to me?" John knew that Jesus had no sins to be washed away. So why should he be baptized?

Then Jesus told John to baptize him anyway. Jesus said, "We must do everything that is right." So John agreed.

After John had baptized him and Jesus was coming up out of the water, the sky above him opened. Something that looked like a dove came down from heaven and sat on him. It was the Holy Spirit. At the same time, God's voice spoke from heaven saying, "This is my Son. I love him very much, and I am very pleased with him."

Satan Tempts Jesus to Sin
Matthew 4; John 1

After Jesus was baptized, he went out into the wilderness alone for forty days and nights. All that time he ate nothing. Afterward he was hungry.

Then the Devil, who is also called Satan, came to Jesus. Way back at the beginning of the world, Satan had tempted Eve to disobey God. She did, and so did her husband, Adam. That caused all the rest of us to have wicked hearts. Well, the Devil saw that Jesus had come to give us new, pure hearts and to make us good. So the Devil thought he would try to stop Jesus by tempting him as he had tempted Eve in the Garden of Eden.

The Devil said, "If you are the Son of God, change these stones into bread. Then you will have food to eat."

But Jesus knew why Satan had come, and he would not turn the stones into bread. He told Satan, "It is written in the Bible that people need more than food to live. They need to believe and obey every word that God has said."

Then the Devil took Jesus into Jerusalem to a very high part of the Temple. "If you are the Son of God," said the Devil, "throw yourself down. For it is written in the Bible that the angels will keep you from hurting yourself."

But Jesus said it is also written in the Bible that we must not put ourselves in danger just to find out if God will help us.

Then the Devil tried again. He took Jesus up on a high mountain and showed him all the kingdoms of the world. He showed Jesus their beautiful cities, their great armies, and all their riches. He said, "I will give you all of these if you will just get down on your knees and worship me." That is what Satan wanted most of all. He wanted to get Jesus to worship and obey him.

But Jesus said, "Get out of here, Satan. It is written in the Bible that you are to worship only the Lord your God and serve no one but him."

When Satan saw that he couldn't make Jesus obey him, he went away. And angels came to care for Jesus.

Then Jesus went back to the Jordan River, where John was baptizing people. John saw him coming and said, "Look! There is the Lamb of God!" He called Jesus the Lamb of God because Jesus would die as a sacrifice for our sins. Until that time real lambs were sacrificed at the Temple.

Two of John's followers heard what he said. Right away they began following Jesus. He talked with them and asked them to come to the place where he was staying. Then one of the men, Andrew, went to get his brother, Peter. The next day two others, Philip and Nathanael, decided to go with Jesus. So now Jesus had five disciples.

The first miracle Jesus did was to turn water into wine at a wedding dinner in the town of Cana.

STORY **119**

Jesus Turns Water into Wine

John 2–3

One day Jesus went to a wedding in the town of Cana. His mother and his disciples went there too. During the wedding supper some of the people needed more wine to drink, but there wasn't any more. Jesus' mother told him about it. Then she told the servants to be sure to do whatever he told them to.

There were six large stone water jars at the house. People would use the water from jars like that to wash their hands before they ate.

Jesus told the servants, "Fill the jars with water." So they did. Then he said to take some to the person in charge of the wedding supper. When they did, the water had become wine!

The man in charge didn't know that Jesus had changed the water to wine, even though the servants did. So when he tasted how good it was, he called the bridegroom over. "I've never known of anyone who saved the best wine to the last!" he said. "Everyone else serves the best first. And after everyone has had enough, they serve the wine that isn't so good."

This was Jesus' first miracle. When his disciples saw what he had done, they believed in him. They knew that no one but the Son of God could have done it.

Now it was time for Jesus to go to Jerusalem for the Passover festival. This was a holiday that the Jewish people celebrated every year. It was a week for everyone to remember when God helped Moses lead the people of Israel out of Egypt.

Nicodemus was one of the leaders of the Jews. After dark one night he came to see Jesus and said, "Teacher, we know God has sent you. You can do miracles, and they show us that God is with you."

Jesus said, "Unless you are born again, you will never see God's Kingdom!"

"What?" Nicodemus asked in surprise. "How can a person be born a second time? Can he go back inside his mother's body as a tiny baby and be born again?"

Then Jesus talked about what he meant by being born again. He said that our parents give us life on this earth. But God the Spirit gives us a new life from heaven. It's a life that will last forever.

Then Jesus said something else that seems very strange at first. He said, "As Moses lifted up the bronze snake in the wilderness, so must I be lifted up." What did he mean? Well, one time when the people of Israel were in the wilderness, God punished them by sending snakes. But then God told Moses to make a bronze snake and put it on a pole. He said to lift up the pole so that everyone with a snakebite could look at it. When they did, they got well.

One dark night Nicodemus came to Jesus to talk to him about the Kingdom of God. Jesus told him that he must be born again to be part of God's Kingdom.

So now Jesus said that he would be lifted up. Jesus was talking about being lifted up on the cross and dying for our sins.

Jesus talked about himself again when he told Nicodemus about God's love. Jesus said God loves the people of the world so much that he sent his only Son into the world to die for them. God did it so that people who look up to Jesus and believe will not be punished for their sins. Instead, they will be forgiven and live forever in heaven after they die.

STORY 120

Jesus Talks to a Woman and Helps a Father

John 4

One day Jesus and his disciples came to a town in Samaria. Just outside the town was a well where people came to get water. It was hot, and Jesus was tired. So he sat down by the well while his disciples went into town to buy food.

A woman carrying an empty jar came from the town to get some water. This woman didn't love God and had done many things that did not please him. Jesus knew this, for he knows everything about us. He told the woman some of the things she had done that did not please God. She was surprised and said, "Sir, I see you are a prophet." She didn't know yet

A woman talked to Jesus beside a well, where she came to get some water. Jesus told her that he could give her life that lasts forever.

that Jesus was God's Son, the Savior. But she thought that he must be a person to whom God told things that other people didn't know.

"I know that the Savior is coming into the world," the woman said to Jesus. "And when he comes, he will tell us everything."

Then Jesus told her, "I am the Savior!"

The woman left her water jar and hurried back to the town. She said to the people, "Come and see a man who told me everything I have ever done! Could this be the Savior?"

The people hurried out to see Jesus. When they heard him, they asked him to please stay for a while. So he stayed in their town for two days, and they listened carefully to what he taught them. Then they said to the woman, "We, too, believe Jesus is the Savior. But it's not just because of what you told us about him. We have heard him for ourselves, and we know now that he is the Savior from heaven."

Jesus now returned to the town of Cana, where he had changed the water into wine. While he was there a rich man from another city came to him and asked him to make his son well. "Please come quickly before my child dies," he said.

But Jesus told the man, "Go home, for your son is already well again!"

The man believed Jesus, so he started back home. But before he got there, his servants met him. They said, "Your son is well!" He asked them what time the child had started to get better. They answered, "Yesterday, at about one o'clock in the afternoon, the fever left him!"

The man knew that this was the same time Jesus had said to him, "Your son is well!" So he and all his family believed in Jesus as the Son of God.

STORY 121
Finding Fish and Finding People
Mark 1; Luke 4–5

Jesus now came to the Sea of Galilee near the town of Capernaum. Big crowds of people came to hear him preach. There were so many people that they almost pushed Jesus into the water. Then he noticed two fishing boats along the shore. Near the boats were the fishermen, washing their nets. So Jesus stepped into one of the boats—it belonged to Peter. And he asked Peter to push his boat out a little way into the water. Then Jesus sat down and taught the people from the boat.

When he had finished, he told Peter and his brother, Andrew, to go out on the lake. He said to let down their nets and they would catch many fish.

Peter answered, "Sir, we fished all night and didn't catch a thing. But if you say so, we'll try again." They were surprised to find out that in just a little while they had caught so many fish that their net broke!

Then they shouted to their partners, James and John, who were in the other boat. They called for their friends to come and help them. They all worked together, filling both boats with fish until they almost sank!

When he saw the miracle Jesus had done, Peter got down on his knees and worshiped him. Jesus said to Peter and Andrew, "Come with me. Now I'll show you how to find people instead of fish." Jesus called James and his brother, John, too! So all four fishermen left their boats, nets, and everything else. They went with Jesus and followed him everywhere, for now they were his disciples.

One day Jesus went to the home of Andrew and Peter. James and John were there too. So was Peter's mother-in-law, but she was sick in bed with a very high fever. The men wanted Jesus to help her. So he went and stood beside her bed. He took her by the hand and helped her to sit up. Right away she was well, so she got up and cooked dinner for everyone!

In the evening, at sunset, a big crowd gathered in front of the house. They brought many sick people to Jesus so he could make them well. They brought people with evil spirits, too. The crowd watched as Jesus made sick people well and sent evil spirits away.

In the morning, getting up long before it was light, Jesus went out to a lonely place in the wilderness to pray. Even though he was God's Son, he was living on the earth as a man. And he needed to pray for God's help just as the rest of us do.

Some men had been fishing all night without catching a thing. Then Jesus told them where to place their nets.

Jesus said to the fishermen, "Come with me.
Now I'll help you find people instead of fish!"
So they followed him.

While he was away, many people looked for Jesus. When they found him, they asked him not to leave. But Jesus said, "I must go and preach the Good News about God's Kingdom in other places too."

STORY 122

Jesus Has Much Work to Do

Matthew 12; Mark 2–3; Luke 5–6; John 5

After Jesus traveled to different places, he came again to the town of Capernaum. Large crowds came to the house where he was staying, and he preached to them.

The house was a one-story building with a flat roof. Among those who came there were four men carrying a sick friend on a mat. They carried him because he couldn't walk. But the crowd was so large that they couldn't get inside. So they went up on the clay roof and dug a hole right through it! They used ropes to let the man on the mat down into the room where Jesus was. The man who couldn't walk landed right in front of Jesus!

Jesus was pleased when he saw how much faith the men had in him. So he said to the man who couldn't walk, "Your sins are forgiven!"

But some teachers of God's laws were sitting there. They said to themselves, "Who does this man think he is, forgiving sins? Only God can do that."

Jesus knew their thoughts and asked them, "Why do you think such thoughts? Is it any harder for me to forgive this man's sins than to help him walk? Now I will make him well." So he said to the sick man, "Stand up, take your mat, and go on home!"

Right away the man jumped up. He picked up his mat and made his way through the crowd! The people who saw it happen just couldn't get over it. They praised God and said, "We've never seen anything like this before!"

One Sabbath day Jesus went into a synagogue, which is what a Jewish church was called. The Sabbath day was the special day when Jewish people worshiped God. No one was to do any work on that day.

Jesus saw a man at the synagogue with a small hand that couldn't be used. The leaders known as the Pharisees watched to see if Jesus would work on the Sabbath by healing the man. But Jesus knew their thoughts. He said to them, "If one of your sheep fell into a well on the Sabbath, wouldn't you pull it out? And a person is much more important than a sheep! So of course it is right to do good on the Sabbath."

Then Jesus said to the man, "Reach out your hand!" When he did, it was fine, just like his other hand!

This made the Jewish leaders very angry, and they began to talk about killing Jesus. So he and his disciples left that place and went away to the Sea of

Galilee. Many people from Jerusalem and Judea and from countries far away came to see him when they heard of the wonderful things he did. The sick people crowded around him to touch him, for when they did, they got well!

After this Jesus went up on a mountain by himself. He stayed there all night, praying to God. When it was morning, he called his disciples to him. He chose twelve of them to be his special friends and helpers who would be with him all the time. He would teach them to preach and do miracles. These twelve were called "apostles," and these were their names:

Peter
Andrew (Peter's brother)
James (son of Zebedee)
John (James's brother)
Philip
Bartholomew
Thomas
Matthew (the tax collector)
James (son of Alphaeus)
Thaddaeus
Simon
Judas Iscariot

The Beatitudes

Matthew 5:3-12

God blesses those who realize their need for him,
for the Kingdom of Heaven is given to them.
God blesses those who mourn,
for they will be comforted.
God blesses those who are gentle and lowly,
for the whole earth will belong to them.
God blesses those who are hungry and thirsty
for justice,
for they will receive it in full.
God blesses those who are merciful,
for they will be shown mercy.
God blesses those whose hearts are pure,
for they will see God.
God blesses those who work for peace,
for they will be called the children of God.
God blesses those who are persecuted because
they live for God,
for the Kingdom of Heaven is theirs.

God blesses you when you are mocked and persecuted
and lied about because you are my followers. Be
happy about it! Be very glad! For a great reward
awaits you in heaven.

The Golden Rule

Luke 6:31

Do for others as you would like them to do for you.

The Lord's Prayer

Matthew 6:9–13

Our Father in heaven,
  may your name be honored.
May your Kingdom come soon.
May your will be done here on earth,
  just as it is in heaven.
Give us our food for today,
and forgive us our sins,
  just as we have forgiven those who have sinned
  against us.
And don't let us yield to temptation,
  but deliver us from the evil one.

Jesus Teaches from a Hill

Matthew 5–7

When Jesus saw crowds of people coming to him, he climbed a hill. He sat there with his disciples, teaching them. You have just read some of the things he said. He talked about the people God blesses and how he blesses them. And Jesus taught his followers how to pray. These are some more things he told them:

When others are unkind to us and hurt us, we must not try to pay them back. Instead we must do good to them and pray for them and love them. Then we will be acting like true children of our Father in heaven. We will be like him, for he is kind even to those who don't obey him or love him.

Jesus told his disciples not to just pretend to be nice so that others would praise them for it, but to please God by really being nice to others. And when we give help to people who are poor, we must not go around bragging about it.

Jesus said we must not want to be rich, but must send our money on ahead to heaven. How do we do this? By giving our money for God's work. We should give to our church and Sunday school and to missionaries and to poor people. Then someday in heaven we will have more things to make us happy than all the money in the world can buy.

In his Sermon on the Mount, Jesus taught the people about God's Kingdom. And he told them how to receive God's blessings.

Jesus said that some people call him Lord and Master but do not obey his Father in heaven. They will not get to heaven. On judgment day Jesus will know who his real followers are. He will send away those who only pretended to be his disciples.

Then Jesus told an important story about two men who built two houses. A wise man built his house on a rock. When he had finished it, a big storm came up. But the rain and wind could not hurt the house because it was built on such a solid rock.

A foolish man built his house on sand. When the storm came, the rain washed away the sand beneath his house, and the wind blew against it. So it fell down with a big crash.

Jesus said that we are either like the wise man or the foolish man. If we listen to his teaching and do what he tells us to do, then we are like the wise man who built his house on the rock. Those who listen to Jesus but don't do what he tells them to are like the foolish man who built his house on the sand. Those who do what Jesus says will be saved. But those who don't obey him will be lost on judgment day.

Perfume and Tears for Jesus

Luke 7–8

One day a Jewish leader named Simon asked Jesus to come to his home for dinner. But as they were eating, a woman came with a beautiful jar of sweet-smelling perfume. She got down on her knees by Jesus' feet, crying because she was sorry for her sins and wanted to be forgiven. Her tears fell on his feet, and she wiped them with her long hair. She kissed them and poured the perfume over them.

Simon knew this woman was a sinner. He said to himself, "If Jesus were really God's Son, he would know how bad this woman is. And he would send her away."

Jesus knew what the man was thinking. So Jesus told him, "Simon, I have something to say to you: Two people owed a man some money. One owed him a lot, and the other owed him only a little. But neither of them had any money to pay him back. So he told them they could forget about it. They didn't have to give him back the money. Tell me now, which of these two men do you think will love him more for being so kind?"

Simon said, "I suppose the one who owed him most."

"You are right," Jesus said. Then he turned to

the woman and said to Simon, "Do you see this woman? When I came into your house, you didn't give me any water to wash my feet. But she has washed my feet with her tears and wiped them with her hair. You didn't give me a kiss to welcome me as you should have, but this woman has kissed my feet again and again. Her many sins have been forgiven, so she has shown me much love. People who haven't been forgiven for so much don't show me as much love."

Then Jesus turned to the woman. He said, "Your sins are forgiven. Go home in peace!"

After this Jesus traveled from place to place, preaching the Good News in the cities and towns. And the twelve apostles were with him.

STORY 125

A Farmer's Seeds and God's Words

Mark 4

Jesus often told stories with lessons about God. These stories are called parables.

One day big crowds followed Jesus as he walked along the shore of the lake. So he got into a boat and taught the people from there. He told them this story:

Jesus told a story about a farmer who planted seeds. Then Jesus said that the seeds are like God's words and people are like the places where the seeds are planted. Some hear God's message but then forget it. Others hear it and remember it and always try to obey it.

A farmer went out into the field to plant some seeds. Some of the seeds fell on a path that ran along the edge of the field. The dirt on the path was hard. So birds flew down and picked those seeds right up from the ground and ate them.

Some of the seeds fell on places where there were

many stones and rocks. The seeds began to grow into little plants. But there wasn't enough dirt on top of the rocks for strong roots to grow down into the earth. So in a few days the little plants dried up and died.

And some of the seeds fell where thorns and other weeds were growing. The seeds began to grow, but the weeds were tall and thick. They shut out the sunshine as they began to take up the space the plants needed. So these little plants soon died too.

But the rest of the seeds fell on good ground. There was plenty of good, soft dirt that had been turned over and was ready for the seeds. The rain watered those seeds and the sun warmed them. Soon they grew bigger and bigger. And after a few months there was a big grain crop. There was a hundred times as much as the farmer had planted!

When Jesus was alone with his disciples, they asked him to explain this parable to them. He told them that the seeds were like God's words. And the farmer is the one who brings God's words to other people.

Some of the people who hear God's words have hard hearts that are like the hard path. They won't believe God's message. Just as the birds ate the seeds that fell on the hard path, these people let Satan come and take God's words away. He can do that by making them think that other things are more important than God.

Other people who hear God's words are happy to hear them at first, and they try to obey him. But it is only for a little while. As soon as they have trouble or hear others laughing at them, they turn away from God. They are like the places with stones and rocks.

Some people hear about God and are glad. But afterward they begin to care more for their homes, their money, and other things than they do for the things of God. All of this crowds out the Good News about Jesus, just as weeds crowded out some of the seeds.

But there are some people who listen carefully to everything God says. They remember it and try every day to obey him and do whatever he tells them to. They are like the good soil, where the seeds grew well and there was a crop of up to a hundred times as much seed as the farmer had planted.

A Storm and Two Thousand Pigs

Mark 4–5

It was evening when Jesus and his disciples got into a boat. They began sailing over to the other side of the Sea of Galilee. But suddenly the wind began to blow very hard, and there was a terrible storm on the lake. High waves came over the sides of the boat. Soon it was filling up with water and beginning to sink. But Jesus was asleep.

"Teacher!" they shouted to him. "Save us! We'll all be drowned!"

Then Jesus stood up and spoke to the wind and the water. He said to them, "Be quiet!"

The wind stopped blowing, and the water became very still and quiet. Then Jesus said to his disciples, "Why were you afraid? How is it that you have so little faith?"

Even though the disciples were Jesus' friends, it was hard for them to understand how Jesus could make the wind and the water obey him.

When they came to the other side of the lake, Jesus got out of the boat. There he saw a man with evil spirits in him. The man had torn off his clothes, and he ran around like a wild man. No one could go near him without getting hurt. People had often tied him with chains, but he broke the chains and went out and lived in a graveyard. All day and all night he shouted and hit himself with stones.

The man saw Jesus and ran to him. The evil spirits in the man were afraid when they saw Jesus, for they knew he could make them go away. He had already said, "Come out of the man."

A terrible storm came up, and the disciples thought their little boat was going to sink. Jesus was asleep, but they shouted to him to wake up and save them all from drowning.

They asked if they could please enter some pigs feeding nearby, and Jesus told them they could. So the evil spirits came out of the man and went into the two thousand pigs. Then all of the pigs ran down the hill and into the lake, where they drowned.

The men who had been taking care of the pigs ran into the city nearby and told everyone what had happened. So all the people hurried out to see Jesus. When they saw the wild man wearing clothes and sitting there quietly, they were afraid. They asked Jesus to go away from their country.

So he got back into the boat to leave. The man asked to go with him. But Jesus said, "No, go home to your friends. And tell them what great things the Lord has done for you." So the man began telling everyone how Jesus had helped him.

STORY **127**

A Woman and a Girl Meet Jesus

Mark 5–6

As soon as Jesus returned to Capernaum, one of the leaders of the Jewish worship place there came to Jesus. The man got down on his knees and said, "My little girl is very sick, and I'm afraid she is going to die. Oh, please come and put your hands on her head so that she will get well again."

The daughter of a Jewish leader had died.
But Jesus brought her back to life. How happy
everyone was!

Jesus and his disciples went with him. A big crowd of people followed along.

In the crowd was a woman who had been sick for twelve years. She had given doctors all the money she had, but she was getting worse instead of better. When the woman heard that Jesus was in town she said to herself, "If I can only touch him, I'll get well." So she pushed her way through the crowd and touched Jesus. As soon as she did, her sickness was gone.

Jesus turned around and asked, "Who touched me?"

The disciples said to him, "The whole crowd is pushing against you and touching you!" But Jesus still kept looking around to see who had done it. The woman knew what had happened. She was shaking as she came to Jesus and told him everything.

"Daughter, don't be afraid," Jesus said to her. "Because of your faith in me you are well."

He was still talking to the woman when a messenger arrived. He came to talk to the father of the little girl they were going to see. He said, "Your child is dead. There is no need for Jesus to come now."

But Jesus told the father, "Don't be afraid. Just trust me."

When they came to the house, Jesus saw the people and heard them crying. He said to them, "Why cry? The child isn't dead; she is only asleep!" He meant that she would soon be alive again, like one waking up from sleep. But the people didn't believe him, so they laughed at him. Then Jesus told the people to go outside. He took just three of his disciples—Peter, James, and John—and the girl's father and mother into the room where she lay. Then he took her by the hand and said, "Get up, little girl!" And the girl, who was twelve years old, jumped up and started walking! Her parents were so happy they didn't know what to do. So Jesus told them to give her something to eat!

Jesus then returned to Nazareth, where he had been brought up. He went into the Jewish worship place on the Sabbath day and taught the people there. They were amazed at his wonderful message. "Where did this man get such great wisdom and power to do such wonderful miracles?" they asked. "Isn't he just a carpenter like Joseph? He is Mary's son. And aren't his brothers and sisters here with us?"

So they would not believe Jesus was anyone special. And because they didn't believe, Jesus did not do any big miracles among them.

STORY 128
Dinner for Five Thousand
Mark 6; John 6

Jesus sent his twelve disciples all through the land to preach the Good News. They went out to the cities and towns, preaching to the people and making sick people well.

When they returned, they told Jesus all they had done. "Let's get away to some quiet place where you can rest for a while," Jesus said.

There were so many people coming and going that Jesus and his twelve special helpers didn't even have time to eat. So they all got into a boat and sailed to the other side of the Sea of Galilee where they could be alone. But many people saw where Jesus was going, so they walked around the lake and met him there.

Jesus saw that the people needed him, just like sheep need a shepherd. So he told them about God. He kept on teaching until late in the day.

Then his disciples came to him. They said, "Send the people away so they can buy food, for it will soon be dark."

"They don't need to go away," Jesus said. "You feed them! Philip, where can we buy bread for everyone?" Jesus already knew what he was going to do, but he wanted to hear what Philip would say.

Philip said, "It would take a lot more money than we have to feed all this crowd!"

Then Peter's brother, Andrew, said that a young boy in the crowd had five loaves of bread and two small fish. But he knew that wouldn't feed many people.

Jesus told the people to sit down in groups on the green grass. So they sat in groups of fifty or a hundred. Then he took the five loaves and two fish, looked up to heaven, and thanked God for the food. He broke the loaves into pieces and gave some

Jesus fed over five thousand hungry people. He used a little boy's lunch of five loaves of bread and two fish to feed them all. And there was food left over!

bread and fish to the disciples. Then they passed the food out to the people. And the strangest thing happened! As the disciples broke off pieces of bread, the loaves were still the same size as before, so there was enough for everyone! And it was the same with the fish.

About five thousand men had dinner that day. The women and children with them had dinner, too. And the food all came from the five loaves and two fish. Everyone had plenty to eat, and there were even twelve baskets of bread left over!

STORY 129

"Should We Forgive Seven Times?"

Matthew 18

Peter asked Jesus one day, "How many times should I forgive someone who hurts me? Should I forgive him as many as seven times?"

"More than that!" Jesus answered. "How many times? Seventy times seven!" He meant that we must always be ready to forgive each other.

Then Jesus told Peter a story to help him understand all about forgiving people.

There was a king and a man who owed the king millions of dollars. But the man couldn't pay the money back. So the king ordered him and his wife and children to be sold as slaves. Then the money for which they were sold would be given to the king. This would pay off the money that the man owed. That was how things were often done in those days.

Then the man got down on his knees in front of the king and asked him to be patient. He asked the king to wait until he could pay the money back. The king was sorry for the man and was kind. He said the man didn't have to pay him back any of the money!

But that same man went out and found another man who owed him only a few dollars. He took hold of the man and said, "Pay me what you owe me!"

The man who owed just a little money got down on his knees and said, "Please have patience with me, and I will pay back everything I owe you." But the first man wouldn't wait. He had the second man put into jail, to be kept there until he paid.

When the king heard about this, he called the first man. "How could you be so wicked?" the king said. "I forgave you all that you owed me just because you asked me to. Shouldn't you have been kind to that other man just as I was kind to you?" Then the angry king sent him away to be punished until he paid back all he owed.

In this story that Jesus told, the king is like God, and the man who owed so much is like us. We have sinned against God many times, and he forgives us when we ask him to. But God will punish us if we don't forgive others, just as the king in the story punished the man who wouldn't forgive.

STORY **130**
The Good Samaritan

Luke 10

One time when Jesus was teaching people, a man who knew God's law very well came to him. The man asked this question to test Jesus: "Teacher, what must I do to live forever?"

"What does God's law say?" Jesus asked him.

The man said, "You must love God with all your heart and all your soul. You must love him with all your strength and all your mind. And you must love your neighbor as much as you love yourself."

"Right!" Jesus replied. "Do that and you will live!"

"But who is my neighbor?" the man asked.

Jesus answered by telling him this story:

A Jewish man was traveling from Jerusalem to Jericho, but some robbers stopped him. They took his clothes and money and beat him up. They left him half dead beside the road.

While he lay there on the ground, too weak to get up, a Jewish priest went by. He was a teacher of God's law. But instead of being kind to the hurt man, he crossed over to the other side of the road. He went on his way, as if he didn't see the man. Next a worship leader from the Temple came along. This Levite saw the man beside the road. But he, too, went to the other side of the road. He kept right on walking without trying to help.

Jesus told a story about a Jewish man who was beaten up by robbers and left for dead. The Jewish priests wouldn't stop to help him, but a Samaritan man did.

But then a Samaritan came by. The Jews and Samaritans didn't like each other. But when the Samaritan saw the hurt Jewish man, he felt sorry for him. The Samaritan put medicine and bandages on the places where the man had been hurt. Then he put the man on the back of his own donkey. He took the man to an inn and took care of him that night. The

Martha was upset! She wanted Mary to help her make dinner instead of just sitting there listening to Jesus. But Mary was doing the best thing.

next day he paid the man's bill. And he asked the person in charge of the inn to take care of the hurt man. He said he would pay the rest of the bill the next time he came to the inn.

At the end of his story Jesus asked, "Which of these three men was a neighbor to the hurt man?"

"The one who helped him," said the man who knew all about God's law.

Then Jesus told him, "Go and do the same to everyone who needs your help."

STORY 131

Mary Listens to Jesus, Her Shepherd

Luke 10; John 10

Jesus and his disciples came to the town of Bethany, which was near Jerusalem. Jesus always liked to stop there to visit two sisters named Martha and Mary. They also had a brother named Lazarus.

After Jesus came, Mary sat at his feet and listened to him. She wanted to hear him tell about God and his Kingdom.

But Martha was worrying about the big dinner she was getting ready. She was angry with her sister for not helping. She said to Jesus, "Lord, don't you even care that Mary has left all the work for me to do? Tell her to come and help me."

But Jesus said, "Martha, Martha, you get upset so easily. Only one thing is important. Mary has chosen it, and I won't tell her to stop. I'll let her keep listening to me."

On another day Jesus was talking to some people about sheep and how they listen to their shepherds. He said, "I am the good shepherd. I know my sheep, and they know me." He meant that he was like a shepherd to his disciples, and they followed him like a flock of sheep. Shepherds stayed with their sheep night and day to keep them from getting lost and to keep them safe from wild animals. Jesus keeps his followers safe from Satan and helps them find their way to heaven.

Jesus went to the Temple another time and talked to the Jewish leaders. They crowded around him and asked, "If you are the Son of God, why don't you say so?"

Jesus answered, "I have, but you wouldn't believe me. That's because you are not my sheep. My sheep listen to my voice and follow me, and I give them life that lasts forever. They will never be lost. My Father gave them to me, and no one can ever take them away from me. My Father and I are one." Jesus meant that he is God—not God the Father, but God the Son. He is as good and as great as God the Father.

Jesus said, "My sheep listen to my voice and follow me. I give them life that lasts forever. They will never be lost, for no one can take them away from me."

Jesus Makes Blind Eyes See

John 8–9

Jesus told the leaders at the Temple in Jerusalem, "Soon I'll be going back to my Father. Then you will look for me but won't be able to find me. And you can't go where I am going because you won't believe that I am the Son of God. So you will die without having your sins forgiven. But if anyone believes me, he will never really die."

As he left the Temple, Jesus saw a man who had been blind ever since he was born. Jesus spit on the ground and made some mud. He put it on the blind man's eyes and said to him, "Go and wash in the pool of Siloam."

So the man did. And when he came back, he could see! His neighbors and many others who knew him when he was blind wondered what had happened. They asked, "Isn't this the blind man who used to sit and beg?"

Some said he was and others said, "No, he just looks like him."

But the man said, "I *am* the same man, but now I can see!"

"Who helped you?" the people asked.

"A man called Jesus made some mud and put it on my eyes. He told me to go and wash it off in the pool of Siloam. When I did, suddenly I could see," he explained.

"Where is Jesus now?" the neighbors asked.

"I don't know," the man answered.

Then they brought the man to the Jewish leaders. They, too, wanted to know how he had been healed.

"Jesus put some mud on my eyes. I washed it off, and now I can see," he said.

Some of the leaders said, "The man who helped you see can't be a good man, because he did it on the Sabbath day!" They said that because God had told his people not to work on the Sabbath. And they were saying that healing was work! Then they asked the man, "Who do you think Jesus is?"

"I think he must be a prophet," the man told them.

But these Jewish leaders wouldn't believe he had been blind. Finally they called in his parents and asked them, "Is this your son? Was he born blind? If he was, how can he see now?"

"Yes, he is our son," they said. "And he was born blind, but we don't know what happened. He is old enough to speak for himself, so ask him." The parents were afraid to say that it was Jesus who had helped their son to see. That's because the Jewish leaders had said they would send people away from their worship place if they said Jesus was the Savior.

Then the leaders talked to the man again. They told him, "Tell the truth about who helped you see, for we know Jesus is a sinner."

"I don't know whether he is a sinner or not," the man said. "But I do know one thing: I used to be blind, and now I see!"

"What did he do to you?" they asked him again.

Then the man got upset. "I told you once," he said. "Why don't you listen? Why do you want to hear it again? Do you want to be his disciples, too?"

The leaders became very angry. They said, "You are his disciple, but we are Moses' disciples. We know that God sent Moses. But as for this man, we don't know anything about who sent him."

"How very strange!" the man replied. "Here's a man who can help blind people see, and yet you don't know who he is! Since the beginning of the world no one has ever been able to help someone see who was born blind. If God didn't send this man, he couldn't have helped me."

"You've been a sinner since you were born," they said angrily. "Are you trying to teach us?" Then they threw him out of their worship place, the Jewish synagogue, and told him never to come back again.

When Jesus heard what had happened, he found the man. Jesus asked him, "Do you believe in God's Son?"

"I want to," the man answered. "Who is he?"

"He is the person talking with you!" Jesus answered.

"Lord, I believe," the man said. And he worshiped Jesus.

STORY 133

A Lost Sheep and a Runaway Boy

Luke 15

When some tax collectors, who cheated people whenever they could, came to hear Jesus, the Jewish leaders were upset. They asked, "Why is Jesus kind to these bad men? He even eats with them!"

This is what Jesus said: "If you have a hundred sheep and lose one of them, don't you leave all the others and hunt for the one that is lost? And when you find it, you put it on your shoulders and joyfully carry it home! After you get home, you tell all your neighbors and friends, and they are happy with you, for you have found your lost sheep. Well, that's the way it is with people who sin. I have come to save them, I haven't come just to help good people."

Then Jesus told this story:

A man had two sons. The younger one said to him, "Father, give me my share of the money you are planning to give my brother and me." So his father did. And soon afterward this younger son took the money and went to a country far away. There he spent it all, doing all sorts of bad things.

*When all the money was gone, there was a famine
in that land. He couldn't get enough food to eat, and
he began to be very hungry. Then he began working
for a farmer who sent him to feed the pigs. He was so
hungry he wanted to eat what the pigs ate. But no one
gave him any food.*

*Finally he said to himself, "At home even the men
who work for my father have plenty to eat. And here
I am with no food. I'll go to my father and tell him that
I have sinned against him and against God. I'll tell
him I'm not good enough to be called his son anymore.
I'll ask him to let me work for him."*

*So he went back home. While he was still far away,
his father saw him and ran out to meet him. Then his
father threw his arms around his son and kissed him.
And his son began his speech: "Father," he said, "I
have sinned against God and you, and I don't deserve
to be called your son anymore. . . ."*

*But his father said to the servants, "Bring out my
best clothes for him, and get him some shoes. Then fix
the best meat we have and let's have a party. This son
of mine was lost, but now he is found." So they had a
big dinner because the father was so glad his son was
home again.*

*When the older son came home from working in
the fields, he heard the music and dancing. So he
called to one of the servants and asked what was
going on.*

*"Your brother's back!" the servant told him. "And
your father is having a big party for him."*

But the older son was angry and wouldn't go in.

Jesus told a story about a boy who ran away from home and was very bad. But when he finally came home, his father loved him anyway.

When his father came out to him, he said, "I've worked hard for you all my life. And in all that time I've always obeyed you. But you never once gave a party for me and my friends. Now this other son of yours comes back after doing all sorts of bad things, and you have a party for him."

The father said, "Son, I've always loved you very much. Everything I have is yours. But it is right that we should be happy, for your brother left us and has come home again. It's as if he came back to life! He was lost and now he has been found."

Jesus told this story to the proud Jewish leaders because they were upset with him for preaching to sinners. Jesus wanted the leaders to know that God loves sinners and is willing to forgive them. He will let them be his children if they will only stop doing bad things and start obeying him.

STORY **134**

Jesus and Lazarus

John 10–11

Jesus left Jerusalem for a while to get away from the Jewish leaders. He was preaching to people on the other side of the Jordan River. Many of the people there believed in him.

About that time Lazarus, who was Mary and Martha's brother, became very sick. His sisters sent a message to Jesus to tell him about it. Jesus loved Lazarus and his sisters very much. But when he heard how sick Lazarus was, he didn't go to help him right away. Instead he stayed where he was for two more days.

Then he said to his disciples, "Now let's go to

Lazarus died and was buried in a cave for four days. When Jesus stood outside the cave and told him to come back to life, he did!

Bethany. Our friend Lazarus is sleeping, and I am going to wake him up." Jesus meant that Lazarus had died and that he was going to bring him back to life again. But his disciples thought he meant Lazarus was resting.

Then Jesus told them plainly, "Lazarus died."

Bethany was just a few miles away from Jerusalem. Many people had gone there to be with Martha and Mary, who were very sad. When Martha heard that Jesus had come, she went out to meet him. But Mary stayed in the house.

Martha said, "Lord, if you had been here, my brother wouldn't have died. But I know that even now God will give you whatever you ask."

Jesus told her, "Your brother will live again."

"Yes, of course," Martha said. "He will live again when everyone else does—at the end of time."

Then Jesus let Martha know that he is the one who brings life. He said, "People who believe in me will live again after they die. Do you believe this?"

Martha said, "Yes, Lord. I believe you are God's Son. And I believe that he sent you into the world."

Then Martha went back to the house. She told Mary that Jesus had come and wanted to see her. So Mary ran out to where he was. She got down on her knees at his feet and said, "Lord, if you had been here, my brother wouldn't have died."

When Jesus saw her and the other people

crying, he was upset. "Where have you buried Lazarus?" Jesus asked them.

"Lord, come and see," they said.

Then Jesus cried.

"See how he loved his friend," the people said. But some of them said, "This man helps blind people see. Couldn't he have saved Lazarus from dying?"

Lazarus's body had been placed in a cave. A stone was rolled across the opening.

"Roll the stone away," Jesus said.

But Martha said, "By this time the smell will be terrible. He has been dead four days."

"Didn't I tell you that if you would only believe in me, you would see how great God's power is?" Jesus asked.

So they rolled the stone away. Then Jesus shouted, "Lazarus, come out!" And he came out, wrapped up in the cloths he had been buried in. "Take the cloths off," Jesus told the people, and they did.

When the people who had come to visit Martha and Mary saw this great miracle, many of them finally believed in Jesus. But some went to the Pharisees and told these Jewish leaders what they had seen.

The Pharisees and chief priests were very upset. They called a meeting to talk about it. "What shall we do?" they asked each other. "We know that this man Jesus does wonderful miracles. But if we leave him alone, everyone will believe he is God's Son. Then the Romans will be angry. They will come and destroy the Temple where we worship. They will take over our whole country!"

From that time on the Jewish leaders began planning how to kill Jesus.

STORY 135

Lepers Thank Jesus, and Children Love Him

Mark 10; Luke 17

Jesus and his disciples were walking along a road one day when ten lepers came to meet Jesus. The men knew they were not supposed to get too close to people. So they stood a little way off and shouted, "Jesus, Master, please care about us and help us."

Jesus heard them shouting to him. He called back to them, "Go and show yourselves to the priests." Jesus said this because if lepers got well, they had to let a priest see them. If he said they were well, they could go back to their families.

As these ten men were going to see the priest, the sores on their skin went away! But only one of them came back to thank Jesus for making him well. That man was a Samaritan.

Jesus asked, "Didn't I make ten men well? Where are the other nine?" Then Jesus told the man, "Stand up and go. You believed in me, and your faith has made you well."

Jesus loves little children.
No one can get into God's Kingdom
without being like a child.

Sick people weren't the only ones who wanted to see Jesus. Some parents knew how special he was, so they brought their little children to him. They wanted him to put his hands on them and bless them. But his disciples sent them away.

Jesus was upset with his disciples. "Let the little children come to me," he said. "Don't tell them not to, for the Kingdom of God belongs to everyone who is like these children." Jesus meant that the only way to get into God's Kingdom is to love him and trust him the way children do.

Then Jesus picked up the children. As he held them in his arms, he placed his hands on them and blessed them.

STORY 136

Zacchaeus Finds a Friend

Luke 18–19

One day Jesus took his twelve disciples to one side. He told them that the time had come again to go to Jerusalem. He explained that when they got there, everything the prophets had said about him would happen. He would be laughed at and whipped. People would spit on him, put him on a cross, and kill him. But the third day he would come back to life again.

Zacchaeus was a tax collector who took more money from people than he should have. He climbed a tree just to see Jesus. But Jesus found him and went home with him!

But the disciples thought Jesus was soon going to be crowned king of the Jews. So they couldn't understand what he was talking about.

When Jesus came to the city of Jericho on the way to Jerusalem, the usual crowds followed him.

A man named Zacchaeus lived in Jericho. He was in charge of collecting taxes in that city. And because he took more money from people than he should have, he was very rich.

As Jesus walked through the streets of the city, Zacchaeus tried to see him. But the crowd was too big and Zacchaeus was too short. So he ran on ahead, climbed up into a sycamore tree, and waited for Jesus.

When Jesus came along the road that went past the tree, he stopped. He looked up into the branches and saw Zacchaeus sitting there. "Come on down, Zacchaeus," Jesus told him. "I want to go to your house today!" So Zacchaeus climbed down. He was very happy to take Jesus home with him.

As soon as Zacchaeus began to talk with Jesus, he felt very sorry for the bad things he had done. He stood beside Jesus and told him that he would give half of his money to people who were poor. And he said that if he had taken more money from people than he should, he would give them back four times as much!

Jesus saw that Zacchaeus was sorry and was ready to do what was right. So he told Zacchaeus that his sins were forgiven.

The other people in the crowd were upset with Jesus for going to a sinner's house. But Jesus said that he had come into the world to look for sinners. He came to save them from being punished for their sins.

Bartimaeus Wants to See

Mark 10; Luke 18

As Jesus and his disciples left Jericho, a big crowd was still following them. A blind man named Bartimaeus was sitting beside the road, begging. When he heard a lot of noise, he wondered what was happening.

"Jesus of Nazareth is coming," someone told him.

As soon as he heard this, he began to shout. He said, "Jesus, please show that you care about me. Please help me!"

"Be quiet!" some of the people told him.

But he just shouted louder, "Jesus, help me!"

As soon as Jesus heard him, he stopped. He said, "Tell that man to come to me."

So the people told Bartimaeus, "He's calling for you!" The blind man jumped up, threw his coat to one side, and went over to Jesus.

Jesus asked, "What do you want me to do for you?"

"Teacher, I want to see," the blind man answered.

"All right," Jesus told him. "Because you have faith in me, you are well!"

Right away the man could see! Then he followed Jesus down the road. And he praised God for the wonderful miracle. Everyone who saw what happened praised God, too!

*Bartimaeus was blind. When he heard that
Jesus was coming down the road, he called for
Jesus to help him. Jesus did! He told the man,
"You are well because you believe in me." And
Bartimaeus could see!*

Jesus Rides a Colt

Matthew 21; Luke 19; John 11–12

It was soon time for the Jewish people to get together for the Passover. It was a happy time to remember how God had helped his people leave Egypt many years before. A lot of people went to Jerusalem for the Passover each year.

Everyone wanted to see Jesus. As the people talked together at the Temple they asked each other, "Do you think he will come?" They knew that they were to tell the Jewish leaders if they saw Jesus. Then the leaders could take him away and have him killed.

Six days before the Passover, Jesus came to Bethany, where Lazarus lived. This was the man Jesus had brought back to life four days after he had died.

Jesus ate supper that night in Bethany with Mary, Martha, and Lazarus.

While he was there, Mary took out a jar of perfume that cost a lot of money. She poured it over Jesus' feet and wiped them with her hair. The perfume made the whole house smell good.

But Judas was upset. He was the disciple who later told the leaders where to find Jesus. "Why wasn't this perfume sold? The money could have been given to the poor people," he said. Judas

didn't really care about poor people. He was the
one who took care of the disciples' money, and
he often took some of it for himself.

Jesus told him, "Leave Mary alone. She has
done a good thing. You will always be able to
help poor people, but I won't be here much
longer."

Then Jesus left Bethany to go to Jerusalem.
When he had come as far as the Mount of Olives,
he sent two of his disciples to a nearby village.

"You'll see a donkey tied there with her young
colt, which has never been ridden," he said.
"Untie the colt, and bring it to me. If anyone
asks what you are doing, just say that the Lord
needs it."

The two disciples found the young donkey just
as Jesus had said. And while they were untying it
the owners asked, "What are you doing?"

"The Lord needs it," the disciples said. Then
the owners let them have the donkey for Jesus to
ride on. The disciples brought the young animal
to Jesus and threw their coats across its back.

Jesus rode the donkey along the road to
Jerusalem. As he did, many people in the crowd
spread their coats on the road in front of him.
Others cut down branches from the trees and
made a green carpet for him to ride over. That is
what people did when a king rode through their
streets. Then the crowd around him began
shouting, "Praise God for sending us a king!"

But Jesus knew that most of the people didn't

Jesus rode into Jerusalem on a young donkey.
The people waved palm branches and shouted,
"Praise God for sending us a king!"

really love him. He knew that in a few days they would be shouting, "Put him on a cross to die. Crucify him!"

When he came to Jerusalem, Jesus went up to the Temple. There he began making people well. He helped people who were blind and people who couldn't walk right. But the Jewish leaders were angry. They didn't like it when they heard some children at the Temple praising God for Jesus, their king. But Jesus said that this was what God wanted the children to do.

STORY **139**

Stories about Heaven

Matthew 24–25

Jesus told his disciples about the end of the world. He told them that he would be living in heaven then, but he would come back. He said he would come in the clouds. "But no one knows when this will be. I don't know, and the angels don't know. Only God the Father knows."

Jesus then told his disciples a story to help them understand the Kingdom of Heaven and how to wait for it.

A man was getting ready for a trip. Before he went, he gave money to his servants. He told them to use it to earn more for him while he was away. He gave five bags of gold to one servant, two bags to another, and one bag to the last.

The servant with the five bags used the gold to buy things. Then he sold these things for more than they cost him. He kept buying and selling like that until he had twice as much money as he started with! The servant with the two bags did the same until he had earned two more bags. But the servant with the one bag didn't use it. He hid it instead.

After a long time the man came back from his trip. He called in his servants to find out how much they had earned with his money.

The servant with the five bags of gold said, "See, I have earned five more." His master was pleased and said he would let this servant do many more things for him.

Then the servant with the two bags of gold came and said, "See, I have earned two more." The master was pleased and said he would let this servant do many more things too.

Then the servant with the one bag of gold came. "Master," he said, "I was afraid I would lose your money, so I hid it. Here is the money that you gave me."

The master was angry. "You lazy servant," he said. "You didn't earn any money at all while I was gone."

The man took back the money and gave it to the servant with the ten bags!

In this story the master is like Christ. He has gone to heaven to stay for a while, but he is coming back. The servants are like all of us left here in this world to work for Jesus. The money is like the things he has given us to work with. Some of us have many abilities and things we can do for Jesus. Some of us can just do a few things, but each of us has some ability God can use. When Jesus comes again, he will reward those who have done what they could for him. But he will punish those who have not done what they could.

Then Jesus told his disciples that when he comes back to earth, he will sit on his throne. All people who have died will come up out of their graves. And they will stand in front of him to be judged. He will separate them as a shepherd separates his sheep from the goats. He will place those who have done what is good at his right. But those who have done what is bad will be at his left.

He will say to those at his right, "Come, children of my Father. Come into the Kingdom that has been waiting for you from the beginning of the world. For when I was hungry, you gave me food. When I was thirsty, you gave me a drink. When I was poor, you gave me clothes. When I was sick, you took care of me. When I was in jail, you came to visit me."

Those who are good will say to him, "Lord, when did we do these things for you?"

Then Jesus told them he would answer, "Whenever you did these things for people from my family who needed help, it was the same as if you did them for me."

Jesus said he will turn to the wicked and say, "Go away, for I was hungry but you didn't feed me. I was thirsty, but you gave me nothing to drink. I had no clothes, but you didn't give me any. I was sick and in prison, but you didn't visit me."

They will ask, "Lord, when did we ever see you hungry or thirsty? When did we see you in need of clothes or sick or in prison? When wouldn't we help you?"

And Jesus said he will answer them, "When you didn't do these things for people from my family who needed help, it was the same as if you didn't do them for me."

Jesus explained that those who wouldn't help others would be punished forever. But those who did what was right would live with him forever.

STORY 140
Fixing Supper and Washing Feet

Luke 22; John 13

The time to get together for the Passover had now come. Peter and John asked Jesus where they should go to fix the Passover lamb and eat it.

"Go into Jerusalem," he told them. "And you will see a man carrying a jar of water. Follow him into the house where he is going. Then say to the man who lives there, 'The Teacher wants to know where he can eat the Passover meal with his disciples.'

He will take you upstairs to a large room all set up for you. Fix the lamb there, for that is where we will eat it."

Peter and John did as Jesus said. And sure enough, they met a man with a jar of water. And he took them to the room Jesus had told them about. There they fixed the lamb.

In the evening Jesus came with his other disciples, and they all sat down for the supper. "I wanted very much to eat this Passover supper with you before my time comes to be hurt," he told them. "I will not eat it again until I have done what I came to do in the Kingdom of God."

But the disciples didn't understand him. They didn't know what he was talking about. They still thought he was going to become king of the Jews, and that the time for this was very near. They began to fight about which of them would be greatest in the Kingdom. Then Jesus told them, "Here in this world the rulers and other important people order others around. But with you it is different. The greatest of you should act the least important. The one who wants to be the leader must be the servant of all!"

Jesus said that most masters eat by a table, and their servants wait on them. "But that's not how it is with me," said Jesus. "I am your servant." Then he showed his disciples what he meant.

He got up from the table and put a towel around his waist. He poured water into a bowl and began to wash his disciples' feet. He wiped them with the towel. Then he came to Peter. But Peter didn't want Jesus to wash his feet, for he didn't want Jesus to act like his servant. Jesus told him, "You don't understand now why I am doing it, but you will later."

"No," Peter told him. "You shall never wash my feet."

Jesus said, "If I don't, you can't be my disciple. You won't belong to me!"

"Then, Lord, don't wash just my feet. Wash my hands and my head, too!" Peter said.

Only servants washed people's feet in Bible times. But Jesus wanted to wash his disciples' feet. He said that the greatest should act the least important.

But Jesus told him, "When you have had a bath, only your feet need to be washed again!"

After he had washed their feet, Jesus came back to the table again. He said, "Do you know what I have done to you? You call me 'Teacher' and 'Lord.' And that is what I am. So if I have washed your feet, you should wash each other's feet. You should follow my example and do as I have done to you."

Eating the Last Supper

Matthew 26; Mark 14; Luke 22; John 13–14; 17

As they ate the Passover supper Jesus looked sad. He said to his disciples, "One of you sitting here eating with me will turn me in to the Jewish leaders."

The disciples were very surprised and sad to hear this. They looked at each other, wondering which one he was talking about. Peter pointed to the disciple sitting next to Jesus. So that disciple asked, "Lord, who will do such a terrible thing?"

"It is the one I give this piece of bread to after I have dipped it in the dish," Jesus answered. Then he gave it to Judas, and Jesus said, "Hurry. Go and do it now."

No one at the table knew what Jesus meant by these words. Some of them thought he was telling Judas to go and buy things they needed. Or maybe Judas was to go and give something to poor people.

Jesus ate with his disciples one last time before he died on the cross. Then he told them to meet together often after he was gone. When they came together they were to eat some bread and drink some wine as they had just done. That would help them remember Jesus until he returns.

After Judas left the room, Jesus said, "I will be with you only a little while longer. So I want to give you this new commandment: Love each other just as I have loved you. Everyone will know that you are my disciples because of your love for one another."

As they were eating, Jesus took a small loaf of bread and asked God to bless it. Then he broke it apart and gave it to his disciples to eat. "This is my body, broken for you," he told them. He meant that his body was soon to be broken when he was put on the cross to die for their sins.

Then Jesus thanked God for the wine and gave it to them. They all drank some of it as he said, "This wine is my blood. I will give it so that God will forgive your sins."

As Jesus and his disciples sat at the supper table, he told them not to be sad that he was leaving them. He was going back to heaven, he said, to get homes ready for them. Then he would come again and take everyone who loves him to be with him forever.

Then he looked up to heaven. He prayed for his disciples and for all those who would believe in him afterward. He prayed that they would be kept safe from sin and that they would love one another.

After that, Jesus told his disciples they would all leave him that night. He said he would die, but then he would come back to life again.

Peter told Jesus, "I will never leave you."

But Jesus said, "Peter, before the rooster crows tomorrow morning you will say three times that you do not know me."

Jesus Is Taken Away

Matthew 26; Mark 14; Luke 22; John 18

Jesus and his disciples sang a song about God. Then they went out to the Mount of Olives, which wasn't far from Jerusalem. There they went into a garden called the Garden of Gethsemane.

"Sit here while I go and pray," Jesus said. Then he went a little farther away and got down on his knees to pray. And now he began to feel terribly sad, for he knew that in a few hours he would be put on a cross to die.

When he went back to his disciples, he found them sleeping. "You're asleep?" he asked. "Get up and pray so that you won't feel like doing what's wrong." Then he went away and prayed again. When he came back he found them sleeping again. He went away a third time. When he returned he asked, "Are you still sleeping? Get up now, for the one who will turn me in is close by."

Judas had seen where Jesus went after the supper. So he told the Jewish leaders that Jesus was alone with his disciples in the Garden of Gethsemane. They sent some men with Judas to get Jesus.

Judas was bringing the men to the garden now. Jesus knew it, but he didn't run. He waited for them to come because it was time for him to die. While he was still talking to his disciples, Judas and the others came. They were carrying swords and clubs.

"The one I kiss on the cheek is the man you want," Judas had told the men. So Judas came up to Jesus and acted as if he was still his friend. He kissed Jesus on the cheek the way men in eastern lands do when they meet. Then the other men grabbed Jesus and held him.

"Lord, shall we use the sword?" the disciples cried out. Then Peter pulled out his sword and cut off an ear of a servant of the high priest.

"Put your sword away," Jesus told him. "Don't you understand that I could pray to my Father to send thousands of angels to fight for me and save me? But then how could the words of the prophets come true? They say that I am to die for the people." Then Jesus touched the man's ear and healed it.

Turning to the men holding him, he asked, "Why the swords and clubs? If I have done wrong things, why didn't you come for me at the Temple? I was there every day."

Then all the disciples ran away.

The men took Jesus to the home of Caiaphas, who was the high priest that year. All the Jewish leaders were there.

Peter followed Jesus, but he didn't get too close. He sat down with the servants beside a fire in the courtyard.

A servant girl came over to him and said, "You were with Jesus of Galilee!" Peter told everyone it wasn't so.

Jesus was very sad as he prayed alone in the garden. He knew that he would soon die for the sins of the whole world.

Judas turned against Jesus and led soldiers to the garden so they could take Jesus away. Judas gave him a "friendly kiss" to show the soldiers which one was Jesus.

Then he went and stood by a gate. Another servant girl saw him there. She said to the others who were standing around, "This man was with Jesus of Nazareth!"

Again Peter said it wasn't so. "I don't even know the man!" he said.

After a while another servant came to Peter. He was a relative of the man whose ear Peter had cut off. This servant said, "Didn't I see you with Jesus in the Garden of Gethsemane?"

For the third time Peter said he didn't know Jesus. Right away he heard a rooster crow, and he saw Jesus turn around and look at him.

Suddenly Peter remembered Jesus' words, "Before the rooster crows tomorrow morning, you will say three times that you don't know me." Then Peter left. He was crying very hard.

STORY 143

A Crown of Thorns and a Cross

Matthew 26–27; Mark 14–15; Luke 22–23; John 18–19

Inside the high priest's house the Jewish leaders asked Jesus, "Are you telling us that you are the Son of God?"

Jesus said, "You are right. I am."

So the Jewish leaders took Jesus to Pilate, the Roman governor. But Pilate found nothing wrong with Jesus. Pilate sent him to King Herod.

Herod and his soldiers made fun of Jesus. They put a purple robe on him because he had said he was a king. Then Herod sent him back to Pilate.

Every year during the Passover, Pilate set a prisoner free. He let one person out of jail that the Jews asked for. A man named Barabbas was in jail for killing someone. Pilate asked the people, "Whom shall I set free? Barabbas or Jesus?"

The crowd said to give them Barabbas. When Pilate asked what he should do with Jesus, everyone shouted, "Kill him! Put him on a cross. Crucify him!"

Pilate washed his hands, as if trying to clean himself up from being blamed for killing Jesus. Then he had his soldiers beat Jesus. They put a purple robe on him again and placed a crown of thorns on his head. They made fun of him and spit on him and hit him.

Then Pilate brought Jesus out to the Jewish leaders. "Take him yourselves and crucify him, for I find no fault in him," Pilate told them.

Judas, the disciple who had turned Jesus in, was afraid because of what he had done. He brought back to the Jewish leaders the thirty pieces of silver they had paid him for telling them where Jesus was. "I have sinned," he said, "for I have turned in a man who did nothing wrong." Judas

Jesus died for our sins. Soldiers put a crown of thorns on his head and nailed him to a cross. Everything became dark because God's Son was dying.

threw down the thirty pieces of silver on the Temple floor and went out to hang himself.

Soldiers took the purple robe from Jesus and gave him his own clothes again. Then they led him away to die on a cross.

Jesus had to carry the heavy wooden cross up a hill outside the city. Along the way a man whose name was Simon was coming in from the country. When the soldiers saw him, they made him carry the cross. A crowd followed Jesus out to a hill called The Skull or Calvary. There the soldiers nailed Jesus' hands and feet to the cross.

Jesus prayed for those who hurt him and for those who let them do it. "Father, forgive them, for they don't know what they are doing," he said. Jesus knew they didn't understand that they were killing the Son of God. Then they tried to give him a sour drink. It would have helped him so he wouldn't have felt the pain quite so much. But Jesus wouldn't drink it.

Two other men were hanging on crosses with Jesus. One was on his right side, and the other was on his left. Both of them had done many wrong things.

It was nine o'clock in the morning when soldiers put Jesus on the cross. He hung there until three o'clock in the afternoon. The soldiers sat down and watched him. They took his clothes and divided them up among themselves. Then they rolled dice to see who would get his coat.

Pilate told the soldiers to place this sign on the

cross above Jesus' head: "Jesus of Nazareth, the King of the Jews." Many people read these words, for his cross was near the city.

The people passing by did not feel sorry for Jesus. They said, "If you are the Son of God, come down from the cross."

And one of the men on a cross next to Jesus made fun of him. He said, "If you are the Christ, show us. Save yourself and us."

But the man on the other cross said, "Jesus, remember me when you come into your Kingdom."

Jesus told him, "Today you will be with me in heaven." Jesus wanted the man to know that his sins were forgiven. He was telling the man that as soon as he died his real self would go where Jesus was going.

Jesus saw his mother and his disciple John standing near the cross. He asked John to take care of his mother, since he was going to die and leave her. After that, John took her to his own home and cared for her just as if she were his own mother.

From twelve o'clock noon until three in the afternoon there was darkness over all the land. God sent the darkness because his Son was being killed by wicked men.

About three o'clock, Jesus called out with a loud voice, "My God, why have you left me?" He said this because God seemed to have turned away from him, and it was true. God had turned away from everyone's sins, for which Jesus was dying.

When one of the men standing there heard his

cry, he ran to get a sponge and filled it with sour wine. He held it up on a stick to Jesus' mouth so that he could drink it. Jesus tasted it and then cried out, "It is finished!" And he bowed his head and died.

At that very moment the earth shook, rocks broke apart, and dead people who had loved God came out of their graves. When the Roman soldiers saw all of this, they were filled with fear. One of them said, "This really was the Son of God!"

STORY 144
Jesus Comes Back to Life
Matthew 27–28; Mark 15–16; Luke 23–24; John 19–20

The Jewish leaders didn't want Jesus and the two men to be hanging on their crosses the next day, for it was the Sabbath. So they talked to Pilate. Then he told the soldiers to break the legs of the men on the crosses to make them die more quickly. So they broke the legs of two of the men. But when they saw that Jesus was already dead, they didn't break his legs. Instead they put a spear into his side. Then everyone knew for sure that Jesus had died.

There was a garden nearby. And in the garden there was a new grave. It was a cave carved out of rock, and it belonged to a rich man named Joseph.

Joseph was one of Jesus' followers. But he had never told anyone for fear of what people would say.

Jesus was buried here in a cave. Some women came with spices for his body, but he was gone. He had come back to life!

Now, though, he went to Pilate and asked for Jesus' body. Pilate said he could take it down and bury it. So Joseph took Jesus' body down from the cross. Nicodemus helped him wrap it in a long cloth. Then they laid it in the cave and rolled a huge stone across the door.

Then the Jewish leaders went to Pilate. They said, "Sir, while Jesus was still alive, he told a lie. He said that after three days he would come back to life. Please send some men to the cave where he is buried. Have them seal up the cave and stay until the third day. Then his disciples can't come in the night to steal his body and tell everyone he has come back to life." So Pilate sent soldiers to the cave.

Early on Sunday morning the angel of the Lord came down from heaven and rolled back the stone from the cave and sat upon it. His face was as bright as lightning, and his clothes were white as snow. The soldiers shook with fear and fell down as if they were dead.

As it was getting light, Mary Magdalene and the other Mary and Salome were walking to the tomb. They were bringing spices to put on Jesus' body. "How can we ever roll away the heavy stone from the door of the cave?" they were wondering. But when they got there, the stone had already been rolled away! They went inside the cave, and there was an angel in a white robe!

The angel surprised the women so much that they felt afraid. But the angel said to them, "Don't be afraid. Are you looking for Jesus? He isn't here.

He has come back to life again! See, that is where his body was. Now go and tell his disciples, including Peter, that he is alive again and that he will meet them in Galilee."

As the women ran from the cave they were filled with fear, but they were also filled with joy. They hurried to find the disciples and give them the angel's message. But as they were running, Jesus met them. "Hello there!" he greeted them. They ran to him and held him by the feet and worshiped him. "Don't be afraid," he said. "Just go and tell my followers to leave for Galilee, and they will see me there."

When Mary told Peter and John what the angel had said, they ran to the cave to see for themselves. John got there first and looked inside. He saw the cloth that Joseph had wrapped around Jesus' body, but he didn't go in the cave. Then Peter came and went right in. So then John went in too, and they finally knew that Jesus had really come back to life again. Before that they hadn't understood that he would be alive again on the third day after he died.

Some of the soldiers who had been at the tomb told the Jewish leaders what had happened during the night. The Jewish leaders gave them money so they would lie about what happened. The leaders told them, "Say that Jesus' disciples came during the night while you were asleep, and they stole Jesus' body! Don't worry about getting in trouble with Pilate. We'll make sure that everything will be all right," they promised.

So the soldiers took the money and said what the Jewish leaders told them to. But of course, it was a lie.

STORY 145
Two Friends Walk to Emmaus

Luke 24

Late that afternoon two of Jesus' friends were walking to the village of Emmaus, which was about seven miles from Jerusalem. They were talking to each other about all the sad things that had happened, for they didn't understand that Jesus had come back to life.

Then Jesus came and walked along with them. But he looked different to them, so they didn't know who he was.

"What are you talking about that makes you so sad?" Jesus asked.

Cleopas answered, "You must be the only person in Jerusalem who hasn't heard all the things that have been happening the last few days."

"What things?" Jesus asked.

"The things that happened to Jesus of Nazareth," they said. "He was a prophet and did great miracles. We thought he was the one who would free Israel from the Romans. But our Jewish

After Jesus came back to life, he came and walked along the road to Emmaus with two of his followers. But they didn't know who he was.

leaders had him put on a cross three days ago, and he died. Early this morning some women who are followers of Jesus, just as we are, went to the cave where he was buried. They came back with the news that his body wasn't there. They said that some angels told them he is alive! Some of our men went to the tomb afterward and found it was as the women had said: Jesus' body wasn't there!"

Then Jesus helped them remember what the prophets had written about Christ—that he would be killed and afterward come back to life again. Jesus began at the beginning of the Bible and explained all that had been written about himself. But still his two friends didn't know who he was.

As they came near the village where they lived, the friends thought that the man with them was going to keep on walking. They invited him to spend the night with them, as it was getting late in the day. So he went home with them.

As they were eating supper together, Jesus took a small loaf of bread. After he had thanked God for it, he broke it and gave it to them. When he did this, suddenly his friends knew who he was. But as soon as they knew him, Jesus wasn't there anymore! Then they said to each other, "Didn't you feel good inside while he was talking with us out there on the road, explaining God's Word?"

They started back to Jerusalem, where they found Jesus' disciples and other followers. The two from Emmaus told how they had seen Jesus and talked with him, and how they knew who he was when he broke the bread at the supper table. Just as they were telling about it, Jesus himself suddenly was standing right there with them! They were afraid, for they thought they were seeing a ghost!

Then Jesus said to them, "Look at the nail marks

in my hands and my feet. Touch me, and you'll know that I'm not a ghost, for a ghost doesn't have a body as you see I have!"

Jesus' followers were full of joy, but they could hardly believe what was happening! "Do you have anything here to eat?" Jesus asked. They gave him some fish and watched him eat it.

Many See Jesus before He Returns to Heaven

Matthew 28; Mark 16; Luke 24; John 21; Acts 1; 1 Corinthians 15

Later Jesus came to his disciples beside the Sea of Galilee. This is the way it happened.

Peter, Thomas, Nathanael, James, John, and two other disciples were there. When Peter said he was going out to fish, the others said they would go along. They did, but they caught nothing all night. Early the next morning Jesus was standing on the shore, but the disciples couldn't see who he was.

"Did you catch any fish?" he asked them.

"No," they said.

"Throw your net out on the right side of the boat, and you'll catch plenty of fish!" Jesus told them.

They did, and soon the net was so full of fish that they couldn't drag it back into the boat! John said,

"It is the Lord." When Peter heard him say that, he jumped right into the water and began swimming to Jesus. The others followed and brought the net full of fish to the shore.

As soon as they came to land, they saw a fire burning. Fish were frying over it, and there was bread.

"Come and have some breakfast," Jesus called.

After breakfast Jesus asked Peter three times, "Do you love me?" Each time Peter said yes.

Then Jesus said to Peter, "Take care of my followers. They are my sheep."

Another time Jesus met his disciples on a mountain in Galilee where he had told them to go. When they saw him, they worshiped him. He said to them, "God has given me all power in heaven and on earth. Go and preach the Good News to the people of every nation. Baptize them in the name of the Father, the Son, and the Holy Spirit. And teach them to obey all the commands I have given you."

Jesus didn't come just to his disciples. One time he let more than five hundred people see him!

Forty days after he came back to life, Jesus came to the disciples at Jerusalem again.

Then he walked with them to a place near the village of Bethany. And while he was blessing them, he began to rise into the air until he went behind a cloud and no one could see him anymore!

While the disciples stood there trying to see him, two angels came. They were dressed in white. The

After his work on earth was done, Jesus went up to heaven to be with his Father. But he will come back!

angels said, "Why stand here looking at the sky? Jesus has gone to heaven. But he will return someday, just as you have seen him go!"

THE
BOOK
about
Jesus'
Friends

Getting Power from the Holy Spirit!

Luke 24; Acts 1–4

After Jesus had gone back to heaven, his disciples returned to Jerusalem. They went there to wait until the Holy Spirit came and filled them with power from heaven. That's what Jesus had told them to do.

It was time for the Jewish holiday called Pentecost, which came fifty days after Passover every year. The disciples were meeting together when suddenly they heard a sound from heaven. It was like the roar of a strong wind. The sound came closer and closer until it was in every room of the house where they were meeting. Then something that looked like small flames or tongues of fire sat on each of them. That's when the Holy Spirit filled them with God's power as Jesus had promised. And they all began to speak in other languages that they had never known before!

At that time there were many Jews in Jerusalem who worshiped God. They had come from other countries for the holiday. These men and women were very surprised to hear their own languages! But other people in the crowd made fun of Jesus' followers and said, "They're drunk."

Peter stepped forward, and the other disciples stood with him. He shouted to the crowd, "No, they aren't drunk. God has sent his Holy Spirit to fill them. You killed Jesus of Nazareth, who did great miracles. But God brought him back to life just as he promised. And we, his disciples, saw him alive again. By coming back to life he showed us that he is the Savior of the world whom the prophets told about. Now he is sitting beside God the Father in heaven. The Father gave him the Holy Spirit, and now he has given that Spirit to us, as you've seen and heard today."

Then many of the people were sad because they had helped kill Jesus. "What can we do now?" they asked Peter and the others.

Peter told them, "Be sorry for your sins and be baptized in Jesus' name. Then he will forgive you, and you'll get the gift of the Holy Spirit. God promised to send him to you and to your children, and to all who will obey him." About three thousand people believed in the Lord Jesus that day and were baptized.

One afternoon Peter and John went to the Temple for the three o'clock time of prayer. They saw a man being carried by his friends and placed at the gate to the Temple called the Beautiful Gate. There he begged for money from all who came to worship, for he had never been able to walk or do any work. When he saw Peter and John about to go into the Temple, he asked them for some money.

Peter looked down at him and said, "Look at us!" The man looked up, hoping to get some money. Peter said, "I have no money! But I'll give you what I have. In the name of Jesus Christ of Nazareth, stand up and walk!"

Then Peter took the man by the right hand and helped him up. Right away his feet and ankle bones got strong. He jumped up and started walking! Then he went into the Temple with Peter and John. He was walking and leaping and praising God!

All the people heard him, and soon they saw that he was the man who often sat begging at the Beautiful Gate. They were filled with wonder at what had happened and crowded around to see him. Then Peter preached this sermon:

"You people of Israel, why be surprised by this? And why look at us as if we had made this man walk? It is Jesus who has given us the power to make the man walk. You let Jesus be killed, but God brought him to life again. Now turn to God and believe in Jesus so that your sins will be forgiven."

There was one group of Jewish leaders who didn't believe that the dead would ever come back to life again. Some of these leaders had Peter and John put in jail that night. But more than five thousand people who had heard Peter's sermon that day already believed in Jesus!

The next day all the leaders met together. Peter and John were brought in. "By what power did you help the man who couldn't walk? Whose name did you call on?" the leaders asked.

The Holy Spirit helped Peter know what to say. He answered, "The man was made well by the name and power of Jesus of Nazareth! He is the one God brought back to life after you killed him on the cross. No one else in all the world except Jesus can save us from being punished for our sins."

The Jewish leaders could see that there was nothing special about Peter and John. They were not trained to speak. But they had been with Jesus. And now they were not afraid to talk about him. They were very bold. That surprised the leaders. But of course they could see that the man had been healed. So they told Peter and John to go out for a little while.

The leaders talked together about what they should do. Finally they called the two disciples back in again. They told the two men that they must never preach about Jesus again.

But Peter and John said, "Do you think God wants us to obey you instead of him? We can't stop telling people about the wonderful things we have seen Jesus do. And we can't stop telling about what we've heard him say."

Then the leaders let them go. They were afraid that people would get upset if Peter and John had to stay in jail. Everyone was praising God for what he had done through these two men.

Peter and John now went to the other people who believed in Jesus. They prayed together, "Help us not to be afraid to preach the Good News, and give us power to do more miracles in Jesus' name."

Then Jesus' disciples went out and preached again. They were not afraid of what the leaders might do to them. Many who heard them believed in Jesus. And all of these new believers joined the others in meeting together and helping each other. Those who owned land or houses sold them and brought the money to the disciples, who gave it to those who were poor. Barnabas was one of the people who did this. He sold a field and gave the money to the disciples so they could share it with those who needed it.

STORY 148

Philip Has Good News for a Man from Ethiopia

Acts 8

In the city of Samaria there was a man named Simon who did wonderful things by magic. Everyone had always listened to whatever he said, for they thought God had given him special powers. Then Philip came to the city and preached the Good News there. Many believed in Jesus and were baptized. Simon was one of them! After that, Simon followed Philip everywhere, watching with surprise all the miracles he did.

Then Peter and John came to Samaria. The new believers were not filled with the power of the Holy Spirit yet, for they had only been baptized in Jesus' name. So Peter and John placed their hands on the people and prayed for them. Then the Holy Spirit came to them.

When Simon saw what the disciples were doing, he said he would pay them if they would give him the power to do this too. But Peter told him how wrong it was to think that God's power could be bought. "Be sorry for your sin and ask God to forgive you," he told Simon. "I can see that you are not right with God at all."

Then Simon said, "Pray that God won't punish me."

Around that time an angel of the Lord told Philip to leave Samaria and go south to a desert road between Jerusalem and Gaza. He obeyed, but he didn't know what he was to do when he got there. As he was walking along the dusty road, a man from the land of Ethiopia rode by in his fancy wagon, which was called a carriage. He was a very important man in his country, for he took care of everything that belonged to the queen of Ethiopia. He had been in Jerusalem to

The Holy Spirit told Philip to go south to a desert road. There in a chariot he saw a man who worked for the queen of Ethiopia. Philip helped the man understand that he was reading about Jesus.

worship at the Temple. And now as he was going home to his own land, he was reading what the prophet Isaiah wrote. He was reading the part where Isaiah said that a Savior was going to come into the world to die for everyone's sins.

The Holy Spirit told Philip to go over to the carriage and talk with the man. When Philip ran over there, he heard the man reading aloud.

"Do you understand what you are reading?" Philip called out to him.

"How can I understand it unless someone explains it to me?" the man said. Then he asked Philip to please come and sit with him in the carriage to talk about it.

As they rode along, the man from Ethiopia asked Philip about Isaiah's words. "What did the prophet mean when he wrote about someone being taken like a sheep to be killed? Was he talking about himself or someone else?"

Philip explained that Isaiah was talking about Jesus. Then he went on to tell more of the Good News about Jesus.

After a while they came to a pool of water beside the road.

The Ethiopian man said, "Look! There is some water! Can't I be baptized?

"I believe that Jesus Christ is the Son of God," continued the man. He ordered his carriage to stop, and they went down into the water. Then Philip baptized him. When they came out again, suddenly Philip was gone. The Holy Spirit took him away! But the Ethiopian went home happy because now he believed in Jesus and was one of his followers.

STORY 149

Saul Sees a Light from Heaven

Acts 9

Saul was a young man who did not believe in Jesus. He went everywhere, looking for followers of Jesus so he could put them in jail or kill them. He went to the high priest in Jerusalem and asked him to write letters to the Jewish leaders in the city of Damascus. He wanted the leaders to help him find people there who were followers of Jesus. Then he would put chains on them and bring them back to Jerusalem. Here they would be sent to jail for believing that Jesus was the Savior.

The high priest gave Saul the letters he wanted. So he left for Damascus. But as he came near the city, suddenly a very bright light from heaven began to shine around him. Saul fell on the ground as he heard a voice saying, "Saul, Saul, why are you trying to hurt me?"

Saul asked, "Who are you, sir?"

The voice answered, "I am Jesus, the one you

are hurting. Now get up and go into Damascus. Someone there will tell you what to do next."

The men who were with Saul didn't know what to say or do. They heard the voice but couldn't understand the words.

When Saul got up, he found out that he couldn't see a thing. Those who were with him had to lead him by the hand to Damascus. For three days he was blind, and he did not eat or drink anything.

There was a man in Damascus named Ananias who believed in the Lord Jesus. The Lord said to him, "Go down to Straight Street and ask at the house of Judas for a man named Saul. He is praying to me right now, and I have let him see in his mind that a man named Ananias will come to him. He knows now that you will put your hands on him and he will be able to see again!"

Ananias said, "Lord, I have heard about this man and all the terrible things he has done to the people in Jerusalem who believe in you. And now he has come here to Damascus to have everyone who believes in you put in jail."

But the Lord said, "Go and do what I say. I want Saul to preach my Good News to kings and Jewish people and Gentiles, too. I want him to tell everyone about me."

So Ananias found Saul and placed his hands on him. He said, "Brother Saul, the Lord Jesus came to you along the road to Damascus. Now he has sent me here so that you can see again and be filled with the Holy Spirit."

When Saul was on his way to Damascus, Jesus talked to him from heaven. Saul was going to Damascus to put Jesus' followers in jail. Instead, Saul became a follower of Jesus himself!

Right away Saul's eyes were able to see again. He got up and was baptized. After that he ate some food and felt strong again.

Saul stayed with the people who believed in Jesus. He went into the Jewish worship places and preached to the Jews, telling them, "Jesus really is the Son of God!"

The people could hardly believe what they heard!

"Isn't this the man who made things hard for Jesus' followers in Jerusalem?" they asked. "And he came here to take those who believe in Jesus back with him in chains."

Saul kept preaching. He made it easy for the Jews to see that Jesus was the Savior.

But the Jewish leaders didn't want the people to believe. They began to talk about killing Saul. He heard that the leaders were watching day and night at the city gates to catch him if he tried to go out.

So Jesus' followers came to help Saul one night. They let him down in a large basket through a hole in the city wall.

Some time later, when Saul was back in Jerusalem, he went to find Jesus' followers. Now, instead of wanting to hurt them, he loved them and wanted to be with them. But they were all afraid of him. They couldn't believe that he had really become one of them. But Barnabas brought Saul to them. He told them that Saul had met Jesus on the road to Damascus and then had preached the Good News in that city.

After that Jesus' disciples let Saul stay with them. He was with them all the time, preaching in Jerusalem.

But some Jewish people from Greece wanted to kill him. So Jesus' followers sent him away to Tarsus, his hometown. After this the people who believed in Jesus had no more trouble for a while. They lived in peace, and many more people began to follow Jesus.

The Good News Is for Everyone

Acts 9–10

Peter went from place to place visiting Jesus' followers. Sometimes he would call on Jesus' name to make people well. Then more people would believe in Jesus as their Savior.

In the town of Joppa, a woman named Dorcas loved Jesus. She was always doing kind things to help poor people. But she became sick and then died.

Her friends heard that Peter was close by. So they sent two men to him. They asked Peter to please hurry and come to the house where the body of Dorcas lay. So he did. All the poor people she had helped were there, crying and showing the coats and other clothes she had made for them.

But Peter asked them all to leave. After they had left the room he got down on his knees and prayed. Then he spoke to Dorcas, telling her to get up! When he did that, she opened her eyes. She saw Peter and sat up! Then he helped her stand up and called her friends to come and see that she was alive.

Peter stayed in Joppa for a long time. He lived at the home of Simon, a man who made things from leather. While he was there an angel told a man in another city about him.

Over in the city of Caesarea was a man named Cornelius, an officer in the Roman army. He was a good man who believed in God. Even though he wasn't a Jew, he taught his family about God. He gave many gifts to poor people, and he prayed to God often. One afternoon God let Cornelius see an angel coming to him and calling him. He was very scared. "What do you want, sir?" he asked.

The angel answered, "God has heard your prayers, and he has seen the gifts you have given to poor people. Now send men to Joppa to find a man named Peter. He is staying by the sea in Simon's house. Have him come to see you."

So Cornelius called for two of his servants and a soldier who loved God. He told them what the angel had said and sent them to Joppa to find Peter.

Cornelius was a Roman army officer. He was baptized after Peter preached at his house and the Holy Spirit came to him.

The next day Peter went up to the flat roof of Simon's house to pray. As he was praying, he grew very hungry. While he was waiting for his lunch, the sky above him seemed to open. In his mind God showed him something like a large sheet coming down. On this sheet were all kinds of wild animals and snakes and birds. Then a voice said, "Kill them and eat them, Peter."

Peter answered, "No, Lord, for I have never eaten anything you have told me not to." Peter was thinking about the laws that God had given to Moses many years before.

Then Peter heard the voice again. This is what he heard: "When God says it is all right, don't say it isn't!"

This happened three times before the sheet was pulled back to heaven.

Peter was trying to understand what he had seen. And just then the three men sent by Cornelius came to the house where Peter was staying. They were outside at the gate, asking if someone named Peter lived there. Then the Holy Spirit said to Peter, "Three men are looking for you. Don't be afraid to go with them, for I have sent them."

So Peter went down to the men and said, "I'm the one you are looking for. Why have you come?"

They answered, "Cornelius sent us. He is a Roman army officer who believes in God and is well thought of by all the Jews. An angel told him to send for you so that you could come and talk to him."

Peter asked the men to come in and stay there that night. The next day he went with them, and some of Jesus' other followers went along.

They came to Caesarea the day after that and found Cornelius waiting for them. He had asked his family and some good friends to come over, so they were waiting when Peter came too. As Peter walked into the house, Cornelius got down and worshiped him. But Peter said, "Stand up! I am only a man like yourself!"

Then Peter said to the people inside, "You know

what the laws of the Jewish people say. It is wrong for Jews to visit people like you who are from other countries and who aren't Jewish. But God has let me see that it's all right. So I came as soon as I was sent for. And now, tell me why you asked me to come."

Cornelius answered, "Four days ago I was praying here in my house. Suddenly I could see an angel in front of me, wearing bright clothes. He told me that God had heard my prayers and had seen the gifts I gave to poor people. He told me to send for Peter in Joppa. So I did. And you have come. It was good of you to do that. Now we want to hear what God has told you to tell us."

Then Peter said, "I understand now that God doesn't love people from one nation more than another. In every nation there are people who worship God and do what is right. God lets them be part of his family.

"God sent Jesus into the world, and he went around doing good. Then the Jewish leaders put him on a cross to die. But God brought him back to life again on the third day and let many of us see him. God has chosen Jesus to be the judge over everyone. He will forgive the sins of all who believe in him."

While Peter was still speaking, the Holy Spirit came to Cornelius and the others who were with him. Then Peter asked the Jewish friends who came with him, "Shouldn't they be baptized? They now have the Holy Spirit just as we do." So

Cornelius and the others were baptized in the name of Jesus. Then they asked Peter to stay with them for several days.

STORY 151

An Angel Gets Peter Out of Jail

Acts 11–12

Some of Jesus' followers were living in the city of Antioch. They began preaching to people who weren't Jews, and God helped many of those people believe in his Son, Jesus.

When the church in Jerusalem heard about this, they sent Barnabas to Antioch. He was glad when he saw how many of the people there believed in Jesus, and he told them to keep on obeying the Lord. Barnabas was a good man who was full of faith and the Holy Spirit. While he was in Antioch many more people believed in Jesus.

Then Barnabas went to the city of Tarsus to look for Saul. When he found him, he brought him back to Antioch. The two of them stayed there a whole year, preaching the Good News. (It was in Antioch that the people who believed in Jesus were first called Christians.)

About that time King Herod began to make trouble for the Christians in Jerusalem. He put

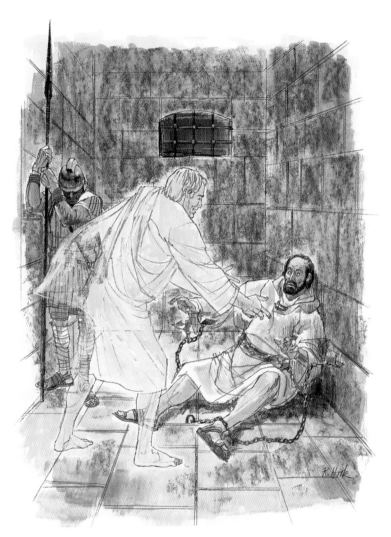

Peter was put in jail for preaching that Jesus came back to life after he died. God sent an angel to save Peter.

Peter in jail and placed soldiers all around him. They guarded him night and day so that he couldn't get away. But the church in Jerusalem kept praying for him.

The night before Peter was to be taken to court, he was sleeping between two soldiers. He was chained to the soldiers, so they knew if he moved even just a little bit!

Suddenly the prison was full of light and an angel was standing there! He tapped Peter on the side to wake him up. "Quick, get up!" he said. The soldiers kept sleeping as the chains fell off Peter's hands! "Dress yourself and put on your shoes," the angel said to him. "Now put on your coat and follow me." Peter did, but he thought it was only a dream! When they had passed the guards and had come to the iron gate that led out of the jail, it opened by itself! They started walking down the street, and suddenly the angel was gone!

Then Peter understood that it wasn't a dream. He said to himself, "It's true! The Lord has sent his angel to save me!" Then he went to the home of Mary, who had a son named Mark. Many Christians were there, praying for Peter. He knocked at the door in the gate, and a girl named Rhoda came to open it. But when she heard Peter's voice, she was so happy that she forgot to let him in. All she could think of doing was running back to tell everyone that Peter was out there!

"Don't be foolish!" they said. "Peter is in jail!" But she told them he really was at the gate.

"Then it must be his angel," they said.

Peter kept on knocking. The people were very surprised when they finally opened the door and saw Peter there! After he got them to quiet down, he told them what had happened. He asked them to tell his other friends about it too. Then he left.

STORY 152
Traveling Missionaries
Acts 13–14

One day while the Christians at Antioch were worshiping the Lord, the Holy Spirit spoke to some of the men. He told them to send Barnabas and Saul away to do the work God had for them in other places. They would be going to many countries, preaching the Good News to people everywhere. The men prayed together. Then they placed their hands on the heads of Barnabas and Saul to bless them. And they sent them away as missionaries.

So Barnabas and Saul left Antioch and sailed away to the island of Cyprus. They took Mark with them as their helper.

On the island they met a Jewish man who didn't want them to preach about Jesus. He talked against them. Then Saul, who was now called Paul, told the man that the Lord would make him blind for a while. And right away everything looked dark to the man. He reached out his hand, asking for someone to lead him. The governor of the island saw what had happened and believed in Jesus.

Paul and his friends now sailed away from Cyprus and came to the land north of there. Mark left and went back to Jerusalem, so Barnabas and Paul went on by themselves. They came to a city where there was a Jewish synagogue. They went into this worship place to teach. After the leaders read what Moses and the prophets had written, they asked Paul and Barnabas to speak to the people.

So Paul stood up and talked to the Jewish people from Israel and all of the other people. He said, "God set the people of Israel free when they were living as slaves in the land of Egypt. Afterward he took care of them for forty years until they came to the land of Canaan.

"And after many years, just as he promised, God sent Jesus. The people of Jerusalem and their leaders didn't know who he really was, and they killed him. But God brought him back to life, and many people talked to him afterward. And now we have come to tell you the Good News that this Jesus is the Savior. He is the one God promised to send. And all of your sins will be forgiven if you believe in him."

The people asked Paul and Barnabas to preach to them again. So the next week almost the entire city came to hear them. But when the Jewish leaders saw the crowds, they were angry. They wanted the people to follow them, not Jesus. So they said bad things about Paul and his message.

Then Paul and Barnabas became very bold. They told the Jews, "It was right for us to preach the Good News to you first. But since you don't want to hear it and don't care to be saved, we will preach it to all the other people instead. We'll tell all the Gentiles about Jesus, for that is what God has told us to do." They said that Jesus is the Savior of all the nations, not just the Jews. Everyone was happy to hear this except the Jewish leaders. They ran Paul and Barnabas out of town. So the two men went to the city of Iconium. But in this city, too, some of the Jews wouldn't believe in Jesus. They stirred up the people until many of them were about to stone Paul and Barnabas to death.

Then the missionaries ran to the city of Lystra and preached there. A man who had never walked believed that Jesus could make him well. Paul knew this, so he shouted, "Stand up!" Then the man jumped up and walked!

When the people of Lystra saw this miracle, they cried out, "These are gods who have come down to us from heaven!"

When Barnabas and Paul saw that the people were going to worship them, they tore their clothes to show how upset they were. They ran among the people shouting, "Why are you doing this? We are just people like yourselves. We have come to preach to you so that you will stop worshiping idols. We want you to worship the true, living God. He is the one who made heaven and earth and the sea, and everything in them."

Just then some Jews came from towns where Paul and Barnabas had been. These people got everyone upset. Almost at once the same people who had just been wanting to worship Paul and Barnabas tried to kill them. They stoned Paul and dragged him out of the city, thinking he was dead. But as Jesus' followers stood around him, he got up and went back into the city!

The next day Paul went with Barnabas to Derbe. After preaching there they went back to all the cities where the people had tried to hurt them. They went to help Jesus' followers keep on believing in the Lord Jesus. They let the people know that they would have times of trouble and sadness as they followed the Lord.

Then Paul and Barnabas chose leaders for the churches in each city.

At last they went back to Antioch to talk about their trip to the church that had sent them out. They called the whole church together and let everyone know that they had told the Good News wherever they went. They said that they preached to the Jews and to other people, too. Then the two missionaries stayed with the Christians in Antioch for a long time.

Paul Meets Young Timothy

Acts 15–16

While Paul and Barnabas were in Antioch, some believers from Jerusalem came to Antioch to teach the new Christians. They said that people who weren't Jews had to become Jewish before they could become Christians. Paul and Barnabas talked with these men and tried to make them understand that this wasn't necessary. But they wouldn't agree. So Paul and Barnabas and some other Christians from Antioch went to Jerusalem to talk with the leaders of the church there.

When Jesus' disciples and other leaders in Jerusalem heard about the problem, they talked about it together for a long time. Then Peter and James both stood up and said that becoming Jewish is not what is important. They said it is by believing in Jesus that people are saved, whether or not they are Jewish.

Then the apostles and other leaders chose two men to go to Antioch and tell the Christians there about the meeting in Jerusalem. They also wrote a letter to be read to the Christians not only at Antioch, but in other cities too.

So Paul, Barnabas, Judas, and Silas went to Antioch. They called together all the believers and gave them the letter from the leaders in Jerusalem. Everyone was glad to hear the message.

After a while Paul said to Barnabas, "Let's go out again and visit the new believers in all the cities where we preached before. Let's see how they are getting along."

Barnabas was ready to go and said he wanted to take Mark with them. But Paul didn't want to take Mark because this young man had left them and gone home the last time they took him with them.

Paul and Barnabas could not agree. So Barnabas took Mark and sailed to the island of Cyprus. Paul chose Silas and went to Derbe and then on to Lystra.

In Lystra, Paul met a young man named Timothy, whose father was Greek and whose mother was Jewish. Timothy was well thought of by the Christians who knew him. So Paul asked the young man to go along with him and Silas. They traveled from town to town, telling people that the leaders in Jerusalem said they didn't have to become Jewish before they became Christians. Many more people believed in Jesus.

Paul and his friends came to the city of Troas, near the sea. That night God helped Paul see in his mind a man from Macedonia. This man was saying, "Please come over here and help us." So Paul and the others with him sailed across the sea. Soon they arrived in Philippi, one of the main cities in Macedonia.

On the Sabbath day they went out of the city and down to the river. They thought that maybe people met to pray there. They found some women by the river, so they sat down and talked with them, telling them about Jesus. A woman named Lydia, who sold fine purple cloth, was very interested in what Paul said. God helped her understand and believe in Jesus. When she and her family had been baptized, she asked Paul and his friends to come and stay at her home.

STORY 154
An Earthquake Shakes a Jail

Acts 16–17

At Philippi Paul and Silas met a slave girl who had an evil spirit in her. The evil spirit helped her know about things that hadn't happened yet. So people paid her to tell them what was going to happen to them. She earned a lot of money for her masters that way.

The girl followed Paul and his friends and shouted, "These men are the servants of God. They will tell you how to be saved." This went on for several days.

Paul didn't like to hear an evil spirit talk about Jesus. At last he turned around and said to the spirit inside the girl, "In the name of Jesus Christ, come out of her." And right away the spirit came out and left her.

When her masters saw that the evil spirit was gone, they were angry. Now the girl could no longer earn money for them by telling people what was going to happen. The men grabbed Paul and Silas and took them to the city leaders. "These Jews are getting everyone in our city upset," they shouted. "They are teaching the people to do things that are against our Roman laws."

A crowd of people became very angry with Paul and Silas. So the city leaders gave an order for the men to get a beating. After that, Paul and Silas were put in jail. The man in charge of the jail was told to be sure they didn't get out. So he took them into a room way inside the prison and put their feet through holes in some blocks of wood, locking them in place.

In the middle of the night Paul and Silas were praying and singing praises to God as the other prisoners listened. Suddenly the earth began to shake, and a great earthquake shook the whole jail. All the doors opened, and everyone's chains fell off! The man in charge woke up and saw that the jail doors were wide open. He was ready to kill himself, for he thought everyone had run away. He was probably afraid that he would be killed anyway for letting that happen. But Paul shouted to him, "Don't hurt yourself. We are all here."

Then the man called for a light and ran into the room where Paul and Silas were. He got down on his knees in front of them and cried out, "Sirs, what must I do to be saved?"

They answered him, "Believe in the Lord Jesus,

Paul and Silas prayed and sang praises to God in jail. God sent an earthquake to open the jail, but the men didn't run away. They told the jailer how to be saved!

and you will be saved. Your family will believe and be saved too." Then they told him and his family about the Savior, preaching the Good News to them. And they all believed and were baptized.

Paul and Silas had received a bad beating, so the jailer washed the blood from their backs. He even gave them a meal in his own house! How happy he and his family were to believe in God and to be Christians.

In the morning the city leaders sent some officers to tell the jailer, "Let those men go."

So the jailer told Paul and Silas they could leave. But Paul said, "The city leaders had no right to beat us, for we are Roman citizens. They put us in jail without even taking us to court to be judged. If they want us to leave, let them come and send us away themselves." Paul wanted everyone to see that the leaders had been wrong to beat them and put them in jail.

When the city leaders heard that Paul and Silas were Romans, the leaders were afraid they would be punished for what they had done. They said they were sorry and asked the two men to leave.

Paul and Silas went back to Lydia's house. After meeting with Jesus' followers there and helping them feel better about everything that was happening, they left Philippi.

From there they went to the city of Thessalonica, and then to Berea. Wherever there was a Jewish synagogue, Paul preached to the people. The Jews in Berea were more willing to learn than those in Thessalonica. They listened to the Good News and then looked at God's Word to see if the things Paul and Silas told them were true. Many people believed in Jesus. Men and women believed, Jewish people believed, and other people believed too.

STORY 155

Paul, the Teacher and Tentmaker

Acts 17–18

When the Jews of Thessalonica learned that Paul was preaching in Berea, they went there to stir up the people against him. Then the Christians decided it would be best if he left the city, but Silas and Timothy stayed there for a while.

Paul and some other men went on to the Greek city of Athens. When they got there, Paul sent the men back with a message for Silas and Timothy to come too.

The people of Athens were known as the best thinkers of that time, and people all over the world had heard about their learning. But they worshiped false gods. They made idols and built beautiful temples and altars in different parts of their city. Even though they had many gods, they thought there might be a god they had never heard of. So they built one altar with these words on it: "To an Unknown God."

As Paul walked through the streets of Athens, he saw their idols everywhere. He preached to the Jews in their synagogue. And every day he went to the marketplace, where the people of the city met to talk. He explained to them the Good News about Jesus, and how he came back to life.

Some of the people in Athens asked, "What is this man talking about?"

Others answered, "He seems to be telling about some new and strange god."

The people asked Paul to come to the center of the city and talk to them some more.

"You are saying some strange things," they said. "And we would like to know what you mean." The people of Athens liked nothing better than to talk about something new.

So Paul stood up and talked to them. He said, "Men of Athens, I see that you think a lot about the gods you worship. As I walked through your city, I saw many altars. One of them had these words written on it: 'To an Unknown God.' Now I want to tell you about this God you worship but don't know."

So Paul told them that God made the world and everything in it. He said that God doesn't live in temples that we have built. God is not like the idols made of gold, silver, and stone. "People haven't known any better than to worship such idols," Paul said. "So God hasn't acted upset with them for doing it. He has given them everything they need. But now God says that everyone must stop worshiping idols. All people must be sorry for their sins and believe in Jesus. That's because God has chosen the time when he will send his Son, Jesus, to judge everyone. And God showed us that it is Jesus who will do this by bringing him back to life."

Some people laughed at Paul. Others wanted him to tell them more later. And several people believed him.

Then Paul left Athens and went to the city of Corinth. There he learned to know a Jew named Aquila and his wife, Priscilla. They were in the business of making tents. Paul was also a tentmaker. Whenever he needed money, he made tents and sold them. So since Aquila, Priscilla, and he were in the same kind of work, Paul went to stay and work with them.

But every Sabbath day he went into the synagogue and taught the people at this Jewish worship place. He tried to help both Jews and Greeks believe in the Savior. After Silas and Timothy came to be with him again, he talked about Jesus all of the time. The Jews wouldn't believe Paul, and they weren't kind to him. So he told them, "I have done what I could to let you know about Jesus. If you won't believe, it's your own problem. From now on I am going to preach to everyone else. I'll tell all the Gentiles about Jesus."

Corinth, like Athens, was a great city, but the people who lived there were very wicked. One night the Lord spoke to Paul, telling him to preach boldly and not to be afraid. God said, "I am with you, and no one will hurt you. Many people in this city already belong to me."

Paul stayed in Corinth for a year and six months, preaching to the people. But at last the Jews who wouldn't believe got together and took him to the governor. They said, "This man teaches the people to worship God in a way that is against our Jewish laws."

Paul started to say this wasn't true. But the governor turned to the Jewish people and said, "If this man had done something wrong, I would need to listen to you. But since it is only a question about your worship, take care of it yourselves. I will not be the judge." And he sent them away.

STORY 156

Going Back to Jerusalem

Acts 20–21

After Paul left Corinth, he traveled to many different places, helping the Christians want to keep on living for Jesus. Several men were traveling with him.

At Philippi, Paul got on a ship that took him to Troas in five days. He stayed there for a week. On Sunday evening the people got together for the Lord's Supper. Paul was planning to leave the next day, so he wanted to tell the people all he could. He kept preaching until midnight. There were many lamps in the upstairs room where the people were meeting. And a young man named Eutychus was sitting on a windowsill listening to Paul. The young man went to sleep and fell to the ground three stories below, where he died. Paul went down and put his arms around Eutychus and said, "It's all right. He is alive." And he was!

Then they all went back upstairs to eat the Lord's Supper together. Paul began preaching again and kept talking until morning. Then he left. Someone took the young man home. He wasn't even hurt, so everyone was happy about that.

Paul and his friends sailed to a place near Ephesus. He didn't want to go to Ephesus at that time, for he was in a hurry to get to Jerusalem. So he sent for the leaders of the Ephesian church to meet him.

When they came he said to them, "You know me well, for I stayed with you three years. I taught in the synagogue and in your own homes, telling both Jews and Gentiles that they must be sorry for their sins and believe in the Lord Jesus Christ.

"And now I am going to Jerusalem. I don't know what will happen to me there. But wherever I go, the Holy Spirit keeps telling me that jail and other bad things will be waiting for me. It doesn't matter, though. The only thing that's important to me is that I keep telling others the Good News about Jesus."

Then Paul said, "I know that none of you will

The leaders of the Ephesian church came to see Paul. He told them that he was going to Jerusalem and that he knew they would never see him again. So they felt very sad when they said good–bye.

ever see me again." When he got down on his knees to pray with them, they all cried together. They felt very sad as they hugged him for the last time. Then they went with him to the ship and watched him sail away.

Paul went to the city of Tyre and stayed there seven days. Then he and his friends sailed on to the city of Caesarea. There they stayed in the home of Philip, who had preached the Good News to the Ethiopian in his carriage.

A prophet named Agabus came and took Paul's belt and tied his own hands and feet with it. Then he said, "The Holy Spirit has told me that the Jews at Jerusalem will tie up the man who owns this belt and turn him over to the Romans."

The Christians cried when they heard this and asked Paul not to go to Jerusalem. But he said to them, "Why do you cry and break my heart? I am not only ready to go to jail, but also to die at Jerusalem."

When they saw they couldn't keep him from going, the people said, "May everything be done the way God wants it to be."

Then Paul and his friends went to Jerusalem, where the church gave them a warm welcome. Then Paul went to the Temple. While he was there, some Jews from Asia saw him and knew who he was. They shouted, "Men of Israel, help! This man teaches people that they don't need to obey Jewish laws. He even brings Gentiles into the Temple!"

Soon the whole city was upset. A mob pulled Paul out of the Temple, trying to kill him. But as they were doing it, someone told the captain of the Roman army.

The captain took some of his soldiers with him and ran down among the people. When the men who were beating Paul saw the soldiers, they stopped. Then the captain took him away from them and gave an order to put chains on Paul. The captain asked who this man was and what he had done. Some of the crowd yelled one thing and some another, so no one could tell what the trouble was.

Then the captain gave orders for Paul to be taken away. As he was being carried up some stairs, the crowd followed him, shouting, "Kill him!"

STORY 157

Paul Isn't Afraid to Talk about Jesus

Act 21–23

Paul talked to the captain who was taking him away from the mob. He said, "I would like to speak to the people." The captain said he could, so Paul stood on the stairs where all of the Jewish people could see him. They saw that he wanted them to be quiet, and they heard him begin to speak in their own language. So they became very quiet.

"I am a Jew who was born in Tarsus and brought up here in Jerusalem. Gamaliel was my teacher, and I learned from him to obey all of the Jewish laws just as you want to do now. I put Christians in jail, both men and women, and even killed some of them. The Jewish leaders can tell you that what I say is true, for they gave me letters to the Jews at Damascus saying I could take all the Christians back to Jerusalem in chains.

"But as I was on my way to Damascus one day about noon, suddenly a bright light from heaven began to shine around me. I fell to the ground and heard a voice saying, 'Saul, Saul, why are you trying to hurt me?'

"I asked who it was.

"He said, 'I am Jesus of Nazareth, the one you are hurting.' The men who were with me saw the light, but they didn't hear the words.

"Then the Lord told me, 'Get up, and go to Damascus, and there you will be told what you must do.'

"I couldn't see, because the light was so bright it made me blind. My friends had to lead me by the hand into Damascus.

"After three days a man there named Ananias came to me. He loved God and was well thought of by all the Jews. As he stood beside me, he said, 'Brother Saul, receive your sight.'

"Right away I could see. And he said to me, 'God

let you see Jesus and hear him speak on the way here so that you can go and tell people from all nations about him.'

"When I came back to Jerusalem and was praying in the Temple, I saw Jesus again in my mind. I heard him say, 'Hurry and get out of Jerusalem, for the Jewish people here will not believe what you tell them about me. I will send you far away to all the other people. You will preach among all these Gentiles.'"

The crowd listened quietly until he said these words about preaching to the Gentiles. Then they began shouting, "Kill him! Kill him! He isn't fit to live."

The captain gave orders for Paul to get a beating so he would tell what wrong things he had done. But as they tied him and got ready to beat him, Paul said to the officer in charge, "Isn't it against the law to beat a Roman before he has been judged to have done wrong?"

The officer ran over to the captain and said, "What are you doing? This man is a Roman."

Then the captain came over and asked Paul, "Tell me, are you a Roman?"

"Yes, I am," he answered.

"I am too," the captain told him. "And I paid a lot of money to become one."

"But I was born a Roman," Paul said. When the men who were about to beat him heard that, they left right away. And the captain was afraid of what might happen to him for having given orders to beat a Roman.

The next day the captain took Paul to the Jewish leaders. He told them to try to find out what the trouble was all about.

Paul looked right at them and said, "Brothers, I know that I have done no wrong." Right away the high priest ordered those who stood near Paul to slap him on the mouth.

Paul said, "God will slap you for pretending to be a good person on the outside when you aren't good at all on the inside. You are a judge, but you break the law yourself by giving orders for me to be hit!"

"Is that the way to talk to the high priest?" the people asked him.

"I didn't know he was the high priest," Paul said. "It is written in God's Word, the Scriptures, that we must not speak against those who rule over us."

Then Paul talked about how he believed that people who are dead will come back to life again someday. Some of the leaders agreed with Paul, but others didn't. Soon there was a lot of shouting. The captain was afraid that Paul would get hurt, so he told his soldiers to take Paul away.

STORY **158**
Paul's Nephew
Saves His Life
Acts 23–25

That night Jesus came to Paul and said, "Don't be afraid, Paul. You have told the people here in Jerusalem about me, and now you must also preach about me in the city of Rome."

The next morning more than forty Jews promised one another that they wouldn't eat or drink until they had killed Paul. Then they went to their leaders and told them about the promise. They said, "We want you to have the captain bring Paul back to you tomorrow. Tell him you want to ask Paul some more questions. But before he gets to you, we will kill him."

Paul's nephew heard about their plan and went to tell Paul. Then Paul called one of the officers and said, "Take this young man to the captain, for he has something to tell him."

So the officer took him to the captain. "Paul, the man in jail, asked me to bring this young man to you," he said.

Then the captain led him to a place where they could be alone and asked what he wanted to tell him. The young man answered, "Some of

Paul's nephew told him that some men were planning to kill him. Then Paul had his nephew tell the captain, who saved Paul's life by sending him to the governor.

the Jews are going to ask you to take Paul to their leaders again tomorrow. But don't do it, for more than forty of them will be hiding along the road, waiting to kill him. They have promised each other that they won't eat or drink until they have done this."

"Don't let anyone know you told me this," the captain said. Then he sent the young man away.

Right away the captain made plans to get Paul out of Jerusalem. He got ready to send Paul to Felix, the Roman governor of Judea. Felix lived by the sea in the city of Caesarea, which was about sixty miles from Jerusalem. The captain told two of his officers to get 470 soldiers ready to go to Caesarea that night. He said that 70 of them were to ride horses and 200 were to have spears. "Have horses ready for Paul to ride, and get him safely to the governor."

Then the captain wrote this letter to Governor Felix. "Some of the Jews wanted to kill the man I am sending you. I had my soldiers keep him safe, for I heard he was a Roman. I wanted to know what he had done, so I took him to the Jewish leaders and learned that he had done nothing that he should die for. When I learned they were still trying to kill him, I sent him to you. Now I have told the Jews to go to you and say what they have against him."

So the soldiers left that night with Paul. The next day they brought him and the letter to the governor. After reading the letter, the governor had Paul put in jail and kept there until the Jewish leaders came.

Five days later the high priest and some of the council came from Jerusalem to Caesarea, bringing with them a lawyer to tell the governor what Paul had done wrong.

"We have found that this man makes trouble wherever he goes, upsetting Jews all over the world. He is a leader among those who believe in Jesus of Nazareth, and he took Gentiles into the Temple! If you talk to him yourself, you'll find out that all of these things are true."

Then Paul answered, "It was only twelve days ago that I went to Jerusalem to worship at the Temple, but I didn't make any trouble or stir up the people. The men here today cannot show that anything they have said about me is true.

"I do worship God in a different way than they do, for I believe in Jesus. But I also believe the Jewish laws and the words that the prophets have written. And just like these Jewish men, I believe that everyone will come back to life again someday. So I always try to do what pleases God."

Governor Felix knew about the people who believed in Jesus. He sent everyone away and asked for the captain to come to him before he would plan what to do with Paul. Felix told the soldiers to keep Paul in jail but to let his friends visit him.

A few days later Felix sent for Paul to come and

talk with him and his wife, who was Jewish. Paul talked to them about Jesus. But then Felix told him to go away and come back at a better time. For two years Felix would often send for Paul and talk with him.

Then Festus became the governor. He asked Paul if he would mind going back to Jerusalem to be judged. But Paul said he wanted to be judged by Caesar, who was the emperor over all of the Romans everywhere.

Shipwrecked but Safe

Acts 27

When the time came for Paul to be sent to Rome, an army captain named Julius was put in charge of him and several other prisoners. They went by ship from Caesarea to the city of Sidon. Julius was kind to Paul, letting him get off the ship to visit some of his friends there.

The next city they came to was Myra. There the captain placed his prisoners on another ship going to Rome.

After sailing slowly for several days they reached a placed called Fair Havens on the island of Crete. It was almost winter, which was the time for storms. So Paul said to the ship's officers, "If we go on, there will be great danger to the ship and to our lives."

But the captain of the ship didn't believe Paul. And since Fair Havens wasn't a good place to keep a ship for the winter, he headed for Phoenix. That was a better place to be for the winter. The wind blew softly from the south that day, so everyone except Paul felt good about leaving.

But soon there was a storm. The wind beat against the ship until the sailors couldn't steer it any longer. So they had to let the ship go with the wind. As they came near a small island, they put

God promised Paul that all the people on the
ship would be safe even though the ship would
go down.

ropes around the ship to keep it from breaking to pieces. The storm grew worse, and the next day they threw out some of the things they were taking with them. They wanted to make the ship lighter to try to keep it from sinking.

The storm kept on day after day. The men on the ship couldn't see the sun, moon, or stars at any time because of the dark clouds that covered the sky. At last they gave up all hope, thinking they would all die. They hadn't eaten anything for many days.

Then Paul stood up and said, "Men, you should have listened to me and stayed at Fair Havens. If you had, you wouldn't have run into all this trouble. But don't be afraid, for no one is going to die even though the ship will go down. I know that this is true because last night God sent an angel to tell me, 'Don't be afraid, Paul, for you will get to Rome safely and be judged by Caesar. And God is good, for he will save the lives of all the men who are with you in the ship.'

"So cheer up," Paul said. "I believe God, and I believe what the angel told me will happen. But our ship will be wrecked on an island."

Two weeks after the storm started, the ship was still being driven along by the wind. But the sailors thought they were near some land. They checked to see how deep the water was and found that they were right. The water was only 120 feet deep. A little later they checked again, and it was only 90 feet deep. They were afraid there were rocks nearby, so they let four anchors down into the water to keep the ship from being driven onto the rocks. Then they prayed for daylight.

When morning came, Paul told everyone to please eat something. "You haven't eaten for two weeks," he said. "Please take some food, and don't worry. Not one of you will be hurt." Then he took some bread, thanked God for it in front of everyone, and began to eat. Suddenly everyone else felt better, and all 276 people began eating. After they were done, they threw some more of their cargo into the sea. They threw out the wheat to lighten the ship even more.

When the next morning came, they saw the shore with a sandy beach. But they didn't know where they were. They cut off the anchors and put the sail up, trying to head the ship toward the shore between the rocks. But before they reached land, the ship ran into some sand at the bottom of the sea. The front part was stuck, while the back part was broken apart by great waves that dashed against it.

The soldiers wanted to kill the prisoners instead of letting them get away. But the captain wanted to save Paul and wouldn't let them do it. He told everyone who could swim to jump into the water and swim to shore. He told the others to hang on to boards broken off from the ship. So everyone reached land safely.

Paul Comes to Rome

Acts 28

Paul and the others from the boat learned that they were on an island called Malta. It was cold and rainy, but the people of the island were kind and helped them build a fire on the beach.

Paul gathered some sticks and laid them on the fire. Suddenly a snake slid out from the sticks and bit him, holding on to his hand. When the people of the island saw the snake hanging there they said, "This man must be a killer. He lived through the storm on the sea, but now he will die for the evil he has done." Then Paul shook off the snake into the fire and was not hurt. The people watched him a long time, thinking that his arm would puff up or that he would fall down and die. When nothing happened to him, they changed their minds and said he was a god.

The governor of the island was a man named Publius. He invited Paul and those with him to his house, and they stayed there three days. The governor's father was sick with a fever, so Paul placed his hands on the man as he prayed, and the man got well. Then all the others on the island who were sick came to Paul, and they got well too. They showed how thankful they were by giving Paul and his friends many presents.

After three months the captain took Paul and the other prisoners onto a ship that had been kept at the island for the winter. They sailed to a city near Rome. Then they had to walk the rest of the way. When the Christians at Rome heard that Paul was coming, they went out to welcome him and walk with him. Paul was happy to see them and thanked God for them.

In Rome the prisoners were turned over to the Roman guards. They let Paul live in a house by himself, but he had a soldier to guard him.

After three days Paul sent for the Jewish leaders who lived in Rome. He said to them, "Brothers, I have done no wrong to our people, and I have not gone against the Jewish laws. But the Jewish leaders in Jerusalem gave me to the Romans as their prisoner. The Romans wanted to let me go because I had done nothing for which I should die. But when some of the Jews still wanted to kill me, I asked to come here so that our emperor, Caesar, could judge me. Now I have sent for you so that I can tell you what I believe. I am in chains because I believe Jesus is the Savior. He is the one our people have been waiting for."

The Jews replied, "We have heard nothing against you. But we know that people everywhere say bad things against Christians. So we would like to hear more about what you believe."

They agreed on another day when they would come back. On that day many Jewish people came to Paul's house. All day long he talked to them about what Moses and the prophets had written about Jesus. Some believed, but some didn't. Paul told them that the prophet Isaiah had spoken the truth when he said that many of the people of Israel wouldn't listen to God's message. He said they would hear it but not understand it because their hearts were wicked. Then he said that the Good News was for everyone, not just Jewish people. He said that when these other people, the Gentiles, heard about Jesus, they would believe in him.

Paul stayed in Rome for two years, living in a house he rented for himself. He welcomed all who came to visit him, and he was brave as he told them about Jesus. No one tried to stop him.

STORY 161
A Letter to Christians in Rome
Romans 1; 3–5; 12–13; 16

Long before Paul knew he would be taken to Rome as a prisoner, he wrote a letter to the believers in the city of Rome. He wanted them to know what he taught. And he wanted them to get to know him by reading the letter, because he was hoping to visit them soon. He told them he didn't care if people thought he was foolish for believing the Good

News about Christ. He said he knew it was God's powerful way to bring all who believe it to heaven.

He helped them remember that all people are sinners. He said, "No one is good, not even one person in all the world. No one has ever really followed God's way, or even wanted to. Everyone has turned away from God. All have gone wrong. No one anywhere has kept on doing what is right, not even one."

That was the bad news. Then Paul wrote about the Good News! He said that if we trust in Jesus Christ to take away our sins, God is kind and sets us free. God sent Jesus to take the punishment for our sins. And God accepts us into his family when we believe that Jesus died for us.

Paul wrote about Abraham to show how this works. He told how the Scriptures, which had been written many years before, said that Abraham believed God. Because he did, everything was right between God and him.

Then Paul said that believing in Jesus not only makes us right with God, but gives us peace of mind. We can be sure that we're God's children and that we'll live with him someday. And the Holy Spirit helps us understand just how much God loves us.

Paul also told about some ways to show love to God and to other people. He said, "Don't be lazy! Be happy to do everything well for the Lord. Wait for God's help when you have trouble, and always keep praying. Do what you can to help God's people, and let others come to your house. Don't act as if you know more than anyone else! And don't try to get back at those who are not kind to you. But do whatever you can to get along with everyone."

Paul said to obey the leaders of the land. He said leaders are put there by God to help us, so we should treat them well. And we should pay our taxes so the leaders can be paid.

At the end of his letter Paul sent his love to all the Christians in Rome. He said, "Give my greetings to all those who meet to worship in Priscilla and Aquila's home. Greet Rufus and his mother, who has been like a mother to me." Paul greeted many others by name because he cared very much for all the people who loved Jesus just as he did.

STORY 162

Good People in a Bad City

1 Corinthians 1–3; 5; 7; 12–13; 2 Corinthians 2; 12

In each of his letters Paul talked about the special problems or needs of the church he was writing to. Corinth was an evil city, and most people who lived there did wicked things. When Corinthians became believers in Jesus Christ, they wanted to change their habits and live the way they should. But their neighbors made it hard for them to change.

Paul wrote that people who aren't Christians can't understand God's thoughts, which the Holy Spirit teaches us. It all sounds foolish to them, because only those who have the Holy Spirit within them can understand what the Holy Spirit means. Others just can't take it in.

Some of the Corinthian Christians could not agree on a lot of things. They began forming different little groups that didn't like each other. Paul said they were acting like babies who just want their own way. He asked, "Don't you realize that all of you together are God's temple, the house where God lives? The Spirit of God lives among you in his house. If anyone hurts God's home by bringing sin into it, God will bring that person down, for God's home is holy. No sin can live there. And remember, you Christians are that home."

Another problem in the Corinthian church was that one man was doing something that was very wrong. Everyone in the church knew about his sin, but no one was doing anything about it. Paul told them they must punish the man by making him leave their church until he understood that he could not keep living that way. The good news is that later on the man was sorry about his sin and stopped doing it. Paul told the Christians to forgive him and love him. And that's what they did, taking him back into the church.

Some of the sins in Corinth had to do with the way men and women acted together. So Paul wrote a lot about what makes a good marriage that is really pleasing to God. He said that no matter if people are married or single, they must be pure like God, and they must obey him. Paul said that people must show their love by putting the feelings of other people ahead of what makes them feel good.

Both to the Corinthians and later to the believers in Ephesus, Paul said God had given each one of them some special ability. Whoever they were or whatever they could do best, there was an important job for them in the church. Paul said that we can think of the church the way we think of a person's body. We all know that each part of our body does something that is special and different from what other parts do. We need our eyes for seeing and our ears for hearing. Our hands do one kind of job, and our feet do something very different. In the same way, each believer is like one special part of the "body" of Jesus Christ. God gives some the ability to be church leaders; others can preach or teach well. Some can do miracles or make sick people well. Some are good at helping others. And some can speak in a special language God gives them.

Paul said that if we think about our bodies, we know that our eyes should not try to do the hearing. And our feet shouldn't think that hands are more important than they are. That would be silly! In the same way, we should be glad for our own gifts in the church body. We should not wish we had someone else's gift.

Then Paul said that even though all these special gifts are good, the greatest gift of all is the gift of love. And we can all have that gift!

Did you know that Paul had a problem with some part of his body? He didn't say just what it was, but some people think he had trouble with his eyes. We do know why he had a problem. He said God gave it to him to keep him from thinking too much of himself. Paul's problem also let God show his strength in Paul's weak body. God said to him, "My power works best in weak people."

The Love Chapter

1 Corinthians 13:4-7, 13

Love is patient and kind.
Love is not jealous or boastful or proud or rude.
Love does not demand its own way.

Love is not irritable,
  and it keeps no record of when it has been
  wronged.
It is never glad about injustice
but rejoices whenever the truth wins out.

Love never gives up,
  never loses faith,
  is always hopeful,
  and endures through every circumstance.

There are three things that will endure—
  faith, hope, and love—
  and the greatest of these is love.

STORY **163**

Free to Love and Help Others

Galatians 1; 3; 5

On one of Paul's missionary trips he went to a
land called Galatia. Many people became
Christians there. But after Paul left, some other
teachers began to tell the new believers that
obeying many Jewish laws was the way to be
saved.

Well, when Paul heard about it, he wrote a letter
to the Galatians. He said he couldn't believe that
they had turned away from the Good News he had
told them. They were following a different "way to
heaven." He let them know that the different way
didn't really lead to heaven at all, and that they
had been fooled by teachers who tried to change
the truth about Jesus. He explained that the Good
News he preached didn't come from ideas that
people made up. Instead, it came from Jesus
Christ himself.

Paul thought some people might ask, "Well,
then, why were the laws given, if we aren't saved
by keeping them?" His answer was that the law
was given so that people could see that they are
sinners. He said that the Jewish law is like a
teacher who gives us rules. The law was a guide

until Christ came to make things right between God and us. Paul added, "Now that Christ has come, we don't need those laws to lead us to him. Now we are all children of God because we believe in Jesus Christ."

Paul wanted all believers to know that we can enjoy freedom. It's not freedom to do wrong, but freedom to love and help each other. After all, the real point of all of God's laws is that we are to love others the same way that we love ourselves.

Then Paul said to do what the Holy Spirit wants. When we do just what we want, we do wrong things. Our thoughts don't please God, and we worship idols instead of the true God. We hate other people and fight with them. We become angry and think only about ourselves. We go to wild parties and get drunk.

But when we let the Holy Spirit control our lives, he helps us to live as we should. We can be like a good fruit tree on which good fruit grows. The Holy Spirit makes many different kinds of fruits grow in our lives: love, joy, peace, patience, kindness, goodness, faithfulness, gentleness, and self-control.

Dressed like Soldiers for God

Ephesians 4–6; Philippians 4; Colossians 2–3

While Paul was a prisoner in Rome, he lived in a house with a soldier guarding him. And he wrote more letters. One letter was to the church at Ephesus.

Paul wanted to tell the Ephesian Christians some things that are helpful to all people who love Jesus. So he said, "You must be new people, holy and good like God. You must never lie to each other. And if you are angry, don't let yourself keep feeling that way. Put a stop to it before the sun goes down."

Then Paul said not to steal, but to work and earn money to share with poor people. He said, "Be kind to each other, and care about everyone. Forgive one another, just as God has forgiven you because you belong to Christ."

Paul told how a happy family can please God. The wife should let her husband lead her in the same way that she lets Jesus lead her. The husband should love his wife the same way that Christ loved the church—enough to die for it! And what should the children do? They should obey their parents. Why? One of God's Ten Commandments says, "If you honor your father and mother, you will live a

Paul told the Ephesians that Christians need to get ready to fight against Satan just as a soldier gets ready to fight his enemy.
Our best weapon is the Word of God, which is like a soldier's sword.

long life filled with God's gifts and care." Paul also said fathers should not make their children angry. Instead, they should show love and kindness as they teach their children to do what's right. They should teach in a way that pleases God.

Then Paul told how everyone can get ready to fight the Devil. Because the Devil, also known as Satan, is our enemy, Paul wrote about dressing like a soldier to fight him. He wrote about what an Ephesian soldier would wear.

First there was a wide belt that kept the middle part of the body safe. Paul said that truth is like that belt. And being right with God is like the metal armor that covers the whole body, even the heart. Faith is the shield that stops the arrows Satan shoots at us, and salvation is the helmet that keeps our head from being hurt. For shoes, we can move quickly if we put on the peace that comes from the Good News. All those things help to keep us safe. Then Paul said the best weapon we can use against Satan is the sword of the Spirit, which is the Word of God, the Bible. And then he told about one more good way to win the battle with Satan: Pray all the time!

Paul talked about prayer in another of his letters—one to the believers in Philippi, the city where he was once in prison with Silas. Paul wrote to the Philippians, "Always be full of joy in the Lord. I say it again—rejoice! Let everyone see how kind you are. And remember that Jesus is coming back soon, so don't worry about anything. Instead, pray about everything. Tell God what you need, and don't forget to thank him for what he has already done." Paul promised that people who do this will have God's peace, which is far more wonderful than anyone's mind can understand.

He also told the Philippians to let their minds think about what is true and good and right. He said to think about things that are pure and lovely, and to focus on the fine, good things in others.

There was another group of believers in the city of Colosse. In his letter to the Colossians, Paul wrote, "I am far away from you, but my heart is with you. I am happy that you are pleasing God by the way you live and that your faith in Jesus is strong. Remember to keep on obeying him. Then your faith and trust in him will grow even stronger. And your thankfulness for all he has done will flow out of you." Paul also said, "Jesus Christ has made your life new, so you should be thinking about heaven. That's where Jesus is now, sitting beside God the Father in a place of honor and power."

Then Paul wrote, "Remember Jesus' words. Let them be part of you so they will make you wise. Use his words to teach each other, and sing all kinds of songs to God. Let everything you say and do show other people what Jesus is like."

Jesus Will Come Again!

1 Thessalonians 4–5; 2 Thessalonians 3

Paul wrote twice to the believers in Thessalonica, and one of the most exciting things he wrote about was what will happen when Jesus returns someday! In his first letter to the Thessalonians, Paul wanted to let Jesus' followers know that we don't need to be worried about what happens to Christians who die. Although their bodies are dead and they are separated from their loved ones for a while, they are safe in God's care. Because we believe that Jesus died and came back to life again, we also believe that when Jesus returns to earth all the Christians who have died will come with him.

Paul said that Jesus will come in the sky and will give a great shout of victory. A special angel and God's trumpet will call everyone. What an exciting thing to see and hear! But something even more exciting will happen next.

The Christians who have already died will rise up out of their graves and be taken up into the sky to meet Jesus. Then all the people who are alive and who love Jesus will be taken up into the sky, too. And from that time on, all of Jesus' followers will live with him forever.

Paul said that these wonderful things will happen

very, very quickly, when people aren't looking for Jesus. He said that if a robber comes during the night, people aren't awake, waiting for him. That's how it will be when Jesus comes. It will happen when people aren't thinking about him.

But we love Jesus, so we don't live in the dark. We know Jesus is coming back, and we should be waiting for him. We should also be helping each other to please Jesus and be happy as we wait.

"Always be joyful," Paul wrote. "Keep on praying. And no matter what happens, always be thankful, for this is what God wants people who love his Son, Jesus, to do."

Paul also said that while we wait for Jesus we shouldn't be lazy. "Work hard just as I have always done," he wrote. "Remember that whoever does not work should not eat. And never get tired of doing good things for other people."

STORY 166
Letters to Friends
1 Timothy 1; 3–5; 2 Timothy 1–2; 4; Titus 1–2; Philemon

Most of Paul's letters were to churches, but he also wrote four letters to individual friends. He wrote two letters to Timothy, one to Titus, and one to Philemon.

Timothy was a very special friend to Paul, who wrote to him, "You are like a son to me in God's Kingdom." Paul told his young friend to fight for the things God wants and to keep believing in Jesus. He told Timothy not to do things that were wrong and that would make him feel bad afterward, but to do what he knew was right.

Then Paul wrote to Timothy about how a church leader should live. He should always be wise and good so no one can say anything bad about him. He must be kind and get along with everyone. He must be good to his wife and teach his children to obey and be kind. He should not be a new Christian or have any bad habits.

Paul also told Timothy to work hard at learning about God and teaching others what he learned. He said it didn't matter that Timothy was young, for he could still show other people how to be like Jesus. But Paul told him that it's important to always be kind and helpful to older people.

Timothy's mother, Eunice, and his grandmother Lois were Christian believers, and they had brought Timothy up to know and love Jesus. Paul knew that, so he told the young man not to be afraid to share the Good News. He said, "God doesn't make you afraid. He gives you power and love, and he helps you do what's right."

Paul was in prison when he wrote to Timothy. He said his young friend should let God make him strong. Then he would be ready if bad things happened to him, too, for preaching about Jesus. Paul said to be like a good soldier for Jesus. He said, "Be a good worker, one who does not need to feel bad when God looks at your work. Know what his Word says and means."

Above all, Paul told Timothy to preach the Word of God at all times. Even when it didn't seem like a good time to do it, he was to keep on showing others what was right so he could bring many people to Christ.

Paul also wrote a short letter to Titus, who was a Christian leader on the island of Crete. Paul said Titus should teach people how to live, showing them how to do all kinds of good things for others.

Paul had a good friend named Philemon. Paul had told him about Jesus, and he had become a believer.

Philemon owned a slave whose name was Onesimus, but his slave ran away. While Paul was a prisoner in Rome, he preached about Jesus. Onesimus heard the Good News and became a Christian. Then he did whatever he could to help Paul.

Onesimus knew he should return to his master, but he was afraid of what would happen to him. So Paul wrote a letter to Philemon for Onesimus to take with him.

In the letter Paul thanked Philemon for being such a good worker in the church. In fact, the church met in his home. Then Paul asked Philemon to do

Living the Christian life is like running a race in which all the Bible heroes of the faith are sitting in the grandstand watching us. We can run a good race if we get rid of our sins and keep our eyes on Jesus.

something for him. He asked him to treat Onesimus with kindness and to forgive him for running away.

Paul said that even though Onesimus hadn't been very useful in the past, from now on he would live up to his name. (The name means "useful.")

Paul said he had wanted to keep Onesimus there with him as his helper, but of course he couldn't do that because Onesimus belonged to Philemon. But now Onesimus was more than a slave. He was also like a brother to Philemon, since both belonged to God because of their faith in Jesus.

Then Paul wrote, "If Onesimus owes you any money, I will pay it for him." But Paul also helped Philemon remember how much he owed Paul. It was Paul who had helped him find Jesus. And there was no way Philemon could ever pay Paul back for that!

At the end of the letter Paul said, "I hope to get out of jail soon and come for a visit. So please keep a room ready for me."

STORY 167
A Letter That Wasn't Signed
Hebrews 9–13

One of the letters in the New Testament is different from all the rest because it is not signed. Paul may have written it, or maybe Luke or Barnabas did. Or maybe it was someone else. It doesn't really matter.

What's important is that it was written to help Christians understand that no one is as special as Jesus.

One message from the writer is that Jesus Christ is like the high priest of the Old Testament. The high priest was the one who could go into the Most Holy Place in the Temple. He took with him the blood from animals that people had given as gifts to God. Then God would forgive the sins of the priest and the other people.

But after Jesus came and died to become our Savior, animals were no longer needed as gifts to God. Jesus died just one time to give his own blood and take away our sins. Now we know that when he comes back, everyone who is waiting for him will be able to live with him forever.

Because Jesus, our Savior, is also the High Priest now, we can go right into God's presence. We can trust God and talk right to him in prayer.

It is faith in Jesus Christ that makes us sure we are saved. The person who wrote the letter explained what faith is. He said it is being sure something is going to happen, even though we are not able to see it happening right now. We sometimes hope and dream about something we wish would happen. But that isn't really faith. Faith is being just as certain of something as if we could see it now!

Then the writer listed many people whose lives showed they had this great gift of faith. As you have been reading this book, you have read stories about these people and you know about the ways they served God. The letter says that some of the people who had faith in God were Abel, Enoch, Noah, Abraham and Sarah, Jacob, and Joseph. Then there were Moses and his parents, the Israelites who followed Moses out of Egypt, and the soldiers who marched around Jericho. The writer also talked about Rahab, Gideon, Samson, David, Samuel, and many others who believed in God and had faith in him.

Near the end of the letter the writer says that it's as if God has put us in a race. And all those Bible heroes of the faith are sitting in the grandstand watching us. So we need to get rid of everything that would slow us down, like the sins that we do over and over again. We need to keep running in the race God has given us. We can do it if we keep our eyes on Jesus, for he is the one who gives us faith from the start to the finish.

We can always count on Jesus because he is the same today as he was yesterday. And he will be the same forever.

STORY 168
John's Letters about Love
1 John 3–5; 2 John; 3 John

Three letters in the New Testament were written by the apostle John. He also wrote one of the four

Gospels, the Gospel of John, in which he told many things about Jesus' life. John and his brother James were fishermen until Jesus asked them to follow him and be his disciples.

When John became an old man and wrote letters to Christian friends, he had a lot to say about love. In his first and longest letter he said that the best way we can show that we love God is to love other people. God is love. So if we are God's children, our lives will be full of love.

John said that if we hate another Christian, we are really killers in our heart. And no one who wants to kill can live forever with Jesus. We know what real love is because Jesus showed us by giving up his life and dying for us. So if we need to, we should give up our lives for our Christian friends too. This might mean actually dying for them, but it can also mean giving up our own way and our own comfort to help them.

John said that some people talk a lot about loving others, but their actions don't show that their love is real. Maybe some Christians have all the money they need, but others don't have enough. How can God's love be in those who have money if they won't share it with those who need things?

Then John said that some teachers might act as if they are Christ's followers, but they teach things about him that aren't true. John explained how to be sure a message is from God. The way to do it is to find out if the teacher believes that

Jesus Christ, God's Son, became a man with a human body. The teachers who believe that is true are the ones whose messages are from God.

John wrote that loving God means doing what he tells us to do. And that isn't hard, for God's children can obey him by trusting Jesus to help them.

God wants us to know that he has given us life that lasts forever. Whoever has God's Son as Savior has that life. But whoever does not have his Son does not have life. John said he wrote his letter so those who believe in the Son of God will know for sure that they have life that will never end.

In his second letter John explained that loving one another means doing what God has told us we must do. He also said that we should have nothing to do with a person who teaches things about Jesus that aren't true.

John's third letter went to his friend Gaius. John praised Gaius for being kind to traveling teachers and missionaries. He said that Christians who help these teachers are partners with them in the Lord's work. Giving them what they need is pleasing to God and helps to share the truth about Jesus.

Letters to Christians Everywhere

James 1–3; 1 Peter 1; 3; 5; 2 Peter 2–3; Jude

Jesus had a half brother whose name was James. This brother wrote a letter to Jewish Christians everywhere. It probably was passed around from one church to another so many people could read it.

James wrote about how important it is for believers to learn how to trust God when they have trouble. He said that the things we learn during hard times help to make us ready for anything.

James said, "If you would like to know what God wants you to do, just ask him. He will be glad to tell you. But when you ask, be sure you believe he will answer you!"

James had two very important messages for the readers of his letter. The first was: If your faith is real, you will show it by your actions. The second was: You must control your tongue.

This is what James wrote about faith. He said it isn't much use to say we are Christians if we don't show it by helping others. If we see people who need food or clothes, we can't just tell them to eat well and stay warm. That wouldn't do any good. So it isn't enough just to have faith. We must also do good things to show that we have faith. James said that if we have faith but don't do good things, our faith is dead. It's of no use to anyone.

Then he talked about the tongue that we have in our mouth. He said that it is one of the smallest parts of our body, but it can hurt people in a big way if we let it get out of control. Just like a tiny spark that can set a whole forest on fire, our tongue can mess up our whole life.

James said that it is harder to tame the tongue than it is to tame wild animals. Sometimes we use our tongue to praise God, but other times we use it to say bad things about the people God made. "This is not right!" said James.

Instead, we should be wise and understand God's ways. Then we'll do good things. And if we're really wise, we won't brag about the good things we do!

Peter, one of Jesus' first disciples, wrote two interesting letters. These were also sent to Christians in many different churches. He told how believers should be like one big, happy family. All of us have had our sins taken away because we have believed the Good News about Jesus. So we should love each other like brothers and sisters. And our love should be a real love that comes from our heart.

Peter also said some good things about marriage, just as Paul did. Wives should let their husbands be in charge. A woman shouldn't worry so much about having beautiful clothes, fine jewels, or fancy hair. She should think more about the kind of beauty that comes from having a gentle, kind heart. And husbands should be kind to their wives, always trying to understand how they feel. In fact, Peter said that if they didn't treat their wives well, God would not answer their prayers.

Peter told Christians to watch out for the Devil, who is our enemy. He is always looking for someone he can tear away from Jesus, just like a hungry, roaring lion looks for something to tear apart.

In his second letter Peter warned Christians about teachers who try to change the truth about Jesus. These were the same kind that Paul had warned the Galatians about. Peter said these teachers promise freedom, but they themselves are slaves to sin. Their lives are controlled by the bad things they want to do.

Then Peter wrote that before Jesus comes back, some people will just laugh about it. They will say, "Well, where is he? Years have gone by, and he still hasn't come. Probably he isn't really going to keep his promise!" Peter said not to listen to people like that. Instead, we should keep waiting for Jesus to come. In God's plans, time isn't the same as it is for people. In fact, Peter said that, to God, a thousand years are like one day. Jesus hasn't come back yet because he wants everyone to have time to be sorry for their sins and turn away from them. But when the right time comes, he *will* come just as he promised.

The letter that Jude wrote is a very short one. Jude, another of Jesus' half brothers, also wrote to tell believers about teachers who give messages that aren't true. Jude said that people like this are like clouds that give no rain. They are like trees with no fruit. And they are like stars that wander away and get lost in a darkness that lasts forever. They are the ones who get Christians upset with one another so they don't get along together. But Jude promised that God is able to help us so that we don't become like those teachers. He can keep us from slipping and falling into a life of sin, doing it through Jesus, our Savior and Lord.

STORY 170
John's Wonderful Vision of Heaven
Revelation 1; 4–5; 14–18; 21–22

When Jesus' disciple John was very old, he was a prisoner on an island called Patmos. He was there for preaching about Jesus.

One day as John was worshiping God, a strange and wonderful thing happened to him. He saw a vision. Even though he was awake, in his mind he saw Jesus in heaven. "His eyes were bright like flames of fire," John wrote. "His feet were as bright as a shiny metal, and his voice made a loud sound

John saw a door standing open in heaven. And a voice from heaven said to him, "Come up here, and I will show you what must happen."

like stormy waves against the seashore. He held seven stars in his right hand and a sword with two sharp edges in his mouth. And his face was as bright as the sun on a day with no clouds."

John fell down in front of Jesus, but Jesus put his hand on John's head and said to him, "Don't be afraid. I am the First and Last, the living one who died but is now alive forever and ever! I hold the keys of death and the grave. And I want you to write down what you are seeing."

As he looked, John saw a door standing open in heaven. The same voice spoke, sounding like a loud trumpet: "Come up here, and I will show you what must happen."

Suddenly John's spirit was in heaven, even though his body did not leave the island! "I saw a king's throne and someone sitting on it. Light flashed from him as from a shiny jewel, and the glow of another shiny jewel made a circle around his throne like a rainbow. Lightning and thunder came from the throne, and spread out in front of it was a shining sea of glass. Around the throne were four living beings. Day and night they kept on saying, 'Holy, holy, holy is the Lord God Almighty. He always was, he is now, and he always will be.'"

Then, in his vision, John heard the singing of millions of angels. They were gathered around the throne, giving praise to Jesus. After that, an angel flew across the heavens, carrying the Good News about Jesus to every nation, tribe, language, and people. "Fear God," the angel shouted. "And praise his greatness. For the time has come when he will sit as judge. Worship him who made heaven and earth, the sea, and all water everywhere."

Then, after seeing many terrible things happen on earth, John saw the holy city, the new Jerusalem, coming down from God out of heaven. It was beautiful to look at. As it came down, John heard a loud shout from the throne in heaven: "Look, the home of God is now among his people. He will live with them, and they will be his people. He will take away their sad tears, and there will be no more death, sadness, crying, or pain. All of that has gone forever."

The city was so filled with the greatness of God that it was like a shiny jewel. John said it was made of pure gold and was as clear as glass!

John heard a very important message about that city. Nothing evil will ever get to go in there. No one can go in who does things that are wrong. The only people who can go in are those whose sins have been taken away because they have asked Jesus to be their Savior. Their names are written in Jesus' Book of Life.

Jesus says, "I am coming soon!"

If we believe Jesus is the Savior, we will be happy to say with John and everyone else in God's family, "Amen! May it be so. Come, Lord Jesus!"

INDEX OF IMPORTANT PEOPLE IN THE BIBLE

(The Stories Where You First Meet Them)

532

NICODEMUS   Jewish leader in Jesus' day   *Story 119*
NOAH   Builder of the Ark   *Story 5*

OBED   Son of Ruth; grandfather of David   *Story 59*
ONESIMUS   Slave of Philemon   *Story 166*
ORPAH   Woman from Moab, married to a son of Naomi   *Story 59*

PAUL   (First called Saul) Missionary   *Story 152*
PETER   An apostle   *Story 121*
PHILEMON   Early Christian leader   *Story 166*
PHILIP   An apostle   *Story 122*
PILATE   A Roman governor of Judea   *Story 143*
POTIPHAR   Egyptian army officer   *Story 21*
PRISCILLA   Tentmaker, wife of Aquila   *Story 155*

RACHEL   Wife of Jacob   *Story 16*
RAHAB   A woman of Jericho   *Story 52*
REBEKAH   Wife of Isaac   *Story 11*
REHOBOAM   First king of Judah   *Story 77*
REUBEN   A son of Jacob   *Story 20*
RUTH   Woman from Moab, married to a son of Naomi   *Story 59*

SALOME   One of the women at the tomb   *Story 144*
SAMSON   A judge of Israel   *Story 57*
SAMUEL   Prophet and judge   *Story 62*
SANBALLAT   Enemy of Nehemiah   *Story 111*
SARAI/SARAH   Wife of Abraham   *Story 7*
SATAN   Wicked spirit who tempts us   *Story 2*
SAUL   First king of Israel   *Story 63*
SAUL   Follower of Jesus, later called Paul   *Story 149*
SHADRACH   Friend of Daniel   *Story 99*
SILAS   Missionary with Paul   *Story 153*
SIMEON   A son of Jacob   *Story 22*
SOLOMON   Third king of Israel   *Story 74*

THADDEUS   An apostle   *Story 122*
THOMAS   An apostle   *Story 122*
TIMOTHY   Missionary with Paul   *Story 153*
TOBIAH   Enemy of Nehemiah   *Story 111*

UZZIAH   Ninth king of Judah   *Story 91*

XERXES   King of Persia   *Story 104*

ZACCHAEUS   A Roman tax collector   *Story 136*
ZECHARIAH   Father of John the Baptist   *Story 114*
ZEDEKIAH   Last king of Judah   *Story 97*